WORLD HISTORY

PUBLISHING

First published in 2008 by Miles Kelly Publishing Ltd
Bardfield Centre, Great Bardfield, Essex, CM7 4SL

Copyright © Miles Kelly Publishing Ltd 2008

The sections in this book are also available as individual titles

2 4 6 8 10 9 7 5 3 1

Editorial Director Belinda Gallagher
Art Director Jo Brewer
Senior Editor Rosie McGuire
Editorial Assistant Chlöe Schroeter
Designers Angela Ashton, Jo Brewer, Michelle Cannatella, Joe Jones,
Sally Lace, Simon Lee, Louisa Leitao, Elaine Wilkinson
Reprints Controller Bethan Ellish
Production Manager Elizabeth Brunwin
Reprographics Ian Paulyn

ISBN 978-1-84236-571-7

Printed in China

British Library Cataloguing-in-Publication Data
A catalogue record for this book is available from the British Library

ACKNOWLEDGEMENTS
All artworks are from the Miles Kelly Artwork Bank
Cover artwork: Mike White

The publishers would like to thank the following
sources for the use of their photographs:

Page 58 Christophe Boisvieux/Corbis; 59(t) Photolibrary Group LTD;
60 Topham Picturepoint TopFoto.co.uk; 62(t/r) The British Museum/HIP/TopFoto.co.uk;
74 TopFoto.co.uk; 75 Topham Picturepoint TopFoto.co.uk; 78 Topham Picturepoint TopFoto.co.uk;
82 Werner Forman Archive/The Greenland Museum; 84(t) Topham Picturepoint TopFoto.co.uk,
84(b) Charles Walker/TopFoto.co.uk; 85 Fortean/Trottmann/TopFoto.co.uk;
86 Remigiusz Sikora/epa/Corbis; 87(t) Charles Walker/TopFoto.co.uk,
87(b) Roger-Viollet/TopFoto.co.uk; 88 TopFoto.co.uk; 89(c) John Malam,
89(b) TopFoto/Fotean/TopFoto.co.uk; 134 Bettman/Corbis; 168 Roger Wood/Corbis;
169 Dreamworks/Universal/Pictorial Press; 170 M Westermann/Corbis;
171 Bryna/Universal/Pictorial Press; 172 Dreamworks/Universal/Pictorial Press;
362 Corbis; 373(t) The Art Archive; 374 Robert Holmes/Corbis

All other photographs are from:

Castrol, Corel, digitalSTOCK, digitalvision, John Foxx, PhotoAlto,
PhotoDisc, PhotoEssentials, PhotoPro, Stockbyte

www.mileskelly.net
info@mileskelly.net

www.factsforprojects.com

WORLD HISTORY

Contents

ANCIENT ROME

GLADIATORS

VIKINGS

KNIGHTS AND CASTLES

PIRATES

ARMS AND ARMOUR

EXPLORERS

Ancient Egypt

Be pharaoh for a day and visit the
magnificent civilization of ancient Egypt.

Temples • Tomb robbers • Gods • Trade • Dynasties
Great Sphinx • Hieroglyphs • Weapons • Kings
Statues • Markets • Underworld • Hunting
Warfare • Kingdoms • Clothing • Pets

The heart of ancient Egypt

Without the waters of the river Nile, the amazing civilization of ancient Egypt might never have existed. The Nile provided water for drinking and for watering crops. Every year its floods left a strip of rich dark soil on both sides of the river. Farmers grew their crops in these fertile strips. The Egyptians called their country Kemet, which means 'black land', after this dark soil. The Nile was also important for transport, it was a trade route for the Egyptians.

▼ The Nile supported many activities of Ancient Egypt such as trade and farming, it was an important water source.

Royal news

The rulers of ancient Egypt were called pharaohs. The word 'pharaoh' means great house. The pharaoh was the most important and powerful person in the country. Many people believed he was a god.

▶ Here the pharaoh is holding the symbols of his rule, the hook and flail. Workers used these tools to separate grain from the stalks.

Ramses II ruled for over 60 years. He was the only pharaoh to carry the title 'the Great' after his name. Ramses was a great builder and a brave soldier. He was also the father of an incredibly large number of children: 96 boys and 60 girls.

Ramses II

◄ These people are paying tribute to the pharaoh. This means that they have come from the surrounding countries to give him presents and tell him how great he is!

▲ On her wedding day, the bride wore a long linen dress or tunic.

The pharaoh often married a close female relative, such as his sister or half-sister. In this way the blood of the royal family remained pure. The title of 'pharaoh' was usually passed on to the eldest son of the pharaoh's most important wife.

I DON'T BELIEVE IT!

On special occasions, women courtiers wore hair cones made of animal fat scented with spices and herbs. The melting fat trickled down their heads, making their hair sweet smelling — and greasy!

Powerful people

Over 30 different dynasties ruled ancient Egypt. A dynasty is a line of rulers from the same family.

More than 7000 years ago, people from central Africa began to arrive in Egypt. They settled in villages along the banks of the Nile and around the Nile Delta. These villages formed the two kingdoms of Upper Egypt (Nile Valley) and Lower Egypt (Nile Delta).

Crown of Lower Egypt

Crown of Upper Egypt

▼ This timeline shows the dates of the dynasties of ancient Egypt.

▶ The double crown of Egypt was made up of two crowns, the bucket-shaped red crown of Lower Egypt and the bottle-shaped white crown of Upper Egypt.

Egypt's first pyramid, the Step Pyramid, was built in 2650 BC.

The Hyksos people invaded in 1670 BC and introduced the chariot.

The tomb of the New Kingdom pharaoh Tutankhamun was discovered in 1922.

2750–2250 BC
OLD KINGDOM
(Dynasties III–VI)

2025–1627 BC
MIDDLE KINGDOM
(Dynasties XI–XIII)

1539–1070 BC
NEW KINGDOM
(Dynasties XVIII–XX)

3100–2750 BC
EARLY DYNASTIC PERIOD
(Dynasties I and II)

2250–2025 BC
FIRST INTERMEDIATE PERIOD
(Dynasties VII–X)

1648–1539 BC
SECOND INTERMEDIATE PERIOD
(Dynasties XIV–XVII)

1070–653 BC
THIRD INTERMEDIATE PERIOD
(Dynasties XXI–XXV)

King Narmer, also called Menes, unites Egypt and records his deeds on what we call the Narmer palette.

As the civilization of Egypt progressed they introduced gods for all different areas of life.

Nilometers were invented to keep track of the height of the river which was very important for the crops.

The god Ra was identified at this time with Amun, and became Amun-Ra, the king of the gods.

The history of ancient Egypt began more than 5000 years ago. The first period was called the Old Kingdom, when the Egyptians built the Great Pyramids. Next came the Middle Kingdom and finally the New Kingdom.

◀ Pharaoh Pepi II (2246–2152 BC), had the longest reign in history – 94 years. He became king when he was only 6 years old.

Queen Cleopatra was the last ruler of the Ptolemaic period.

332–30 BC
PTOLEMAIC PERIOD

664–332 BC
LATE PERIOD
(Dynasties
XXVI–XXXI)

In 332 BC Alexander the Great conquered Egypt and founded the famous city of Alexandria.

30 BC–AD 395
ROMAN PERIOD

The Roman Emperor Octavian conquered Egypt in 30 BC.

▲ This vizier is checking the sacks of grain that have been brought in from the harvest while a criminal awaits his punishment. The viziers of ancient Egypt were among the most important people in the country.

Officials called viziers helped the pharaoh to govern Egypt. Each ruler appointed two viziers – one each for Upper and Lower Egypt. Viziers were powerful men. Each vizier was in charge of a number of royal overseers. Each overseer was responsible for a particular area of government, for example the army or granaries where the grain was stored. The pharaoh, though, was in charge of everyone.

I DON'T BELIEVE IT!
Farmers tried to bribe tax collectors by offering them gifts of goats or ducks in exchange for a smaller tax charge.

17

Magnificent monuments

The three pyramids at the town of Giza are more than 4500 years old. They were built for three kings: Khufu, Khafre and Menkaure. The biggest, the Great Pyramid, took more than 20 years to build. Around 4000 stonemasons and thousands of other workers were needed to complete the job.

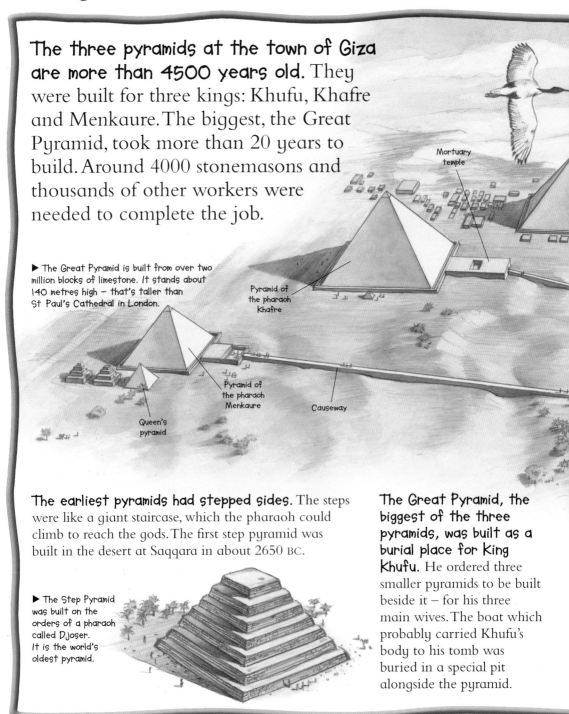

▶ The Great Pyramid is built from over two million blocks of limestone. It stands about 140 metres high – that's taller than St Paul's Cathedral in London.

Mortuary temple

Pyramid of the pharaoh Khafre

Pyramid of the pharaoh Menkaure

Causeway

Queen's pyramid

The earliest pyramids had stepped sides. The steps were like a giant staircase, which the pharaoh could climb to reach the gods. The first step pyramid was built in the desert at Saqqara in about 2650 BC.

▶ The Step Pyramid was built on the orders of a pharaoh called Djoser. It is the world's oldest pyramid.

The Great Pyramid, the biggest of the three pyramids, was built as a burial place for King Khufu. He ordered three smaller pyramids to be built beside it – for his three main wives. The boat which probably carried Khufu's body to his tomb was buried in a special pit alongside the pyramid.

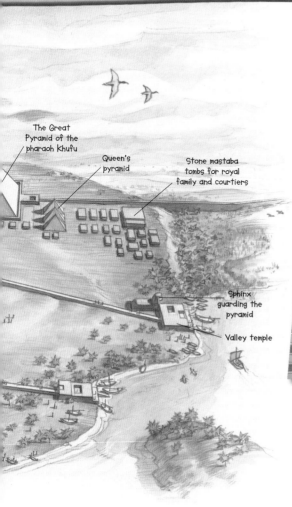

The Great Pyramid of the pharaoh Khufu

Queen's pyramid

Stone mastaba tombs for royal family and courtiers

Sphinx guarding the pyramid

Valley temple

The Great Sphinx at Giza guards the way to the Great Pyramid. It is a huge stone statue with the body of a lion and the head of a human. The features on the face were carved to look like the pharaoh Khafre.

I DON'T BELIEVE IT!

A special handbook for tomb robbers called 'The Book of Buried Pearls' gave details of hidden treasures and tips for sneaking past the spirits that guarded the dead!

Tomb robbers broke into the pyramids to steal the fabulous treasures inside. To make things difficult for the robbers, pyramid builders added heavy doors of granite and built false corridors inside the pyramids.

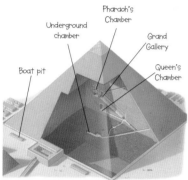

Pharaoh's Chamber

Underground chamber

Grand Gallery

Boat pit

Queen's Chamber

Inside the Great Pyramid were two large burial rooms, one each for the pharaoh and queen. The Pharaoh's Chamber was reached by a corridor called the Grand Gallery, with a roof more than 8 metres above the floor, four times higher than a normal ceiling. Once the king's body was inside the burial chamber, the entrance was sealed with stone blocks. The last workers had to leave by specially built escape passages.

Supreme beings

The ancient Egyptians worshipped more than 1000 different gods and goddesses. The most important god of all was Ra, the sun god. People believed that he was swallowed up each evening by the sky goddess Nut. During the night Ra travelled through the underworld and was born again each morning.

◀ The sun god Ra later became Amun-Ra. He was combined with another god to make a new king of the gods.

A god was often shown as an animal, or as half-human, half-animal. Sobek was a god of the river Nile. Crocodiles were kept in pools next to Sobek's temples. Bastet was the goddess of cats, musicians and dancers. The cat was a sacred animal in ancient Egypt. When a pet cat died, the body would be wrapped and laid in a cat-shaped coffin before burial in the city's cat cemetery. The moon god Thoth usually had the head of an ibis, but he was sometimes shown as a baboon. The ancient Egyptians believed that hieroglyphic writing came from Thoth.

▼ Some of the well-known gods that were represented by animals.

Sobek   Bastet   Thoth

As god of the dead, Osiris was in charge of the underworld. Ancient Egyptians believed that dead people travelled to the kingdom of the underworld below the Earth. Osiris and his wife Isis were the parents of the god Horus, protector of the pharaoh.

Isis   Osiris   Horus

Anubis was in charge of preparing bodies to be mummified. This work was known as embalming. Because jackals were often found near cemeteries, Anubis, who watched over the dead, was given the form of a jackal. Egyptian priests often wore Anubis masks when preparing mummies.

▶ Anubis preparing a body for mummificiation.

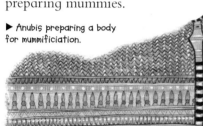

QUIZ

1. Who was buried inside the Great Pyramid?

2. Describe the crown of Upper Egypt.

3. What was a vizier?

4. Which pharaoh ruled for more than 90 years?

5. What is the Great Sphinx?

Answers:
1. King Khufu 2. A bottle-shaped white crown 3. An important governor 4. Pepi II 5. An animal with the body of a lion and the head of a human

A pharaoh called Amenhotep IV changed his name to Akhenaten, after the sun god Aten. During his reign Akhenaten made Aten the king of all the gods.

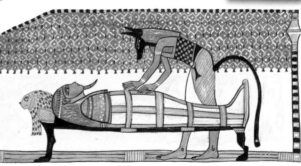

In tombs and temples

From about 2150 BC pharaohs were not buried in pyramids, but in tombs in the Valley of the Kings. At that time it was a fairly remote place, surrounded by steep cliffs lying on the west bank of the Nile opposite the city of Thebes. Some of the tombs were cut into the cliffside, others were built deep underground.

▲ Robbers looted everything from the royal tombs – gold, silver, precious stones, furniture, clothing, pots – sometimes they even stole the dead ruler's body!

Like the pyramids, the riches in the royal tombs attracted robbers. The entrance to the Valley of the Kings was guarded, but robbers had broken into every tomb except one within 1000 years. The only one they missed was the tomb of the boy king Tutankhamun, and even this had been partially robbed and re-sealed.

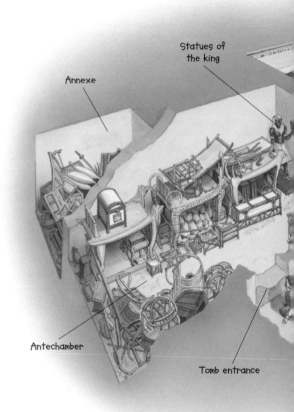

Statues of the king

Annexe

Antechamber

Tomb entrance

▲ The solid gold death mask of Tutankhamun found in the Valley of the Kings. The young king's tomb was discovered, with its contents untouched, about 80 years ago.

Archaeologist Howard Carter discovered the tomb of Tutankhamun in 1922. An archaeologist is someone who searches for historical objects. Tutankhamun's body was found inside a nest of three mummy cases in a sarcophagus (stone coffin). The sarcophagus was inside a set of four wooden shrines big enough to contain a modern car.

I DON'T BELIEVE IT!

Temple visitors had to shave off their hair and eyebrows before they were allowed to enter the sacred buildings.

The ancient Egyptians built fabulous temples to worship their gods. Powerful priests ruled over the temples, and the riches and lands attached to them. Many of the finest temples were dedicated to Amun-Ra, king of the gods.

The temple at Abu Simbel, in the south of Egypt, is carved out of sandstone rock. It was built on the orders of Ramses II. The temple was built in such a way that on two days each year (22 February and 22 October) the Sun's first rays shine on the back of the inner room, lighting up statues of the gods.

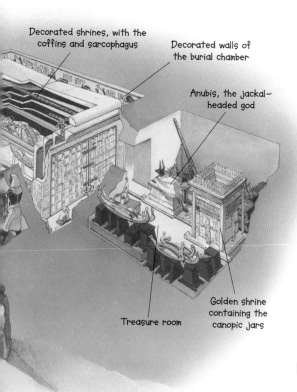

Decorated shrines, with the coffins and sarcophagus

Decorated walls of the burial chamber

Anubis, the jackal-headed god

Golden shrine containing the canopic jars

Treasure room

▲ Carter, and his sponsor Lord Carnarvon, finally found Tutankhamun's tomb after five years of archaeological exploration in Egypt. Carnarvon died just four months after he first entered the tomb. Some people said he was the victim of Tutankhamun's 'curse' because he had disturbed the pharaoh's body. In fact Carnarvon died from an infected mosquito bite.

▲ Four enormous statues of Ramses II, each over 20 metres high, guard the temple entrance at Abu Simbel.

Big building blocks!

Each block used to build the Great Pyramid weighed as much as two and a half adult elephants! Labourers used copper chisels and saws to cut and shape the stones before dragging them on wooden sledges to the base of the pyramid.

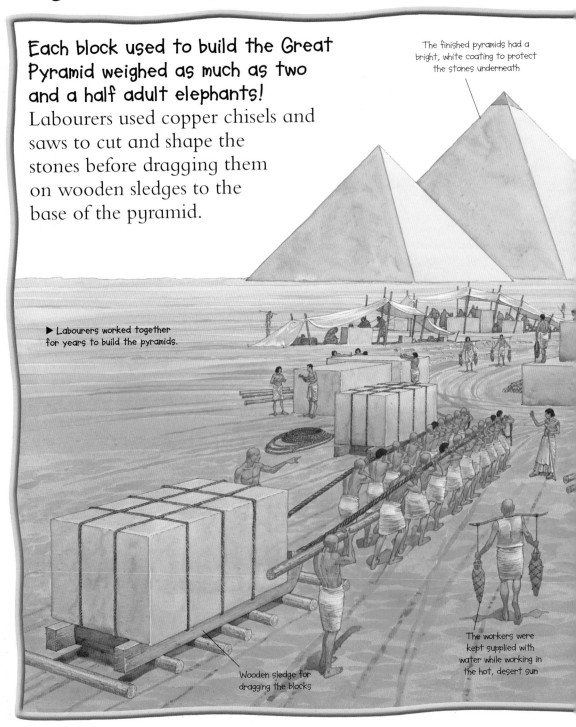

The finished pyramids had a bright, white coating to protect the stones underneath

▶ Labourers worked together for years to build the pyramids.

Wooden sledge for dragging the blocks

The workers were kept supplied with water while working in the hot, desert sun

The huge stones had to be levered into exactly the right position

Up to two million of these blocks could be used to make one pyramid. It could take as long as 20 years

Teams of workers had to drag the stones up the slopes

Steep ramps of earth and mud brick were built to raise the stones onto the pyramid structure. As each new layer of stones was laid in position, the ramps were lengthened to allow workers to build the next layer.

I DON'T BELIEVE IT!

Imhotep, the architect of the Step Pyramid at Saqqara, was a busy man — he was also a vizier, a doctor, a scribe, a high priest and a poet! He served under a total of four different kings.

War and enemies

Foot soldiers carried metal swords and spears, with shields made of wood or ox hide. Later, soldiers were protected by body armour made from strips of leather.

Specially trained soldiers fired arrows from their bows while riding in horse-drawn chariots. Each chariot carried two soldiers and was pulled by a pair of horses. During the time of the New Kingdom (around 3500 years ago), this new kind of war weapon helped the Egyptians to defeat several invading armies.

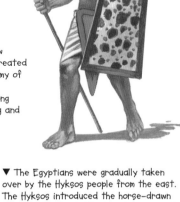

▶ During the New Kingdom, Egypt created a professional army of trained soldiers. Soldiers had strong shields and a long and deadly spear.

▼ The Egyptians were gradually taken over by the Hyksos people from the east. The Hyksos introduced the horse-drawn chariot into Egypt. The Egyptians copied the chariot and eventually used it to defeat the Hyksos and drive them out.

The Sea People attacked Egypt during the reign of Ramses III. These raiders came from the northeastern corner of the Mediterranean. Ramses sent a fleet of warships to defeat them.

▼ Ramses III fought off three separate lots of invaders, including the Sea People. Warships were used by Ramses to defeat the Sea People.

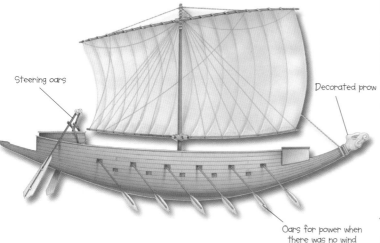

Steering oars

Decorated prow

Oars for power when there was no wind

▼ The Hyksos invaders conquered Lower Egypt during the 1700s BC. They did not reach Thebes, but made their capital at Avaris.

Sea People
Tarsus
Antioch
MEDITERRANEAN SEA   Hyksos
Jerusalem
Alexandria   Tanis
           Avaris
Memphis

Thebes

Abu Simbel

A general called Ptolemy won control of Egypt in 323 BC. He was the first of several rulers who made up the Ptolemaic dynasty. Under the Ptolemies, the city of Alexandria, on the Mediterranean Sea, became the new Egyptian capital and an important city for art and culture.

▶ The great harbours at Alexandria were guarded by the huge Pharos, the first lighthouse in the world (and one of the Seven Wonders of the Ancient World). The city also had a museum and a vast library containing up to 500,000 books.

The Hyksos people conquered Egypt in about 1700 BC. They ruled the Egyptians for 200 years. They introduced the horse, the chariot and other new weapons which the Egyptians eventually used to conquer an empire.

I DON'T BELIEVE IT!

Soldiers who fought bravely in battle were awarded golden fly medals — for 'buzzing' the enemy so successfully!

Bartering and buying

Egyptian traders did not use money to buy and sell goods. Instead they bartered (exchanged goods) with other traders. Merchants visited the countries bordering the Mediterranean Sea as well as those lands to the south. The Egyptians offered goods such as gold, a kind of paper called papyrus, and cattle.

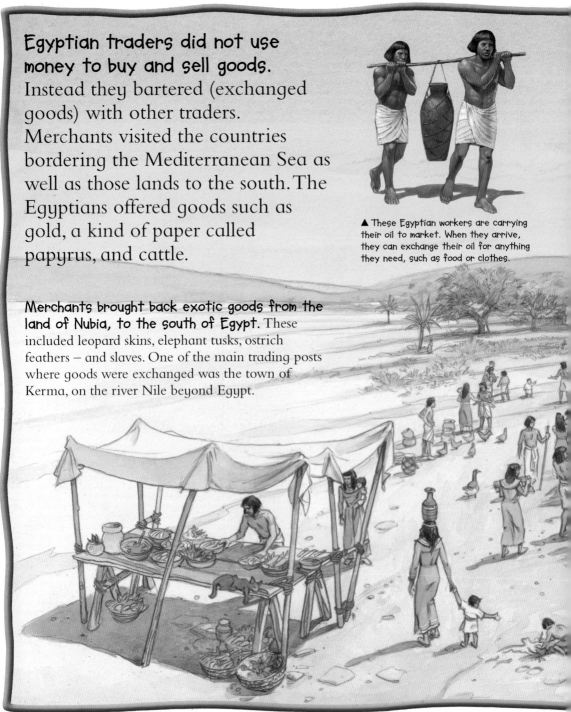

▲ These Egyptian workers are carrying their oil to market. When they arrive, they can exchange their oil for anything they need, such as food or clothes.

Merchants brought back exotic goods from the land of Nubia, to the south of Egypt. These included leopard skins, elephant tusks, ostrich feathers – and slaves. One of the main trading posts where goods were exchanged was the town of Kerma, on the river Nile beyond Egypt.

Egyptians traded with a large number of countries in the Middle East and Africa. Traders brought back silver from Syria, cedar wood, oils and horses from Lebanon, copper from Cyprus, a gem called lapis lazuli from Afghanistan, and ebony wood and ivory from central Africa.

I DON'T BELIEVE IT!
Fly swatters made from giraffe tails were a popular fashion item in ancient Egypt.

▲ A busy Egyptian trading market with people bartering for goods.

When goods were sold they were weighed using a balance and special copper weights called deben. An item could be exchanged for its equivalent weight in copper. A bed, for example, had a value of 25 deben. Pieces of gold and silver were also weighed and used as payment.

The farmer's year

The farming year was divided into three seasons: the flood, the growing period and the harvest. Most people worked on the land, but farmers could not work between July and November because the land was covered by flood waters. Instead, they went off to help build the pyramids and royal palaces.

▲ Water was lifted from the Nile using a shaduf. It was a long pole with a wooden bucket hanging from a rope at one end, and a weight at the other. One person working alone could operate a shaduf.

The river Nile used to flood its banks in July each year. The flood waters left a strip of rich black soil, about 10 kilometres wide, along each bank. Apart from these fertile strips and a few scattered oases, pools of water in the desert, the rest of the land was mainly just sand.

▼ Almost no rain fell on the dry, dusty farmland of ancient Egypt. No crops would grow properly without the water from the Nile.

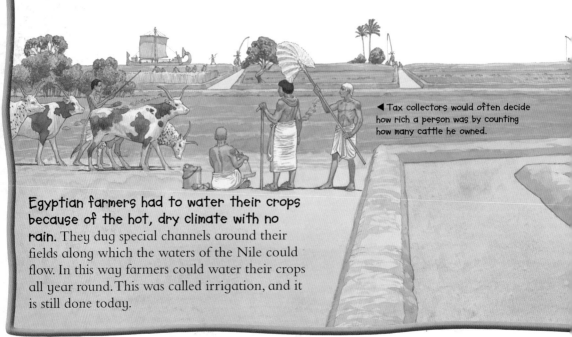

◄ Tax collectors would often decide how rich a person was by counting how many cattle he owned.

Egyptian farmers had to water their crops because of the hot, dry climate with no rain. They dug special channels around their fields along which the waters of the Nile could flow. In this way farmers could water their crops all year round. This was called irrigation, and it is still done today.

Farmers used wooden ploughs pulled by oxen to prepare the soil for planting. They also had wooden hoes. The seeds were mainly planted by hand. At harvest time, wooden sickles edged with stone teeth were used to cut the crops.

Harvesting the grain was only the start of the process. In the threshing room people would beat the grain to separate it from the chaff, the shell, of the grain. It was then winnowed. Men would throw the grain and chaff up into the air and fan away the chaff. The heavier grain dropped straight to the floor. The grain was then gathered up and taken to the granary to be stored.

Wheat and barley (for bread and beer) were the two main crops grown by the ancient Egyptians. They also grew grapes (for wine) and flax (to make linen). A huge variety of fruits and vegetables grew in the fertile soil, including dates, figs, cucumbers, melons, onions, peas, leeks and lettuces.

I DON'T BELIEVE IT!

Instead of using scarecrows, Egyptian farmers hired young boys to scare away the birds — they had to have a loud voice and a good aim with a slingshot!

▲ Winnowers separate the grain from the chaff.

◄ Farmers had to hand over part of their harvest each year as a tax payment. It was usually given to the local temple in exchange for use of the temple's land.

Egyptian farmers kept cattle as well as goats, sheep, ducks and geese. Some farmers kept bees to produce honey, which was used for sweetening cakes and other foods.

Getting around

The main method of transport in ancient Egypt was by boat along the river Nile. The Nile is the world's longest river. It flows across the entire length of the desert lands of Egypt.

The earliest kinds of boat were made from papyrus reeds. They were propelled by a long pole and, later on, by oars. Gradually, wooden boats replaced the reed ones, and sails were added.

▲ These early boats were made of bundles of reeds tied together.

Alexandria
Tanis
Avaris
Giza
Saqqara
Memphis
El-Amarna
Valley of the Kings
Karnak
Thebes
Luxor
LOWER NUBIA
Aswan
Abu Simbel
UPPER NUBIA
Kerma KUSH
RED SEA
Blue Nile
White Nile

▲ The total length of the river Nile is around 6670 kilometres. To the south of Egypt, the Nile has two main branches – the White Nile and the Blue Nile.

A magnificent carved boat was built to carry the body of King Khufu at his funeral. More than 43 metres long, it was built from planks of cedar wood. The boat was buried in a special pit next to the Great Pyramid.

▼ The cabin on board Khufu's funerary boat was decorated with carved flowers. Other traditional designs were carved into the boat. The joints were held together with strips of leather.

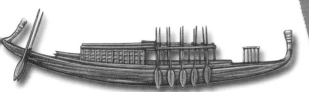

Wooden barges carried blocks of limestone across the river Nile for the pyramids and temples. The stone came from quarries on the opposite bank to the site of the pyramids. The granite used to build the insides of the pyramids came from much farther away – from quarries at Aswan 800 kilometres upstream.

▼ Simple wooden barges were essential for the building work that went on in Egypt.

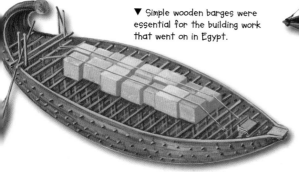

QUIZ

How well do you know your gods and goddesses? Can you name these:
1. This god has a jackal's head and hangs around dead bodies.
2. This god's magic eye will protect you from evil.
3. Cats are really fond of this goddess.
4. This god is a bit of a snappy character!

Answers:
1. Anubis 2. Horus 3. Bastet 4. Sobek

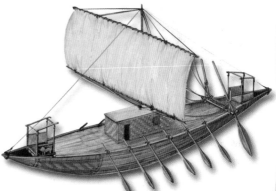

Wooden–built trading ships were propelled by a combination of sail and oar power. Wide-bodied cargo boats were used to ferry cattle across the Nile. The animals stood on deck during the crossing.

Who's who in ancient Egypt

The people of ancient Egypt were organized into three classes: upper, middle and lower. The royal family, government officials, senior priests and priestesses, scribes and doctors made up the upper class. Traders, merchants and craftworkers were middle class. The biggest group of people by far – the unskilled workers – made up the lower class.

◄ The arrangement of Egyptian society can be shown as a pyramid shape. The pharaoh sits at the top of the pyramid, with the huge mass of unskilled labourers at the bottom.

Viziers and priests

Scribes and noblemen

Craftworkers and dancers

Peasant workers

The man was the head of any Egyptian household. On his father's death, the eldest son inherited the family's land and riches. Egyptian women had rights and privileges too. They could own property and carry out businesses deals, and women from wealthy families could become doctors or priestesses.

Egypt, Old kingdom

Egypt, Middle kingdom

Egypt, New kingdom

▲ These maps show the extent of the Egyptian empire in the three kingdoms.

Most ancient Egyptians lived along the banks of the river Nile or in the river valley. As Egypt became more powerful they spread out, up along the river Nile and around the Mediterranean Sea. Others lived by oases, pools of water in the desert.

Rich families had several servants, who worked as maids, cooks and gardeners. In large houses the servants had their own quarters separate from those of the family.

▼ Family life played an important role in ancient Egypt. Couples could adopt children if they were unable to have their own.

Dogs and cats were the main family pets. Egyptians also kept pet monkeys and sometimes flocks of tame doves. Some people trained their pet baboons to climb fig trees and pick the ripe fruits.

Young children played with wooden and clay toys. Popular toys were carved animals – often with moving parts – spinning tops, toy horses, dolls and clay balls. Children also played games that are still played today, such as leapfrog and tug-o'-war.

I DON'T BELIEVE IT!

Wealthy Egyptians wanted servants in the afterlife too. They were buried with models of servants, called shabtis, that were meant to come to life and look after their dead owner!

Home sweet home

Egyptian houses were made from mud bricks dried in the sun. Mud was taken from the river Nile, and straw and pebbles were added to make it stronger. The trunks of palm trees supported the flat roofs. The inside walls of houses were covered with plaster, and often painted. Wealthy Egyptians lived in large houses with several storeys. A poorer family, though, might live in a crowded single room.

◄ A mixture of mud, straw and stones was poured into wooden frames or shaped into bricks and left to harden in the sun.

In most Egyptian homes there was a small shrine. Here, members of the family worshipped their household god.

◄ The dwarf god, Bes, was the ancient Egyptian god of children and the home.

Egyptians furnished their homes with wooden stools, chairs, tables, storage chests and carved beds. A low three- or four-legged footstool was one of the most popular items of furniture. Mats of woven reeds covered the floors.

Rich families lived in spacious villas in the countryside. A typical villa had a pond filled with fish, a walled garden and an orchard of fruit trees.

▼ Family life in ancient Egypt with children playing board games.

They cooked their food in a clay oven or over an open fire. Most kitchens were equipped with a cylinder-shaped oven made from bricks of baked clay. They burned either charcoal or wood as fuel. They cooked food in two-handled pottery saucepans.

QUIZ

1. Why did the Egyptians bury a boat next to their pharaoh?

2. Which part of the body was left inside a mummy?

3. Who was Howard Carter?

4. Why did farmworkers have nothing to do between July and November each year?

Answers:
1. So he can use it in the next life 2. The heart 3. The man who discovered the tomb of Tutankhamun 4. The river Nile had flooded the farmland

Pottery lamps provided the lighting in Egyptian homes. They filled the container with oil and burned a wick made of cotton or flax. Houses had very small windows, and sometimes none at all, so there was often very little natural light. Small windows kept out the strong sunlight, helping to keep houses cool.

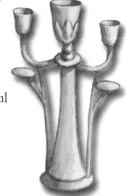

In Egypt it was good to eat with your fingers! In rich households, servants would even bring jugs of water between courses so that people could rinse their hands.

Dressing up

Egyptians wore lucky charms called amulets. The charms were meant to protect the wearer from evil spirits and to bring good luck. One of the most popular ones was the eye of the god Horus. Children wore amulets shaped like fish to protect them from drowning in the river Nile.

▼ The eye of Horus was thought to protect everything behind it. The god Horus had his eye torn out while defending the throne of Egypt. Later, the eye was magically repaired.

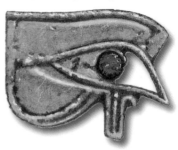

In Egypt, men and women both wore eye make-up. A special black eye make-up, called kohl, was made from ground-up raw metals mixed with oil. The Egyptians believed it had magical healing powers and could restore bad eyesight and fight eye infections. Egyptians also used face rouge for the cheeks and lips, face powder, paint for fingernails and hair dyes.

◄ A wealthy woman applying eye make up before putting on her wig.

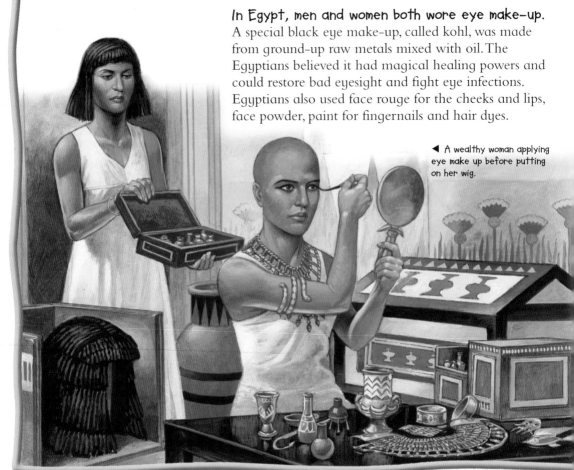

Most clothes were made from light-coloured linen. Women wore long dresses, often with pleated cloaks. Noblewomen's dresses were made of the best cloth with beads sewn onto it. Men wore either robes or kilt-like skirts, a piece of linen wrapped around the waist and tied in a decorative knot.

▶ This fine long dress is worn with a see-through cloak. Clothes like these made sure that the people of Egypt kept cool in the hot weather.

Wealthy people wore wigs made from human hair or sheep's wool which they kept in special boxes on stands at home. Girls wore their hair in pigtails, while boys mostly had shaved heads, sometimes with a plaited lock on one side.

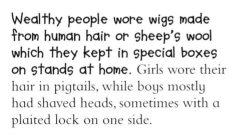

Comb

Hair pins

Wigs

Comb

▲ Wigs were often long and elaborate and needed a lot of attention. Egyptians cared for their wigs with combs made of wood and ivory. They sometimes used curling tongs as well.

MAKE A MAGIC EYE CHARM

You will need:

self-hardening modelling clay
a length of leather strip or thick cord
a pencil   poster paints
a paintbrush   varnish

1. Knead the clay until soft and then shape into the charm.
2. Add extra clay for the pupil of the eye and at the top of the charm. Use the pencil to make the top piece into a loop.
3. Leave the clay to harden. Paint in bright colours and leave to dry.
4. Varnish, then thread the leather strip or cord through the loop and wear your charm for extra luck.

Sandals were made from papyrus and other reeds. Rich people, courtiers and kings and queens wore padded leather ones. Footwear was a luxury item, and most ordinary people walked around barefoot. Colourful pictures of sandals were even painted onto the feet of mummies!

Leather sandals

Reed sandals

Baking and brewing

Bread was the most important food in the diet of ancient Egypt. Harvested grain was stored in huge granaries until needed. The Egyptians' favourite drink was beer. It was very thick and had to be strained before drinking. Models of brewers were even left in tombs to make sure the dead person had a plentiful supply of beer in the next world!

▼ An Egyptian banquet was a real occasion! Rich people could afford the best food and drink, but they would also have servants, as well as musicians and dancers.

DESIGN A BANQUET MENU

A huge choice of foods was served at banquets for wealthy Egyptians. Meats such as duck, goose, gazelle and heron, fresh fruits and vegetables, sweet pastries and cakes, with lots of beer and grape or date wine to drink.

Choose the foods for a banquet and design a decorative menu for your guests.

A rough kind of bread was baked from either wheat or barley. The bread often contained gritty pieces that wore down the teeth of the Egyptians. Historians have discovered this by studying the teeth of mummies.

Hard day's work

Scribes were very important people in ancient Egypt. These highly skilled men kept records of everything that happened from day to day. They recorded all the materials used for building work, the numbers of cattle, and the crops that had been gathered for the royal family, the government and the temples.

▼ Craftworkers produced statues and furniture for the pharoah. Workers such as these often had their own areas within a town. The village of Deir el-Medina was built specially for those who worked on tombs in the Valley of the Kings.

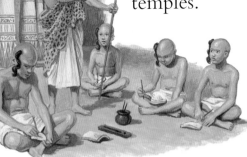

◄ Only the sons of scribes could undergo the strict scribe training, which began as early as the age of nine.

The libraries of ancient Egypt held thousands of papyrus scrolls. They covered subjects such as astronomy, medicine, geography and law. Most ordinary Egyptians could not read or write, so the libraries were used only by educated people such as scribes and doctors.

Imagine if there were 700 letters in the alphabet! That was how many hieroglyphs Egyptian schoolchildren had to learn! Hieroglyphs were symbols that the Egyptians used for writing. Some symbols stood for words and some for sounds. Children went to schools for scribes where they first learned how to read and write hieroglyphs.

Most people worked as craftworkers or farm labourers.
Craftworkers included carpenters, potters, weavers, jewellers, shoemakers, glassblowers and perfume makers. Many sold their goods from small shops in the towns. They were kept busy making items for the pharaoh and wealthy people.

A typical lunch for a worker consisted of bread and onions. They may also have had a cucumber, washed down with a drink of beer.

QUIZ

Can you name the following items from life in ancient Egypt?

1.

2.

3.

4.

Answers:
1. The dwarf god Bes 2. A canopic jar
3. A hair comb 4. An amulet

The base of the Great Pyramid takes up almost as much space as five football pitches! Huge quantities of stone were needed to build these monuments. The Egyptians quarried limestone, sandstone and granite for their buildings. In the surrounding desert they mined gold for decorations.

Slaves were often prisoners who had been captured from Egypt's enemies. They also came from the neighbouring countries of Kush and Nubia. Life as a slave was not all bad. A slave could own land and buy goods – he could even buy his freedom!

Clever Egyptians

The insides of many Egyptian tombs were decorated with brightly coloured wall paintings. They often depicted scenes from the dead person's life, showing him or her as a healthy young person. The Egyptians believed that these scenes would come to life in the next world.

Sunken relief

▶ The Egyptians produced raised reliefs by cutting away the background, and sunken relief by cutting stone from inside the outline.

Raised relief

Egyptian sculptors carved enormous stone statues of their pharaohs and gods. These were often placed outside a tomb or temple to guard the entrance. Scenes, called reliefs, were carved into the walls of temples and tombs. These often showed the person as they were when they were young, enjoying scenes from daily life. This was so that when the god Osiris brought the dead person and the tomb paintings back to life, the tomb owners would have a good time in the afterlife.

The ancient Egyptians had three different calendars: an everyday farming one, an astronomical and a lunar (Moon) calendar. The 365-day farming calendar was made up of three seasons of four months. The astronomical calendar was based on observations of the star Sirius, which reappeared each year at the start of the flood season. Priests kept a calendar based on the movements of the Moon which told them when to perform ceremonies for to the moon god Khonsu.

▲ The days on this calendar are written in black and red. Black days are ordinary, but the red days are unlucky.

◀ Several artists worked on the tomb paintings. A junior artist drew the outlines of the scene, which were then checked and corrected by a more senior artist. Next, painters filled in the outlines in colour.

Astronomers recorded their observations of the night skies. The Egyptian calendar was based on the movement of Sirius, the brightest star in the sky. The Egyptians used their knowledge of astronomy to build temples that lined up with certain stars or with the movement of the Sun.

Egyptian doctors knew how to set broken bones and treat illnesses such as fevers. They used medicines made from plants such as garlic and juniper to treat sick people. The Egyptians had a good knowledge of the basic workings of the human body.

I DON'T BELIEVE IT!

Bulbs of garlic were used to ward off snakes and to get rid of tapeworms from people's bodies.

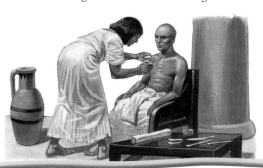

The Egyptians used a device called a nilometer to measure the depth of the river Nile. They inserted measuring posts into the riverbed at intervals along the bank so they could check the water levels at the start of each flood season.

From pictures to words

The Egyptians had no paper — they wrote on papyrus. It was made from the tall papyrus reeds that grew on the banks of the Nile. At first papyrus was sold as long strips, or scrolls, tied with string. Later the Egyptians put the papyrus sheets into books. Papyrus is very long lasting; sheets of papyrus have survived 3000 years to the present day.

Ink was made by mixing water with soot, charcoal or coloured minerals. Scribes wrote in ink on papyrus scrolls, using reed brushes with specially shaped ends.

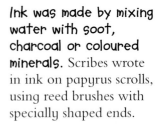

1. Papyrus was expensive because it took a long time to make. First people had to cut down the papyrus stems, and cut them up into lots of thin strips.

2. Then someone laid these strips in rows on a frame to form layers.

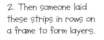

3. The papyrus strips were then pressed under weights. This squeezed out the water and squashed the layers together.

4. Finally, when the papyrus was dry, a man with a stone rubbed the surface smooth for writing.

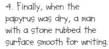

The Rosetta Stone was found in 1799 by a French soldier in Egypt. It is a large slab of stone onto which three different kinds of writing have been carved: hieroglyphics, a simpler form of hieroglyphics called demotic and Greek. All three sets of writing give an account of the coronation of King Ptolemy V. By translating the Greek, scholars could understand the Egyptian writing for the first time.

The ancient Egyptians used a system of picture writing called hieroglyphics. Each hieroglyph represented an object or a sound. For example, the picture of a lion represented the sound 'l'; a basket represented the word 'lord'. Altogether there were about 700 different hieroglyphs. Scribes wrote them on papyrus scrolls or carved them into stone.

In the 5th century BC a Greek historian called Herodotus wrote about life in ancient Egypt. As he travelled across the country he observed and wrote about people's daily lives, and their religion and customs such as embalming and mummification – he even wrote about cats!

WRITE YOUR NAME IN HIEROGLYPHICS

Below you will see the hieroglyphic alphabet. I have written my name in hieroglyphs. Can you write yours?

J A N E

A B C D E F G H
I J K L M N O P
Q R S T U V W X Y Z

◄ A junior artist's work was checked by a senior artist, who then painted over the work in black paint.

The hieroglyphs of a ruler's name were written inside an oval-shaped frame called a cartouche. The pharaoh's cartouche was carved on pillars and temple walls, painted on tomb walls and mummy cases and written on official documents.

Heroes and heroines

Ramses II built more temples than any other Egyptian ruler. Two of his greatest achievements are the huge rock-cut temple at Abu Simbel and the Great Hall at Karnak. He also finished building the mortuary temple of Seti I at Luxor. After his death a further nine pharaohs were given the name Ramses.

The Great Hall at Karnak

Queen Hatshepsut was often depicted wearing men's clothing and a false beard. She was the wife of Thutmose II. On his death Hatshepsut took the title of pharaoh and adopted the royal symbols of the double crown, the crook, the flail (whip) – and also the ceremonial beard!

▶ During her 20-year reign Hatshepsut sent an expedition of five ships to Punt on the coast of the Red Sea. The ships brought back incense, copper and ivory.

Mark Antony   Cleopatra

Queen Cleopatra VII was one of the last rulers of ancient Egypt. She fell in love with the Roman emperor Julius Caesar, and later married the Roman general Mark Antony. Cleopatra killed herself in 30 BC when the Romans conquered Egypt.

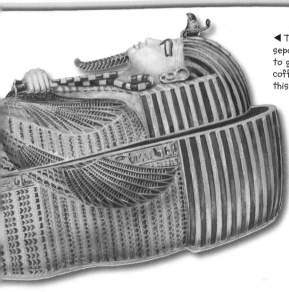

◄ The pharaoh Tutankhamun was buried in three separate coffins. Each coffin was specially made to go around the one inside. This is the middle coffin. Like all the coffins, it is made of gold, but this one is also inlaid with a gem called lapis lazuli.

Narmer palette

Tutankhamun is probably the most famous pharaoh of all. His tomb, with its fabulous treasure of over 5000 objects, was discovered complete in 1922. Tutankhamun was only nine years old when he became ruler, and he died at the young age of about 17. He was buried in the Valley of the Kings.

King Menes was the first ruler of a united Egypt. He joined together the kingdoms of Upper and Lower Egypt, under one government, in around 3100 BC. Menes was also called Narmer. Archaeologists have found a slate tablet, called the Narmer Palette, that shows him beating his enemies in battle.

Thutmose's giant granite obelisk

Thutmose III was a clever general who added new lands to ancient Egypt. Under his leadership, Egypt's armies seized territory in Syria to the north and Palestine to the east. During his reign Thutmose ordered a giant obelisk made of granite to be placed at Heliopolis – it now stands on the bank of the river Thames in London.

QUIZ

1. Name two popular drinks in ancient Egypt.
2. What is a cartouche?
3. What is the Rosetta Stone?
4. What is senet?

Answers:
1. Beer and wine 2. An oval plaque on which the pharaoh's name was written. 3. The stone that enabled historians to read hieroglyphs. 4. An ancient Egyptian game.

Mummies

Unravel the secrets surrounding mummies
and find out about the civilizations around the
world that made them.

Afterlife • Curses • Bog bodies • Amulets • Masks
Tombs • Sacrifices • Pharoahs • Iceman • Relics
Spells • Charms • Animals • Curses • Myths
Coffins • Jewellery

What is a mummy?

A mummy is a dead body that has not rotted away. Natural mummies are accidents of nature, made by freezing, drying or waterlogging. Artificial mummies are made on purpose, by people who have used different ways to preserve bodies. The best-known artificial mummies were made in ancient Egypt. Long ago, travellers from Persia (modern-day Iran) thought that a sticky black substance, called bitumen, was used to make Egyptian mummies. The Persian word for bitumen was *mummia*, and from this comes the English word 'mummy'.

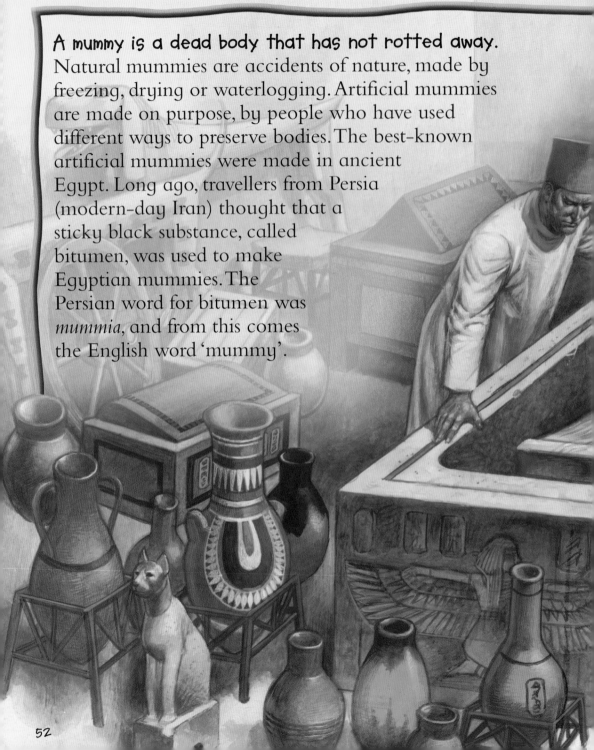

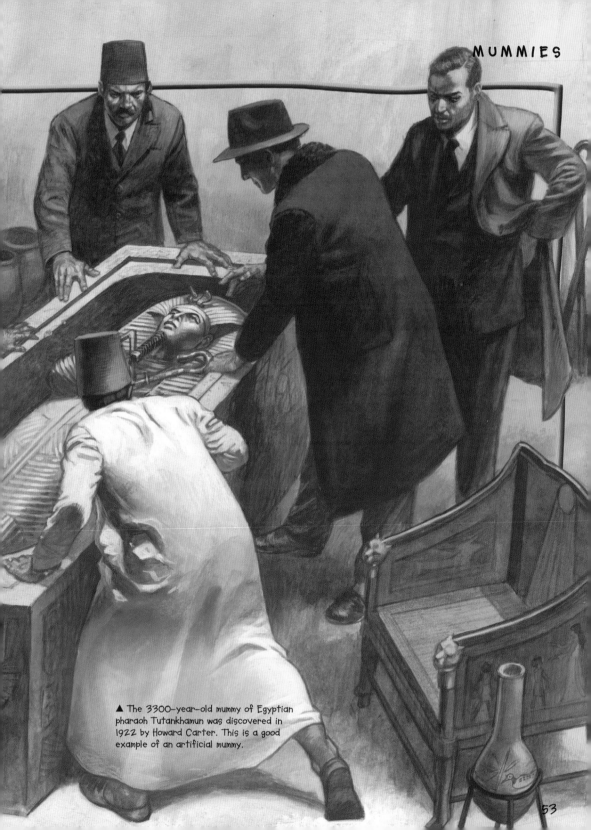

▲ The 3300-year-old mummy of Egyptian pharaoh Tutankhamun was discovered in 1922 by Howard Carter. This is a good example of an artificial mummy.

The first mummies

The first artificial mummies were made 7000 years ago by the Chinchorro people of South America. These people are named after a place in Chile. Here, scientists discovered traces of the way the Chinchorro lived. They were a fishing people who lived in small groups along the coast of the Pacific Ocean.

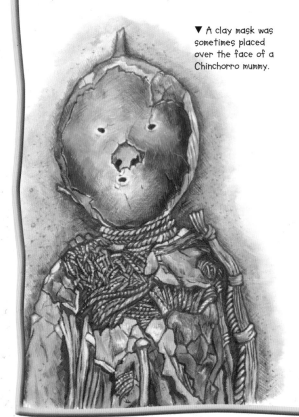

▼ A clay mask was sometimes placed over the face of a Chinchorro mummy.

It is thought that the Chinchorro made mummies because they believed in life after death. They tried to make a mummy look as lifelike as possible, which shows they did not want the person's body to rot away. Perhaps they thought the dead could live again if their bodies were preserved.

To make a mummy, the Chinchorro first removed all of a dead person's insides. The skin and flesh were then taken off the bones, which were left to dry. Then sticks were tied to the arm, leg and spine bones to hold them together. White mud was spread over the skeleton to build a body shape. The face skin was put back in place, and patches of skin were added to the body. When the mud was dry, it was painted black or red.

▼ Once the Chinchorro had removed all the skin and soft tissue, the body was rebuilt with sticks, mud and paint.

The Chinchorro made mummies for about 3000 years. Early mummies were painted black, but by the time of the last mummies, 4000 years ago, the Chinchorro were painting them red.

The first Chinchorro mummies were discovered in 1917, when 12 were found buried in northern Chile. In 1983, builders uncovered more of this ancient burial ground. About 100 ancient Chinchorro mummies were dug up at this site, and more have been found elsewhere in Chile.

Iceman of Europe

Europe's oldest human mummy is known as the Iceman. He died about 5300 years ago, at the end of the Stone Age. His mummy was discovered by hikers in northern Italy in 1991. They found it lying face down in an icy glacier.

When the Iceman was alive, arrows had sharp points made from flint (a type of stone). It was a flint arrowhead that injured the Iceman, piercing his clothes and entering his left shoulder. This arrow caused a deep wound. The Iceman pulled the long arrow shaft out, but the arrowhead remained inside his body. This injury would have made the Iceman weak, eventually causing him to die.

◀ The Iceman is the oldest complete human mummy ever to be found. He is so well preserved, even his eyes are still visible.

The Iceman mummy was found high up in the mountains, where it is very cold. At first, people thought that he was a shepherd, or a hunter on the search for food – or even a traveller on a journey. Then in 2001, an arrowhead was found in the Iceman's left shoulder. He might have fled into the mountains to escape danger.

The mummy's clothes were also preserved by the ice. For the first time, scientists saw how a Stone Age person actually dressed. The Iceman wore leggings and shoes made from leather, a goatskin coat, a bearskin hat and a cape made from woven grass. These would have kept the Iceman warm in the cold climate.

Equipment used by the Iceman was also found with him. He carried a copper axe, a flint dagger, and a bow and quiver with 14 arrows. He also had a leather pouch filled with dried grass, which he would have used for starting fires. If the Iceman had been a hunter, he would have killed animals, such as the mountain ibex (a type of goat), with his arrows.

Today, the Iceman mummy and his clothes and equipment are kept at a museum in northern Italy. Visitors are able to peep through a tiny window to see the Iceman, who is kept frozen inside a special room. The mummy must never be allowed to thaw, as this would cause it to rot.

Quiver to hold arrows

Leather pouch

Flint dagger

▶ This reconstruction of the Iceman shows how he would have looked on the day he died.

Copper axe

Shoes stuffed with grass for warmth

I DON'T BELIEVE IT!

At first, the Iceman was thought to be a modern person who had died in a recent accident on the mountain.

Bog bodies

Lots of mummies have been found in the peat bogs of northern Europe. Peat is a soily substance that is formed from plants that have fallen into pools of water. The plants sink to the bottom and are slowly turned into peat. If a dead body is placed in a bog, it may be preserved as a mummy. This is because there is little oxygen or bacteria to rot the body.

I DON'T BELIEVE IT!

When Tollund Man was found, scientists could only save his head. His body was left to dry until only the bones were left.

Bog bodies, or mummies, are usually found when peat is dug up. One of the best-known bodies was dug up at Tollund, Denmark, in 1950. Tollund Man, as he is known, died 2300 years ago. Around his neck was a leather noose. He was hanged, perhaps as a sacrifice to his gods, and then thrown in the bog. Over the years his face was perfectly preserved, right down to the whiskers on his chin!

▶ The face of Tollund Man is so well preserved, he looks as if he is sleeping.

Grauballe Man was also found in a peat bog in Denmark. He was discovered by peat workers near the village of Grauballe in 1852. About 2300 years ago, the man's throat was cut and he bled to death. His body was thrown into a bog, where it was preserved until its discovery.

▲ The head of Grauballe Man. Like all bog bodies, his skin has turned brown due to the acids in the bog.

Bog bodies have also been discovered in Germany. At Windeby, the body of a teenage girl was found. The girl, who died 1900 years ago, was wearing a blindfold. It seems she was taken to the bog, her eyes were covered, and then she was drowned. A heavy rock and branches were put on top of her body, so it sank to the bottom of the bog.

▶ The mummy of Windeby Girl revealed that some of her hair had been cut off, or shaved, at the time of her death.

From the Netherlands comes the bog body of another teenage girl. Known as Yde (*ay-de*) Girl, she was stabbed, strangled and then dumped in a bog around 1900 years ago. A medical artist made a copy of her skull, then covered it with wax to rebuild her face. The model shows scientists how Yde Girl may have looked when she was alive.

Lindow Man

A bog body of a man was found in north-west England in 1984. It was discovered by peat cutters at Lindow Moss, Cheshire. The mummy was named 'Lindow Man', but a local newspaper nicknamed it 'Pete Marsh' because a peat bog is a wet, marshy place! Lindow Man is now on display at the British Museum, London.

Lindow Man was about 20 years old when he died. His short life came to an end around 1900 years ago. After his death, his body was put in a bog, where it sank without trace until its discovery by the peat cutters.

▼ The body of Lindow Man was squashed flat by the weight of the peat on top of it.

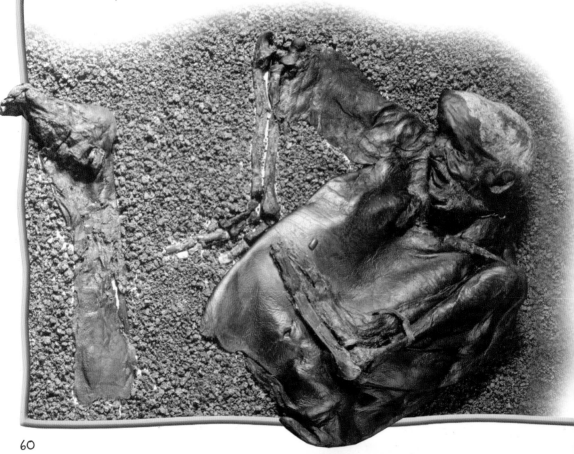

Lindow Man did not die peacefully. Before he died, he ate food with poisonous mistletoe in it. It's impossible to say if the poison was put there on purpose, or by accident. The marks on his body tell the story of his last moments alive. Someone hit him hard on the head, a cord was tightened around his neck and he was strangled. Then, to make sure he was dead, his throat was cut.

It took four years to find most of Lindow Man's body. The machine used to cut the peat had sliced it into pieces, which were found at different times. His top half, from the waist up, was found in 1984, and four years later his left leg turned up. His right leg is missing, possibly still buried in the peat bog.

▲ In this reconstruction, Lindow Man eats a meal containing burnt bread. This may have been part of a ceremony in which he was sacrificed to the gods.

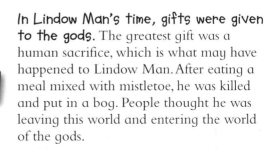

I DON'T BELIEVE IT!

Visitors to the British Museum have come up with names for Lindow Man, including Sludge Man and Man in the Toilet!

In Lindow Man's time, gifts were given to the gods. The greatest gift was a human sacrifice, which is what may have happened to Lindow Man. After eating a meal mixed with mistletoe, he was killed and put in a bog. People thought he was leaving this world and entering the world of the gods.

Mummies of ancient Egypt

▲ Even pet dogs were mummified in ancient Egypt.

The most famous mummies were made in ancient Egypt. The Egyptians were skilled embalmers (mummy-makers). Pharaohs (rulers of Egypt) and ordinary people were made into mummies, along with many kinds of animal.

▲ Two people walk through the Field of Reeds, which was the ancient Egyptian name for paradise.

Mummies were made because the Egyptians thought that the dead needed their bodies in a new life after death. They believed a person would live forever in paradise, but only if their body was saved. Every Egyptian wanted to travel to paradise after death. This is why they went to such trouble to preserve the bodies of the dead.

Ancient Egypt's first mummies were made by nature. When a person died, their body was buried in a pit in the desert sand. The person was buried with objects to use in the next life. Because the sand was hot and dry, the flesh did not rot. Instead, the flesh and skin dried and shrivelled until they were stretched over the bones. The body had been mummified. Egypt's natural mummies date from around 3500 BC.

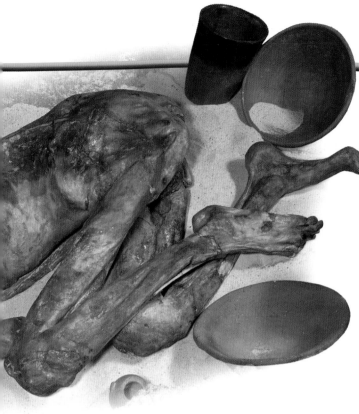

The ancient Egyptians made their first artificial mummies around 3400 BC. The last mummies were made around AD 400. This means the Egyptians were making mummies for 4000 years! They stopped making them because as the Christian religion spread to Egypt, mummy-making came to be seen as a pagan (non-Christian) practice.

◀ This man died 5200 years ago in Egypt. His body slowly dried out in the hot, desert conditions, and became a natural mummy.

When an old grave was found, perhaps by robbers who wanted to steal the grave goods, they got a surprise. Instead of digging up a skeleton, they uncovered a dried-up body that still looked like a person! This might have started the ancient Egyptians thinking – could they find a way to preserve bodies themselves?

▶ Many Egyptian coffins were shaped like a person and beautifully painted and decorated.

Egypt's first mummy

The ancient Egyptians told a myth about how the very first mummy was made. The story was about Osiris, who was ruler of Egypt. It explained how Osiris became the first mummy, and because it had happened to him, people wanted to follow his example and be mummified when they died.

The story begins with the murder of Osiris. He had a wicked brother called Seth, and one day Seth tricked Osiris into lying inside a box. The box was really a coffin. Seth shut the lid and threw the coffin into the river Nile, and Osiris drowned. Seth killed his brother because he was jealous of him – he felt the people of Egypt did not love him as much as they loved Osiris.

Isis was married to Osiris, and she could not bear to be parted from him. She searched throughout Egypt for his body, and when she found it, she brought it home. Isis knew that Seth would be angry if he found out what she had done, and so she hid the dead body of Osiris.

QUIZ

1. Who killed Osiris?
2. Who was the wife of Osiris?
3. How many pieces did Seth cut Osiris into?
4. Which three gods helped Isis?
5. What did Osiris become in the afterlife?

Answers:
1. Seth 2. Isis 3. 14
4. Ra, Anubis, Thoth
5. King of the dead

▶ Isis, Anubis and Thoth rebuild the body of Osiris to make the first mummy.

However Seth found out, and he took the body of Osiris from its hiding place. Seth cut Osiris into 14 pieces, which he scattered far and wide across Egypt. At last, he thought, he had finally got rid of Osiris.

Seth might have destroyed Osiris, but he could not destroy the love that Isis had for him. Once again, Isis searched for Osiris. She turned herself into a kite (a bird of prey), and flew high above Egypt so she could look down upon the land to see where Seth had hidden the body parts of Osiris. One by one, Isis found the pieces of her husband's body, except for one, which was eaten by a fish.

Isis brought the pieces together. She wept at the sight of her husband's body. When Ra, the sun god, saw her tears, he sent the gods Anubis and Thoth to help her. Anubis wrapped the pieces of Osiris' body in cloth. Then Isis, Anubis and Thoth laid them out in the shape of Osiris and wrapped the whole body. The first mummy had been made. Isis kissed the mummy and Osiris was reborn, not to live in this world, but to live forever in the afterlife as king of the dead.

A very messy job

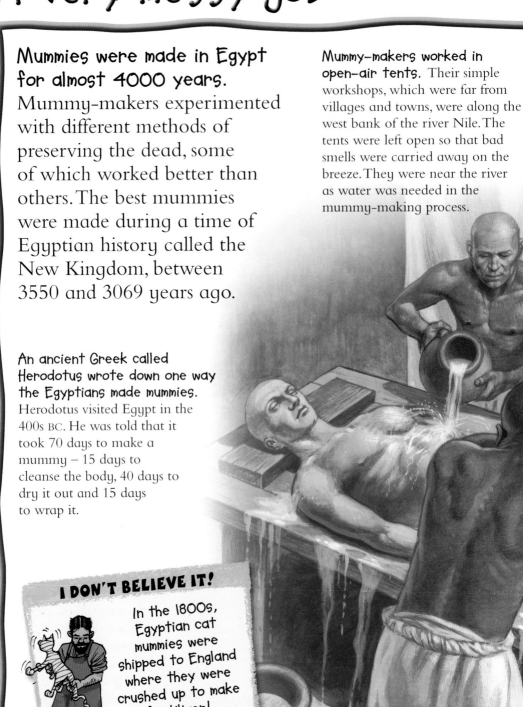

Mummies were made in Egypt for almost 4000 years. Mummy-makers experimented with different methods of preserving the dead, some of which worked better than others. The best mummies were made during a time of Egyptian history called the New Kingdom, between 3550 and 3069 years ago.

Mummy-makers worked in open-air tents. Their simple workshops, which were far from villages and towns, were along the west bank of the river Nile. The tents were left open so that bad smells were carried away on the breeze. They were near the river as water was needed in the mummy-making process.

An ancient Greek called Herodotus wrote down one way the Egyptians made mummies. Herodotus visited Egypt in the 400s BC. He was told that it took 70 days to make a mummy – 15 days to cleanse the body, 40 days to dry it out and 15 days to wrap it.

I DON'T BELIEVE IT!

In the 1800s, Egyptian cat mummies were shipped to England where they were crushed up to make fertilizer!

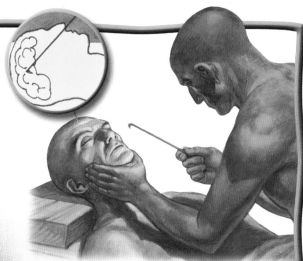

▶ To remove the brain, a metal hook was pushed up through the left nostril. It was then used to pull the brain out through the nose.

Mummy–making skills were handed down from one generation to the next. It was a job for men only, and it was a father's duty to train his son. A boy learned by watching his father at work. If his father worked as a slitter – the man who made the first cut in the body – his son also became a slitter.

The first 15 days of making a mummy involved cleaning the body. In the Place of Purification tent, the body was washed with salty water. It was then taken to the House of Beauty tent. Here, the brain was removed and thrown away. Then a slit was made in the left side of the body and the liver, lungs, intestines and stomach were taken out and kept.

The heart was left inside the body. The Egyptians thought the heart was the centre of intelligence. They believed it was needed to guide the person in the next life. If the heart was removed by mistake, it was put back inside. The kidneys were also left inside the body.

◀ A dead body was carefully washed with salty water before its organs were removed.

Drying the body

After the insides had been taken out, the body was dried. Mummy-makers used a special salt called natron to do the drying. The salt was a powdery-white mixture and was found along the edges of lakes in the north of Egypt. The natron was put into baskets, then taken to the mummy-makers.

The liver, lungs, intestines and stomach were also dried. Each of these organs was placed in a separate pottery bowl, and natron was piled on top. Just like the body, these organs were also left for 40 days, during which time the natron dried them out.

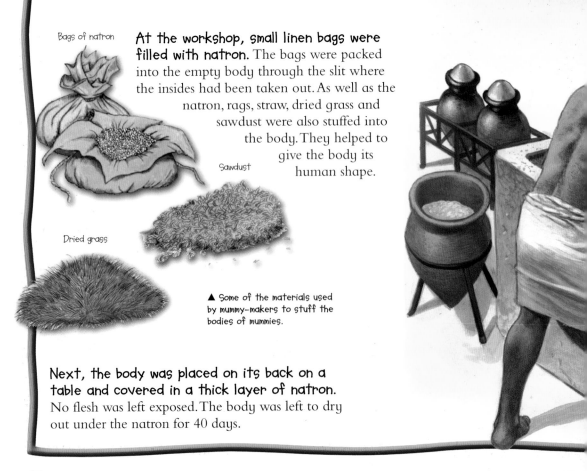

Bags of natron

Sawdust

Dried grass

At the workshop, small linen bags were filled with natron. The bags were packed into the empty body through the slit where the insides had been taken out. As well as the natron, rags, straw, dried grass and sawdust were also stuffed into the body. They helped to give the body its human shape.

▲ Some of the materials used by mummy-makers to stuff the bodies of mummies.

Next, the body was placed on its back on a table and covered in a thick layer of natron. No flesh was left exposed. The body was left to dry out under the natron for 40 days.

Fisherman first used natron to dry the fish they caught. They realized that natron's salty crystals sucked juices out of dead flesh, leaving it dry. Dried, or salted, fish did not rot. This was why the mummy-makers began to use natron to preserve the dead.

During the 40 days of drying, the natron absorbed the body's juices. At the end of this time, the mummy-makers scraped away the natron and removed the materials used to stuff the body. The dried body had lost about three-quarters of its original weight and was shrivelled, hard and blue-black in colour. It hardly looked like a body at all.

▲ The body was covered in natron, a kind of salt, to dry it out. Up to 225 kilograms were needed.

Wrapped from head to toe

The next job was to make the body appear lifelike. The body cavity was filled and the skin was rubbed with oil and spices to make it soft and sweet-smelling. Then it was given false eyes and a wig, and make-up was applied. Lastly, tree resin was poured over it. This set into a hard layer to stop mould growing.

The cut on the left side of the body was rarely stitched up. Instead, it was covered with a wax plaque. On the plaque was a design known as the Eye of Horus. The Egyptians believed it had the power to see evil and stop it from entering the body through the cut.

The dried-out organs were wrapped in linen, then put into containers called canopic jars. The container with the baboon head (the god Hapi) held the lungs, and the stomach was put into the jackal-headed jar (the god Duamutef). The human-headed jar (the god Imseti) protected the liver, and the intestines were placed in the falcon-headed jar (the god Qebehsenuef).

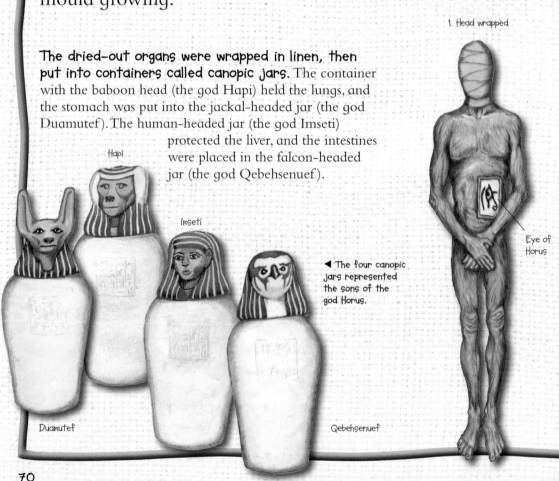

Hapi

Imseti

◄ The four canopic jars represented the sons of the god Horus.

Duamutef

Qebehsenuef

1. Head wrapped

Eye of Horus

In the final part of the process, the body was wrapped. It took 11 days to do this. The body was wrapped in strips of linen, 6 to 20 centimetres wide. There was a set way of wrapping the body, which always started with the head. Lastly, the body was covered with a sheet of linen, tied with linen bands.

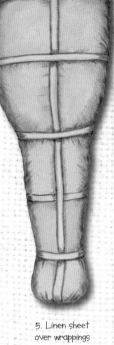

5. Linen sheet over wrappings

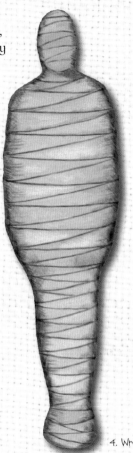

4. Wrapping complete

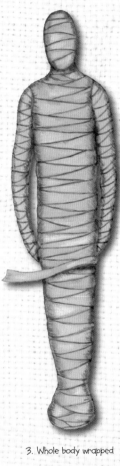

3. Whole body wrapped

▲ There was a five-stage sequence for wrapping the body, which always started with the head.

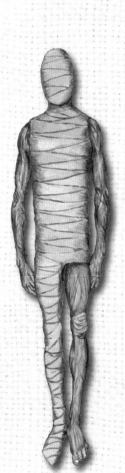

2. Limbs and torso wrapped

During the wrapping, amulets (lucky charms) were placed between the layers of linen. These protected the person from harm on their journey to the afterlife. Magic spells written on the wrappings were another form of protection. After it was wrapped, resin was poured over the mummy to make it waterproof. Last of all, it was given a face mask.

Tombs and tomb robbers

The body was placed in a wooden coffin. Simple coffins were made from planks of wood, and expensive ones were shaped like a person. They were decorated with spells. A picture on the inside of the coffin showed the route to the afterlife.

The earliest pharaohs (kings) were buried in pyramid tombs. The first pyramid was built about 2650 BC, for Pharaoh Djoser. For the next 800 years, all pharaohs were buried in pyramids. However robbers found their way into all of them. Later pharaohs were buried in tombs cut into a rocky valley, known as the Valley of the Kings. Robbers found many of these tombs too, but not all.

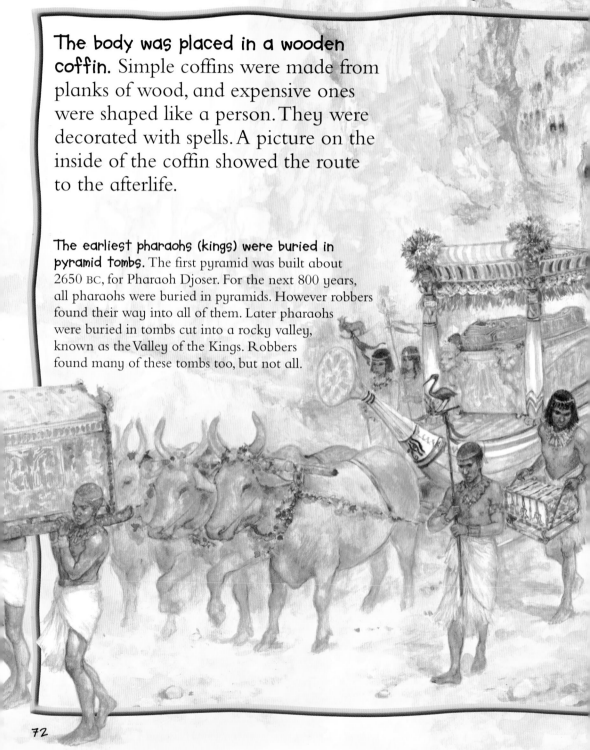

On the day of burial, the mummy was lifted out of its coffin and stood upright. A priest used a Y-shaped stone tool to touch the mummy's mouth, eyes, nose and ears. This was the Opening of the Mouth ceremony. It was done so that the person's speech, sight, hearing and smell came back to them for use in the next life.

▲ A priest (right) about to touch a mummy (left) in the Opening of the Mouth ceremony.

Mummies were buried with grave goods. These were items for the person to use in the next life. Ordinary people were buried with basic items, such as food and drink. Pharaohs and wealthy people were buried with everything they would need in their next life, such as furniture, clothes, weapons, jewellery and musical instruments.

Tombs were tempting places to robbers. They knew what was inside them, and took great risks to break in and steal the goods. Not even a mummy was safe – the tomb robbers smashed coffins open, and cut their way through the layers of linen wrappings to get at the masks, amulets and jewellery. Tomb robbery was a major crime, and if a robber was caught he was put to death.

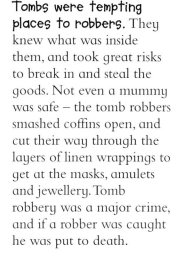

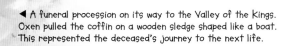

◀ A funeral procession on its way to the Valley of the Kings. Oxen pulled the coffin on a wooden sledge shaped like a boat. This represented the deceased's journey to the next life.

Tutankhamun, the boy-king

Tutankhamun is one of Egypt's most famous pharaohs. He became king in 1334 BC when he was eight years old. Because he was too young to carry out the important work of ruling Egypt, two of his ministers took charge. They were Ay, chief minister, and Horemheb, head of the army. They made decisions on Tutankhamun's behalf.

◀ This model of Tutankhamun was buried with him in his tomb.

Tutankhamun was pharaoh for about nine years. He died when he was 17 years old. His body was mummified and buried in a tomb cut into the side of a valley. Many pharaohs were laid to rest in this valley, known as the Valley of the Kings. Tutankhamun was buried with valuables for use in the next life.

The tombs in the Valley of the Kings were meant to be secret. However robbers found them, and stole the precious items buried there. They found Tutankhamun's tomb, but were caught before they could do much damage. Years later, when the tomb of Rameses VI was being dug, rubble rolled down the valley and blocked the entrance to Tutankhamun's tomb. After that, it was forgotten about.

In 1922, British archaeologist Howard Carter discovered the tomb of Tutankhamun. He had spent years searching for it. Other archaeologists thought he was wasting his time. They said all the tombs in the valley had already been found. Carter refused to give up, and in November 1922 he found a stairway that led to the door of a tomb.

◄ Found covering the head and shoulders of Tutankhamun's mummy, this beautiful mask features a royal cobra and a vulture's head, representing the unification of Upper and Lower Egypt.

▲ Tutankhamun's throne. The back is decorated with a picture of the pharaoh, who is seated, and a princess.

Behind the door was a corridor. At the end of it was a second door, which Carter made a hole in. He peered through the hole, and said he could see 'wonderful things'. It took ten years to remove all the objects from the tomb – jewellery and a gold throne were among the treasures. A gold mask covered the king's head and shoulders. It was made of 10 kilograms of pure gold.

Magnificent mummies!

The mummy of pharaoh Rameses II was found in 1871. It had been buried in a tomb, but had been moved to prevent robbers finding it. Rameses II had bad teeth, probably caused by eating gritty bread. He was in his eighties when he died and had arthritis, which would have given him painful joints. In 1976 his mummy was sent to France for treatment to stop mould from damaging it.

Mummy 1770 is in the Manchester Museum, in the UK. This is a mummy of a teenage girl, whose real name is not known. Her lower legs and feet are missing, and the mummy-makers had given her false ones to make her appear whole. It's a mystery what happened to her, but she might have been bitten by a crocodile, or even a hippo, as she paddled in the river Nile 3000 years ago.

▼ The mummy of Rameses II. Scientific studies have shown that particularly fine linen was used to stuff and bandage the body.

A trapped donkey led to the discovery of thousands of mummies! It happened in 1996, when a donkey slipped into a hole at Egypt's Bahariya Oasis. The owner freed it, then climbed down into an underground system of chambers lined with thousands of mummies of ordinary people. The site is called the Valley of the Golden Mummies, as many of the mummies have golden masks over their faces. They are about 2000 years old.

Djedmaatesankh – Djed for short – is an Egyptian mummy in the Royal Ontario Museum, Toronto, Canada. She lived around 850 BC, and in 1977 she entered the history books as the first Egyptian mummy to have a whole-body CAT scan (computerized axial tomography). The CAT images revealed that Djed had a serious infection in her jaw, which may have caused her death.

QUIZ

1. What was damaging Rameses II?
2. What is false about Mummy 1770?
3. What did a donkey help to find?
4. Which mummy had the first CAT scan?

Answers:
1. Mould 2. Her legs and feet 3. The Valley of the Golden Mummies 4. Djed

Mummies of Peru

Mummies were made in Peru, South America, for hundreds of years.
The first were made in the 400s BC, and the last probably in the early 1500s. A body was put into a sitting position, with its knees tucked under its chin. Layers of cloth were wrapped around it to make a 'mummy bundle'. The body was preserved by the dry, cold environment.

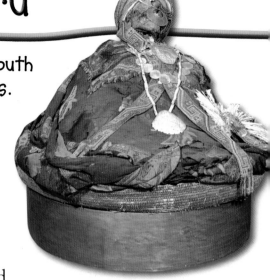

▲ This mummy from Peru is more than 500 years old. It was covered in cloth to make a 'mummy bundle'.

In the 1500s, the mummies of Inca emperors were paraded through the streets of Cuzco, Peru. People thought that by doing this the souls of the dead were well-cared for, and this helped them on their journey into the afterlife. People also believed that this practice pleased the gods, who then ensured that living people were healthy and happy.

▲ Mummies of emperors were carried through the streets and put on display to the public.

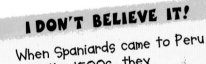

I DON'T BELIEVE IT!

When Spaniards came to Peru in the 1500s, they destroyed thousands of Inca mummies – they got rid of 1365 in just four years!

The Incas sacrificed children to their gods.
They hoped that in return the gods would
provide rain for crops, good health and
prosperity. The children's bodies were left at the
tops of freezing mountains, where they slowly
turned into natural mummies.

In 1995, the mummy of
a teenage Inca girl
was found. She was led
to her death 500 years
ago, as a sacrifice to the
gods. Her body was left
6300 metres up Mount
Ampato, Peru, with
offerings of cloth, food,
gold and silver. The icy
conditions preserved
her body.

▶ Inca children stand in front of a priest
as they prepare to be sacrificed to the
gods in a religious ceremony.

Mummies from Asia

More than 2500 years ago, the Pazyryk people of Siberia, Russia, buried their leaders in the region's frozen ground. In 1993, a Pazyryk burial mound was dug up, and inside was the frozen mummy of the 'Ice Princess'. She was dressed in clothes made from silk and wool, and she wore a pair of riding boots. When her body thawed from the ice, pictures of deer were found tattooed on her skin.

▲ The Pazyryk people tattooed images of snow leopards, eagles and reindeer onto their bodies. Those found on the 'Ice Princess' may have been a mark of her importance, or rank.

Lady Ch'eng is one of the world's best-preserved mummies. She was found in China, and is 2100 years old. Her body had been placed inside a coffin filled with a strange liquid that contained mercury (a silvery liquid metal, also known as quicksilver). The coffin was sealed and placed inside another, and then another. The coffins were buried under a mound of charcoal and clay, and in this watertight, airtight tomb, her body was preserved.

◀ This artist's impression shows how Lady Ch'eng may have looked when she was alive more than 2000 years ago.

QUIZ

1. What country did Vu khac Minh come from?
2. What metal was in Lady Ch'eng's coffin?
3. What was on the skin of the Ice Princess?
4. How old are the Taklamakan mummies?

Answers:
1. Vietnam 2. Mercury 3. Tattoos 4. 3000 years

Vu khac Minh was a Buddhist monk from Vietnam. In 1639, when he was near the end of his life, he locked himself in his room. He told his fellow monks to leave him alone for 100 days while he meditated (prayed). When this time was up, the monks found that he had died. His body was perfectly preserved and was put on view for all to see.

Mummies have been found in China's Taklamakan Desert. It hardly rains here, and the salty sand means that human bodies do not rot. It was a surprise when mummies were found in this remote place. They are about 3000 years old, and look Indo-European, not Chinese. It seems that long ago, a group of tall, light-skinned people settled in the east, where they died and were buried.

◀ Cherchen Man was just one of the many mummies found in the Taklamakan Desert.

North American mummies

At 9000 years old, Spirit Cave Man is one of the oldest mummies. The mummy was found in Spirit Cave, Nevada, USA, in 1940. It was wearing a cloak of animal skins, leather moccasins on its feet, and was wrapped inside mats made of tough grass. The cool, dry air in the cave had dried the body, turning it into a natural mummy.

▲ The mummy of Spirit Cave Man. Although it was discovered in 1940, the mummy's actual age was not determined until 1994.

I DON'T BELIEVE IT!

Hazel Farris, like Elmer McCurdy, was another American outlaw whose mummified body was put on show at funfairs.

A mummy family was found on Greenland in 1972. The bodies of six Inuit women and two children had been placed on a rocky ledge, in about 1475. The cold conditions had preserved them, slowly freeze-drying their bodies.

The mummy of the North American Iceman no longer exists. It was found in 1999, in Canada. The Iceman had died in the 1400s, and was preserved in a glacier. Native North Americans claimed that the man was their ancestor, so the mummy was handed to them. It was cremated, and the ashes buried near where the mummy had been found.

▲ An Inuit mummy of a baby boy. He was killed so that he could stay with his mother in the afterlife.

Elmer McCurdy was an American outlaw who became a mummy! He was shot dead in 1911 after robbing a train. His body was taken to an undertakers where it was preserved, but no one claimed the body. Eventually, McCurdy's mummy was sold to a fairground. In 1976, a TV programme was being filmed at a ghost ride, and a 'dummy' turned out to be the mummy of Elmer McCurdy! He was finally buried in 1977.

The mummies of three British sailors lie in the frozen ground of the Arctic. They are John Torrington, John Hartnell and William Braine, who died in 1845 during a voyage from England to find a sea route across the Arctic Ocean. Their bodies were examined in 1984, and it was discovered that they had suffered from lead poisoning, caused by eating contaminated food. The sailors were reburied, and the Arctic began to freeze their bodies again.

▼ The crew of HMS *Terror* try to dig their ship out of the Arctic ice. The men eventually died, and some of their remains were mummified in the freezing conditions.

Worldwide mummies

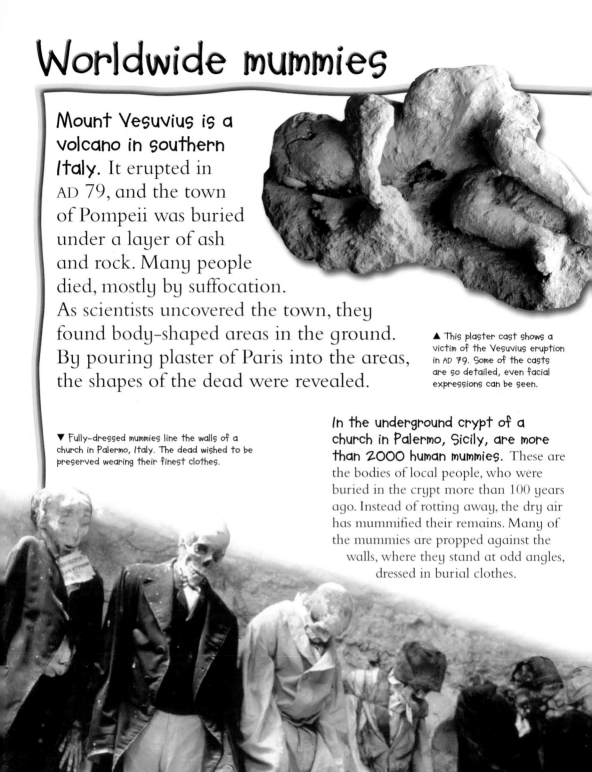

Mount Vesuvius is a volcano in southern Italy. It erupted in AD 79, and the town of Pompeii was buried under a layer of ash and rock. Many people died, mostly by suffocation. As scientists uncovered the town, they found body-shaped areas in the ground. By pouring plaster of Paris into the areas, the shapes of the dead were revealed.

▲ This plaster cast shows a victim of the Vesuvius eruption in AD 79. Some of the casts are so detailed, even facial expressions can be seen.

▼ Fully-dressed mummies line the walls of a church in Palermo, Italy. The dead wished to be preserved wearing their finest clothes.

In the underground crypt of a church in Palermo, Sicily, are more than 2000 human mummies. These are the bodies of local people, who were buried in the crypt more than 100 years ago. Instead of rotting away, the dry air has mummified their remains. Many of the mummies are propped against the walls, where they stand at odd angles, dressed in burial clothes.

The mummies of saints are displayed in many Roman Catholic churches. It isn't always the whole body that is on show, sometimes it is just a body part, called a 'relic'. Many of the mummies are natural, and are the result of being in a dry environment for many years. A few are artificial, and have been preserved on purpose. However, the Catholic Church believes that some saints have been preserved by God, and are evidence of miracles.

▲ The body of Saint Bernadette Soubirous (1844–1879) at Lourdes, France. Her body was exhumed (dug up) from her grave three times, and had not decomposed. People believed that she had been preserved by God.

In Japan, there are about 20 mummies of Buddhist priests. The mummy of Tetsumonkai is one of them. He died in 1829, and a few years before his death he started to prepare his body for mummification. He ate less, and stopped eating rice, barley, wheat, beans and millet, as he believed that they harmed the body. After he died, his fellow priests put him in a sitting position with his legs crossed, and then dried out his body.

◀ The mummy of Tetsumonkai. His fellow priests dried his body by placing burning candles around it.

Mummies have been made on the island of Papua New Guinea for generations. When a person died, they were put into a squatting position and their body was left to dry in the sun, or smoke-dried over a fire. Because the body was preserved, islanders believed their dead relatives were still living with them.

Studying mummies

Until recently, mummies were studied by opening them up. Unwrapping Egyptian mummies was popular in the 1800s, and was often done in front of an audience. Thomas Pettigrew (1791–1865) was an English surgeon who unwrapped many mummies at this time. He wrote some of the finest books about Egyptian mummies.

▲ An audience looks on as a mummy is unwrapped in the 1800s. This process destroyed lots of historical evidence.

There is no need to open up mummies today. Instead, mummies are studied by taking X-rays of bones, while scans reveal soft tissue in great detail. Mummies can even be tested to work out which families they came from.

▼ A Polish scientist prepares a 3000-year-old Egyptian mummy for an X-ray.

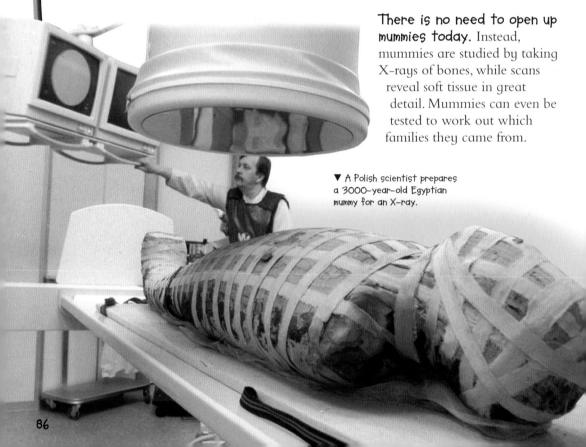

▶ This X-ray of a mummy's skull reveals that a fractured skull was the cause of death.

We can learn about the diseases and injuries people suffered by studying mummies. Egyptian mummies have been studied the most. We can tell they had problems with their health. Gritty bread damaged their teeth, parasites (worms) entered their bodies when they drank polluted water, insect bites caused fevers, and hard work led to problems with their joints and bones.

French emperor Napoleon Bonaparte was fascinated by mummies. After defeating the British in 1798, Napoleon and his troops became stranded in Egypt. With Napoleon were 150 scientists, who began to study Egypt and its mummies.

▼ When Napoleon left Egypt in 1799, he left behind a team of historians and scientists to study Egypt for him.

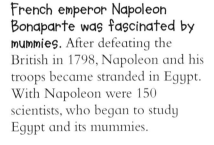

Animal mummies

Animals were mummified in ancient Egypt, too!
Birds and fish were mummified as food for a dead person in the next life. Pet cats, dogs and monkeys became mummies so they could keep their dead owners company. Some bulls were believed to be holy as it was thought the spirits of the gods lived inside them. When they died, the bulls were mummified and buried in an underground tomb.

▲ Crocodiles were sacred to the Egyptian god Sobek. They were probably mummified in the same way as humans, then wrapped up.

▼ Red fur is still visible around the feet of Dima, the baby mammoth.

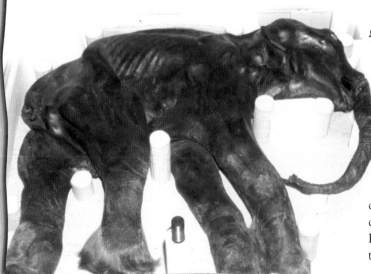

A baby mammoth was found in the frozen ground of Siberia in 1977. Many of these ancient elephant-like animals have been found in this part of Russia. What made this one special was the near-perfect state of its body. The animal was about a year old when it died, and was named Dima, after a stream close to where it was discovered.

QUIZ

1. How old is Dima?
2. Which animal is linked to the goddess Bastet?
3. What did Charles Sternberg find?
4. Did the Egyptians mummify crocodiles?

Answers:
1. 40,000 years old 2. Cat
3. A mummy of a dinosaur 4. Yes

The world's oldest mummy is a dinosaur! It is the fossil of an *Edmontosaurus*, which was found in Wyoming, USA, in 1908. This dinosaur died 65 million years ago, but instead of becoming a skeleton, its body was baked dry by the sun. When US fossil hunter Charles Sternberg discovered it, the skin and insides had been fossilized, as well as the bones.

▲ This frog was naturally mummified in 2006 when it died in a plant pot. The sun baked it dry.

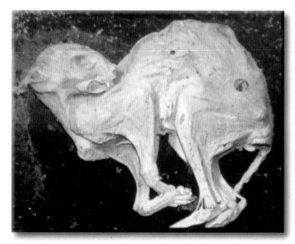

▲ This mummified cat was found in 1971 in Sudbury, Suffolk, UK. It had been walled up in an old mill to protect the building from harm.

Cats have been made into mummies for thousands of years. In ancient Egypt, cats were linked to the goddess, Bastet. They were bred to be killed as religious offerings at temples. Cat mummies are sometimes found behind the walls of old houses in Europe. It was believed a cat could bring good fortune, so a cat's body was sometimes walled up, after which it dried out until it was a natural mummy.

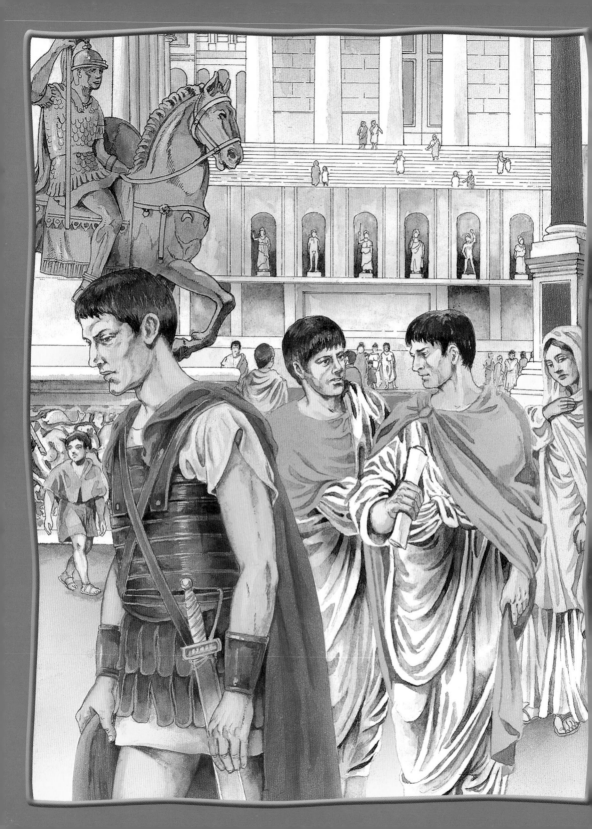

Ancient Rome

Discover a time when the mighty Romans ruled a vast empire. Take your seat in the arena and let the games begin!

Gladiators • Army • Food • Slaves • Religion
Chariots • Power • School • Empire • Medicine
Emperors • Language • Roads • Laws • Clothes
Farming • Sacrifices • Cities • Religion

The centre of an empire

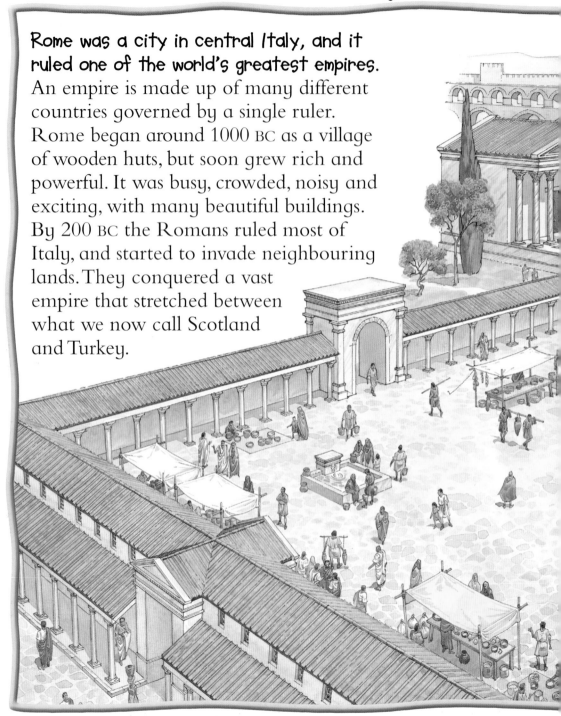

Rome was a city in central Italy, and it ruled one of the world's greatest empires. An empire is made up of many different countries governed by a single ruler. Rome began around 1000 BC as a village of wooden huts, but soon grew rich and powerful. It was busy, crowded, noisy and exciting, with many beautiful buildings. By 200 BC the Romans ruled most of Italy, and started to invade neighbouring lands. They conquered a vast empire that stretched between what we now call Scotland and Turkey.

Capital city

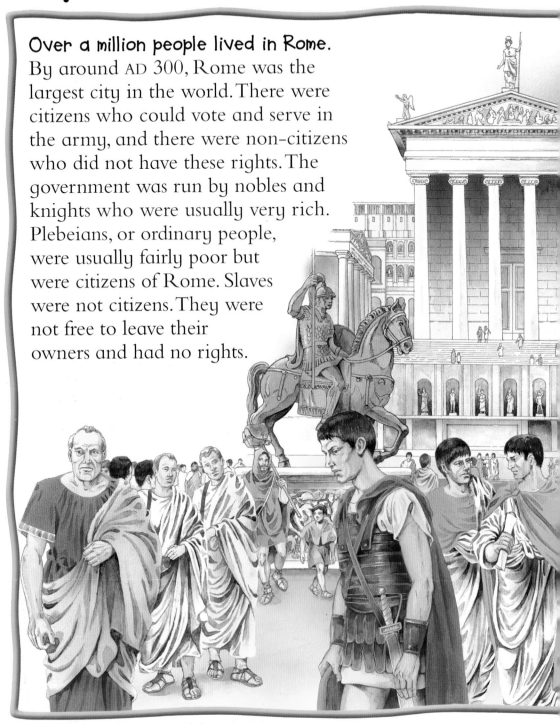

Over a million people lived in Rome.
By around AD 300, Rome was the
largest city in the world. There were
citizens who could vote and serve in
the army, and there were non–citizens
who did not have these rights. The
government was run by nobles and
knights who were usually very rich.
Plebeians, or ordinary people,
were usually fairly poor but
were citizens of Rome. Slaves
were not citizens. They were
not free to leave their
owners and had no rights.

▼ The Forum was the government district in Rome. People went there to meet their friends and business colleagues, discuss politics, and to listen to famous orators who made speeches in the open air.

The Romans were great water engineers. They designed aqueducts, rasied channels to carry water from streams in far-away hills and mountains to the city. The richest Roman homes were supplied with constant running water carried in lead pipes. Ordinary people had to drink from public fountains.

Rome relied on its drains. Rome was so crowded that good drains were essential. Otherwise, the citizens could have caught diseases from sewage and died. The largest sewer, called the 'cloaca maxima', was so high and so wide that a horse and cart could drive through it.

Rome was a well-protected city. It was surrounded by 50 kilometres of strong stone walls, to keep out attackers. All visitors had to enter the city through one of its 37 gates, which were guarded by soldiers and watchmen.

I DON'T BELIEVE IT!

Roman engineers also designed public lavatories. These lavatories were convenient, but not private. Users sat on rows of seats, side by side!

City life

The Romans built the world's first high-rise apartments. Most of the people who lived in Ostia, a busy port close to Rome, had jobs connected with trade, such as shipbuilders and money-changers. They lived in blocks of flats known as 'insulae'. A typical block was three or four storeys high, with up to a hundred small, dirty, crowded rooms.

Rich Romans had more than one home. Rome was stuffy, dirty and smelly, especially in summer time. Wealthy Roman families liked to get away from the city to cleaner, more peaceful surroundings. They purchased a house (a 'villa urbana') just outside the city, or a big house surrounded by farmland (a 'villa rustica') in the countryside far away from Rome.

Many Roman homes had a pool, but it was not used for swimming! Pools were built for decoration, in the central courtyards of large Roman homes. They were surrounded by plants and statues. Some pools had a fountain; others had mosaics – pictures made of tiny coloured stones or squares of glass – covering the floor.

MAKE A PAPER MOSAIC

You will need:

large sheet of paper   scissors
pencil   glue
scraps of coloured and textured paper

Draw the outlines of your design on a large sheet of paper. Plan which colours to use for different parts of the mosaic.

Cut the paper scraps into small squares, all roughly the same size. The simplest way to do this is to cut strips, then snip the strips into squares.

Stick the paper squares onto the large sheet of paper following the outlines of your design.

Fortunate families had hot feet.

Homes belonging to wealthy families had underfloor central heating. Blasts of hot air, warmed by a wood-burning furnace, circulated in channels built beneath the floor. The furnace was kept burning by slaves who chopped wood and stoked the fire.

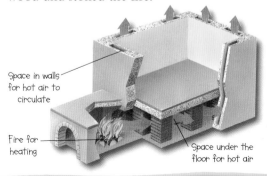

Space in walls for hot air to circulate

Fire for heating

Space under the floor for hot air

Rome had its own fire brigade. The
7000 firemen were all specially trained freed slaves. Ordinary families could not afford central heating, so they warmed their rooms with fires in big clay pots which often set the house alight.

Going shopping

Rome housed the world's first shopping mall. It was called Trajan's Market, and was built on five different levels on the slopes of the Quirinal Hill in the centre of Rome. It contained over 150 different shops together with a large main hall.

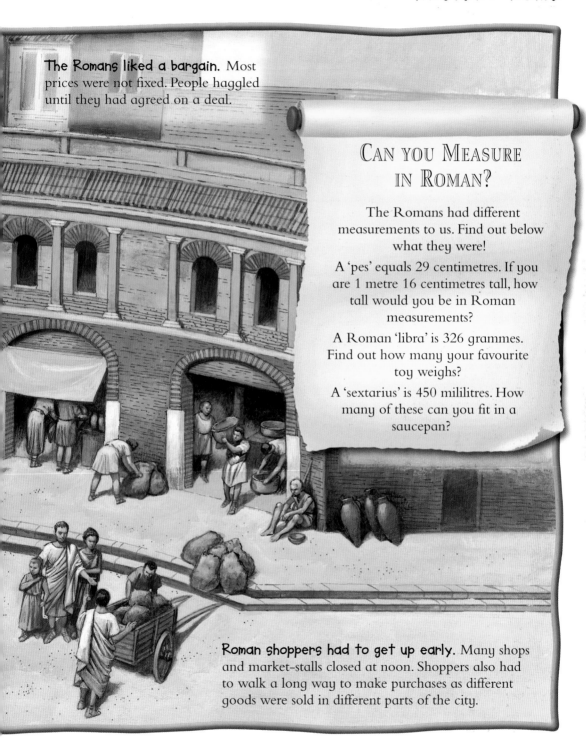

The Romans liked a bargain. Most prices were not fixed. People haggled until they had agreed on a deal.

CAN YOU MEASURE IN ROMAN?

The Romans had different measurements to us. Find out below what they were!

A 'pes' equals 29 centimetres. If you are 1 metre 16 centimetres tall, how tall would you be in Roman measurements?

A Roman 'libra' is 326 grammes. Find out how many your favourite toy weighs?

A 'sextarius' is 450 mililitres. How many of these can you fit in a saucepan?

Roman shoppers had to get up early. Many shops and market-stalls closed at noon. Shoppers also had to walk a long way to make purchases as different goods were sold in different parts of the city.

Eating and drinking

Most Romans ate very little during the day. They had bread and water for breakfast and a light snack of bread, cheese or fruit around midday. They ate their main meal at about 4 o'clock. In rich people's homes, a meal would have three separate courses, and could last for up to three hours! Poor people ate much simpler foods, such as soups made with lentils and onions, barley porridge, peas, cabbage and tough, cheap cuts of meat stewed in vinegar.

Only rich Roman people had their own kitchen. They could afford to employ a chef with slaves to help him in the kitchen. Ordinary people went to 'popinae' (cheap eating houses) for their main meal, or bought ready-cooked snacks from roadside fast food stalls.

At parties, the Romans ate lying down. Men and women lay on long couches arranged round a table. They also often wore crowns of flowers, and took off their sandals before entering the dining room.

REAL ROMAN FOOD!

PATINA DE PIRIS (Pear Soufflé)
Ingredients:

1kg pears (peeled and cored)	a little bit of oil
	pinch of salt
	½ tsp cumin
6 eggs (beaten)	ground pepper
4 tbsp honey	to taste

Make sure that you ask an adult to help you with this recipe. Mash the pears together with the pepper, cumin, honey, and a bit of oil. Add the beaten eggs and put into a casserole. Cook for approximately 30 minutes in a moderate oven. Serve with a little bit of pepper sprinkled on top.

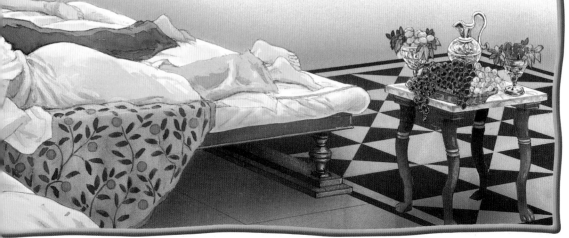

◄ Dishes served at a Roman banquet might include shellfish, roast meat, eggs, vegetables, fresh fruits, pastries and honeyed wine. The Romans enjoyed strong-flavoured, spicy food, and also sweet-sour flavours.

School days

Roman boys learned how to speak well. Roman schools taught three main subjects, reading, maths – and public speaking. Boys needed all three skills for their future careers. There were no newspapers or television, so politicians, army leaders and government officials all had to make speeches in public, explaining their plans and policies to Roman crowds. Boys went to school from around seven years old and left aged 16.

▼ Roman schoolboys practise reading with their slave schoolmaster.

▼ A girl is taught to play the lyre.

Roman girls did not go to school. They mostly stayed at home, where their mothers, or women slaves, taught them how to cook, clean, weave cloth and look after children. Girls from rich families, or families who ran a business, also learned to read, write and keep accounts.

Many of the best teachers were slaves. Schoolmasters and private tutors often came from Greece. They were purchased by wealthy people who wanted to give their sons a good education. The Greeks had a long tradition of learning, which the Romans admired.

The Romans wrote a lot — but not on paper. They used thin slices of wood for letters and day-to-day business. For notes Romans used flat wooden boards covered with wax, as the wax could be smoothed over and used again. For important documents that they wanted to keep, the Romans used cleaned and polished calfskin, or papyrus.

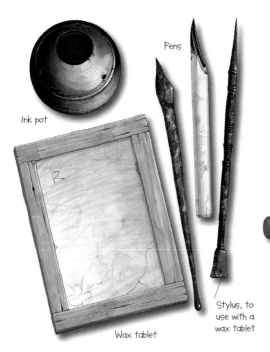

Pens

Ink pot

Wax tablet

Stylus, to use with a wax tablet

Romans made ink from soot. To make black ink, the Romans mixed soot from wood fires with vinegar and a sticky gum that oozed from the bark of trees. This sounds like a strange mixture, but some Roman writing has survived for almost 2000 years.

Rome had many libraries. Some were public, and open to everyone, others belonged to rich families and were kept shut away in their houses. It was fashionable to sponsor writers and collect their works.

Many Romans read standing up — it was easier that way. It took time and patience to learn how to read from a papyrus scroll. Most were at least 10 metres long. Readers held the scroll in their right hand, and a stick in their left hand. They unrolled a small section of the scroll at a time.

LEARN SOME ROMAN WORDS!

The Romans spoke a language called Latin. It forms the basis of many languages today, and below you can learn some Latin for yourself!

liber = book   epistola = letter

bibliotheca = library

vellum = calfskin

stylus = writing stick
(used with wax tablets)

librarii = slaves who work in a library

grammaticus = schoolmaster

paedagogus = private tutor

Father knows best!

A Roman father had the power of life and death over his family. According to Roman law, each family had to be headed by a man. He was known as the 'paterfamilias' (father of a family), and was usually the oldest surviving male. The buildings of the house and its contents belonged to him, and he had the right to punish any family members who misbehaved. Even his mother and other older female relatives were expected to obey him.

▲ The Romans gave a good luck charm, called a bulla, to their babies.

Roman families included more than blood relations. To the Romans, a 'family' meant all the people living and working together in the same household. So families included many different slaves and servants, as well as a husband and wife and their children.

▲ This carving shows a Roman wedding. The bride and groom are in the centre, with a priestess behind them.

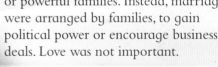

I DON'T BELIEVE IT!

The Romans invented Valentine's Day, but called it Lupercalia. Boys picked a girl's name from a hat, and she was meant to be their girlfriend for the year!

Sons were valued more than daughters.
The Romans preferred boys to girls. Boys would grow up to carry on the family name. They might also bring fame and honour to a family by achievements in government, politics and war. They might marry a rich wife, which helped to make the whole family richer, or win friends among powerful people.

Childhood was short for a Roman girl.
Roman law allowed girls to get married at 12 years old, and many had become mothers by the time they were 15. Roman girls could not choose whom to marry, especially if they came from rich or powerful families. Instead, marriages were arranged by families, to gain political power or encourage business deals. Love was not important.

Roman families liked to keep pets.
Roman statues and paintings show many children playing with their pets. Dogs, cats and doves were all popular. Some families also kept ornamental fish and tame deer.

Roman style

Most Roman clothes were made without sewing. Roman men and women wore loose-fitting robes, made of long strips of cloth. They were draped round the body, and held in place by pins, brooches or belts. Most women wore several layers. These were a thin shift, a 'tunica', a long, sleeveless dress called a 'stola', and a thick cloak called a 'palla'. Men wore a knee-length tunic, a 'colobium', with a semi-circular cloak, a 'toga', over the top.

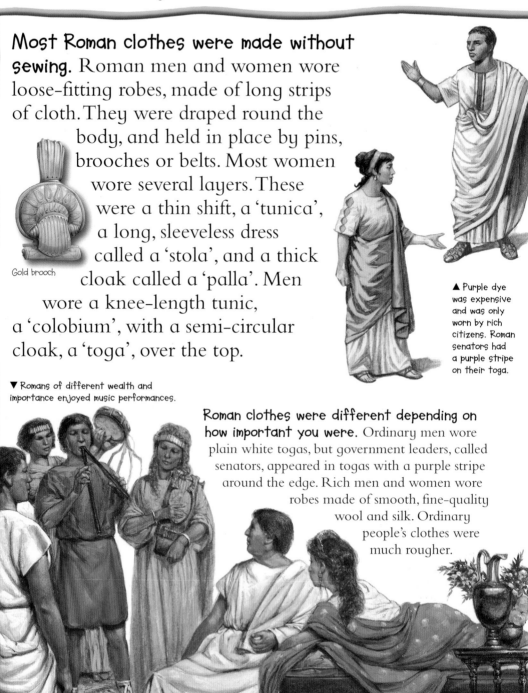

Gold brooch

▲ Purple dye was expensive and was only worn by rich citizens. Roman senators had a purple stripe on their toga.

▼ Romans of different wealth and importance enjoyed music performances.

Roman clothes were different depending on how important you were. Ordinary men wore plain white togas, but government leaders, called senators, appeared in togas with a purple stripe around the edge. Rich men and women wore robes made of smooth, fine-quality wool and silk. Ordinary people's clothes were much rougher.

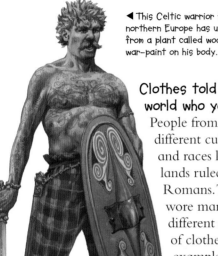

◄ This Celtic warrior from northern Europe has used dye from a plant called woad as war-paint on his body.

Clothes told the world who you were.

People from many different cultures and races lived in lands ruled by the Romans. They wore many different styles of clothes. For example, men from Egypt wore wigs and short linen kilts. Celtic women from northern Europe wore long woollen shawls, woven in brightly coloured checks. Celtic men wore trousers.

▼ These Roman sandals have metal studs in the soles to make sure that they don't wear down too quickly!

DRESS LIKE A ROMAN!

You can wear your very own toga! Ask an adult for a blanket or a sheet, then follow the instructions below!

First ask an adult to find you a blanket or sheet. White is best, like the Romans.

Drape your sheet over your left shoulder. Now pass the rest behind your back.

Pull the sheet across your front, so that you're wrapped up in it. You're almost a Roman now!

Finally, drape the last end over your right hand and there you have it, a Roman toga!

Roman boots were made for walking!

Roman soldiers and travellers wore lace-up boots with thick leather soles studded with iron nails. Other Roman footwear included 'socci', loose-fitting slippers to wear indoors. Farmers wore shoes made of a single piece of ox-hide wrapped round the foot, called 'carbatinae'. There were also 'crepidae', comfortable lace-up sandals with open toes.

Looking good

Just like today, hairstyles changed according to fashion. All free-born Roman women grew their hair long as short hair was a sign of slavery. In early Roman times the fashion was for plain and simple styles. Later on, most women wore their hair smoothed down and tied back tightly. Roman men usually wore short hair, and were mostly clean-shaven, except when they were old.

◄ Rich women spent a lot of time on their hair. Pins of ivory and bone were used to keep some elaborate styles in place.

The Romans painted their faces. The Romans admired pale, smooth skin. Women, and some men, used stick-on patches of cloth called 'splenia' to cover spots, and wore lots of make-up. They used crushed chalk or white lead as face-powder, red ochre (crumbly earth) for blusher, plant juice for lipstick and wood-ash or powdered antimony (a silvery metal) as eye-liner.

Blonde hair was highly prized. Most Romans were born with wiry dark brown hair. Some fashionable people admired delicate blonde hair because it was unusual. Roman women used vinegar and lye (an early form of soap, made from urine and wood-ash) to bleach their own hair.

QUIZ

If you had to dress up as a Roman, what clothes would you wear? Use the information on this and the previous page to help you draw a picture of the clothes you would need and how you might arrange your hair. Will you be a rich governor, a Celtic warrior or a soldier?

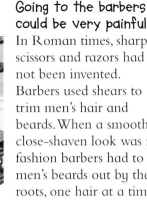

Going to the barbers could be very painful. In Roman times, sharp scissors and razors had not been invented. Barbers used shears to trim men's hair and beards. When a smooth, close-shaven look was in fashion barbers had to pull men's beards out by the roots, one hair at a time!

Olive oil

Flowers to make perfume

Bark used for perfume

Star anise to make perfume

Olives

Saffron for eyeshadow

Ash to darken eyelids

Perfume bottle made of onyx, a kind of black stone

Romans liked to smell sweet. They used olive oil (made from the crushed fruit of the olive tree) to cleanse and soften their skins, and perfumes to scent their bodies. Ingredients for perfume came from many different lands – flowers came from southern Europe, spices came from India and Africa, and sweet-smelling bark and resin came from Arabia.

Roman combs were made from bone, ivory or wood. Like combs today, they were designed to smooth and untangle hair, and were sometimes worn as hair ornaments. But they had another, less pleasant, purpose – they were used for combing out all the little nits and lice!

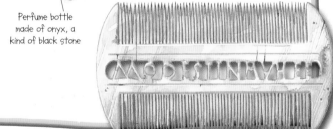

Bath time

The Romans went to the public baths in order to relax.
These huge buildings were more than a place to get clean.
They were also fitness centres and places to meet friends.
Visitors could take part in sports, such as wrestling, do
exercises, have a massage or a haircut. They could buy
scented oils and perfumes, read a book, eat a snack or
admire works of art in the baths own sculpture gallery!

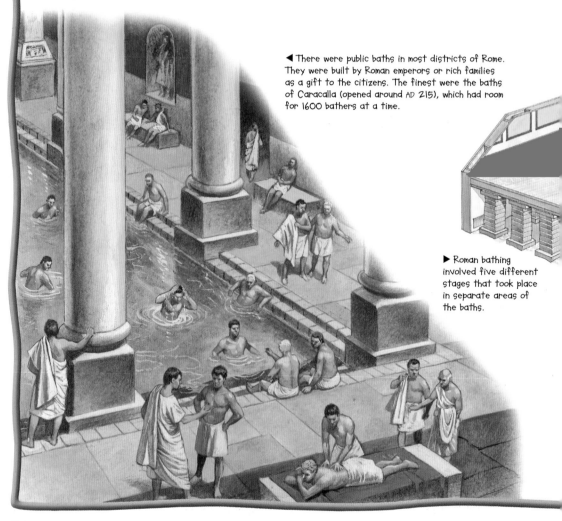

◀ There were public baths in most districts of Rome.
They were built by Roman emperors or rich families
as a gift to the citizens. The finest were the baths
of Caracalla (opened around AD 215), which had room
for 1600 bathers at a time.

▶ Roman bathing
involved five different
stages that took place
in separate areas of
the baths.

Men and women could not bathe together. Women usually went to the baths in the mornings, while most men were at work. Men went to the baths in the afternoons.

I DON'T BELIEVE IT!

Although the Romans liked bathing, they only visited the baths once in every nine days!

The 'frigidarium' had the coldest pool

The 'tepidarium' had a cool, or tepid, pool

The hot room was called the 'caldarium'

Fires heat the water for the hot rooms

Bathing wasn't simple. There were five separate stages to taking a bath Roman-style. After changing, bathers went into a very hot room, which was full of steam where they sat for a while. Then they went into a hot, dry room, where a slave removed all the sweat and dirt from their skin, using a metal scraper and olive oil. To cool off, they went for a swim in a tepid pool. Finally, they jumped into a bracing cold pool.

Having fun

The Romans liked music and dancing. Groups of buskers played in the streets, or could be hired to perform at private parties. Among ordinary families, favourite instruments included pipes, flutes, cymbals, castanets and horns. Rich, well-educated people, though, thought the noise they made was vulgar. They preferred the quieter, gentler sound of the lyre, which was played to accompany poets and singers.

▲ Roman buskers play music in the street.

Scenery could be very complicated, so it was moved around by complex machinery

Stage, or 'pulpitum'

Romans theatre-goers preferred comedies to tragedies. Comic plays had happy endings, and made audiences laugh. Tragedies were more serious, and ended with misery and suffering. The Romans also liked clowns, and invented mime, a story told without words, through gestures, acrobatic movements and dance.

Plays were originally part of religious festivals. Many famous dramas showed scenes from ancient myths and legends, and were designed to make people think about morals and politics. Later, plays were written on all sorts of topics – including politics and current affairs. Some were paid for by rich politicians, to spread their political message. They handed out free tickets to Roman citizens, hoping to win votes.

Roman actors all wore masks. Masks helped the audience in big theatres see what each character was feeling. They were carved and painted in bright colours, with larger than life features and exaggerated expressions. Some masks were happy, some were frightened, some were sad.

◀ All the parts in Roman plays were performed by men. For women's roles, men wore masks and dressed in female costume. Women could not be actors, except in mime.

Other favourite pastimes included games of skill and chance. Roman adults and children enjoyed dice and knucklebones, which needed nimble fingers, and draughts which relied on luck and quick thinking. They played these for fun, but adults also made bets on who would win.

Theatres were huge well-built structures. One of the best preserved Roman theatres is at Orange, in southern France. It has seats for almost 10,000 people. It is so cleverly designed, that the audience can hear the actors even from the back row.

I DON'T BELIEVE IT!

Roman actors were almost all men. Some were as popular as TV stars today. Women couldn't sit near the stage, in case they tried to arrange a date with one of the stars!

Let the games begin!

Romans admired gladiators for their strength, bravery and skill. However, gladiators' lives were short and their deaths were horrible. They were sent to the arena to fight – and suffer – until they died.

Large fork, called a trident

Net to trap opponent

Gladius, a gladiator's sword

Greaves to protect the legs

Most gladiators did not choose to fight. They were either prisoners-of-war or criminals who were sold to fight-trainers who organized gladiator shows. Some were specially trained, so that they would survive for longer and provide better entertainment for the watching crowds.

Gladiators fought wild beasts, as well as each other. Fierce wild animals were brought from distant parts of the Roman empire to be killed by gladiators in the arenas in Rome. So many lions were taken from North Africa that they became extinct there.

The Colosseum was an amazing building for its time. Also known as the Flavian Amphitheatre, the Colosseum was a huge oval arena in the centre of Rome, used for gladiator fights and mock sea-battles. It opened in AD 80, and could seat 50,000 people. It was built of stone, concrete and marble and had 80 separate entrances. Outside, it was decorated with statues of famous Roman heroes.

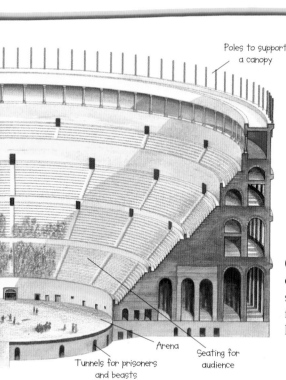

Poles to support a canopy

Arena

Tunnels for prisoners and beasts

Seating for audience

▲ The Colosseum was the largest amphitheatre in the Roman empire.

Chariots often collided and overturned. Each charioteer carried a sharp knife, called a 'falx', to cut himself free from the wreckage. Even so, many horses and charioteers were killed.

I DON'T BELIEVE IT!

Some gladiators became so popular that people used to write graffiti about them on the walls of buildings around Rome!

Some Romans preferred a day at the races. Horses pulled fast chariots round race-tracks, called 'circuses'. The most famous was the Circus Maximus in Rome, which had room for 250,000 spectators. There could be up to 24 races each day. Twelve chariots took part in each race, running seven times round the oval track – a total distance of about 8 kilometres.

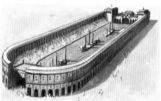

The Circus Maximus

Racing rivalries sometimes led to riots. Races were organized by four separate teams – the Reds, Blues, Greens and Whites. Charioteers wore tunics in their teams' colours. Each team had a keen – and violent – group of fans.

Ruling Rome

Rome used to be ruled by kings.
According to legend, the first king was Romulus, who came to power in 753 BC. Six more kings ruled after him, but they were unjust and cruel. The last king, Tarquin the Proud, was overthrown in 509 BC. After that, Rome became a republic, a state without a king. Every year the people chose two senior lawyers called consuls to head the government. Many other officials were elected, or chosen by the people, too. The republic lasted for over 400 years.

▼ Senators were men from leading citizen families who had served the Roman republic as judges or state officials. They made new laws and discussed government plans.

▲ Roman coin showing the emperor Constantine.

In 47 BC a successful general called Julius Caesar declared himself dictator.
This meant that he wanted to rule on his own for life. Many people feared that he was trying to end the republic, and rule like the old kings. Caesar was murdered in 44 BC by a group of his political enemies. After this, there were many years of civil war.

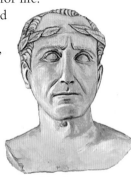

Julius Caesar

In 27 BC an army general called Octavian seized power in Rome.
He declared himself 'First Citizen', and said he would bring back peace and good government to Rome. He ended the civil war, and introduced many strong new laws. But he also changed the Roman government for ever. He took a new name, 'Augustus' and became the first emperor of Rome.

Octavian

◀ Roman courts were busy places. There was a public gallery where people could watch cases that interested them. People who were accused of crime and refused to go to court, could be made by force to attend. Lawyers called advocatus spoke on their behalf.

The Romans were proud of their laws. Everyone in Rome, from the emperor to the poorest beggar, was expected to obey the law. The first rules of the Roman legal system were recorded in 450 BC in a document called the Twelve Tables. Roman laws were strict but fair. Everyone was considered innocent until they had been proved guilty in an open trial. The Roman system forms the basis of many legal systems today.

I DON'T BELIEVE IT!

Some Roman emperors were mad and dangerous. The Emperor Nero was said to have laughed and played music while watching a terrible fire that destroyed a large part of Rome.

In the army

Being a soldier was a good career, if you did not get killed! Roman soldiers were well paid and well cared for. The empire needed troops to defend its land against enemy attack. A man who fought in the Roman army received a thorough training in battle skills. If he showed promise, he might be promoted and receive extra pay. When he retired after 20 or 25 years of service, he was given money or land to help him start a business.

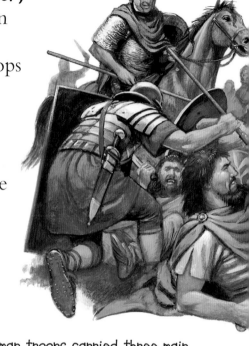

The Roman army contained citizens and 'helpers'. Roman citizens joined the regular army, which was organized into legions of around 5000 men. Men who were not citizens could also fight for Rome. They were known as auxiliaries, or helpers, and were organized in special legions of their own.

Roman troops carried three main weapons. They fought with javelins, swords and daggers. Each man had to buy his own set. He looked after them carefully – one day, his life might depend on them.

▶ Soldiers used their shields to make a protective shell. It was called a 'testudo', or tortoise.

▼ Roman troops defended the empire from attack, they were well paid but it was a dangerous job.

The army advanced 30 kilometres every day. When they were hurrying to put down a rebellion, or moving from fort to fort, Roman soldiers travelled quickly, on foot. Troops marched along straight, well-made army roads. On the march, each soldier had to carry a heavy pack. It contained weapons, armour, tools for building a camp, cooking pots, dried food and spare clothes.

Soldiers needed many skills. In enemy territory, soldiers had to find or make everything they needed to survive. When they first arrived they built camps of tents, but soon afterwards they built permanent forts defended by strong walls. Each legion contained men with a wide range of skills, such as cooks, builders, carpenters, doctors, blacksmiths and engineers – but they all had to fight!

Barracks, where soldiers sleep

Exercise yard

Gate

Protective wall

Soldiers worshipped their own special god. At forts and army camps, Roman soldiers built temples where they honoured Mithras, their own god. They believed he protected them, and gave them life after death.

Ruled by Rome

More than 50 million people were ruled by Rome. Celts, Germans, Iberians, Dacians and many other peoples lived in territory conquered by Roman armies. They spoke many different languages, and had different customs and beliefs. Roman rulers sent armies to occupy their lands, and governors to rule them. They forced conquered peoples to pay Roman taxes and obey Roman laws.

▲ A Roman tax collector assesses a farmer for taxes.

▼ Boudica, Queen of the Iceni tribe, led a revolt against the Romans.

A few conquered kings and queens refused to accept Roman rule. For example, in AD 60 Boudicca, queen of the Iceni tribe who lived in eastern England, led a rebellion against the Romans in Britain. Her army marched on the city of London and set fire to it, before being defeated by Roman soldiers. Boudicca survived the battle, but killed herself by taking poison so that she would not be captured by Roman troops.

Cleopatra used beauty and charm to stop the Romans invading. Cleopatra was queen of Egypt, in North Africa. Cleopatra knew that the Egyptian army would not be able to defeat Roman soldiers. Two Roman army generals, Julius Caesar and Mark Antony, fell in love with her. She stopped the Romans invading for many years, but Egypt was eventually conquered.

Cleopatra

▼ A carving from Trajan's column of Roman legionaries boarding ships.

Trajan's column

PAINT YOURSELF LIKE A CELTIC WARRIOR!

Roman writers reported how Celtic warriors decorated their faces and bodies with patterns before going into battle. They believed that the paint was magic, and would protect them. The Celts used a deep-blue dye made from a plant called woad. If you have some special face-painting make-up (make sure you ask an adult), then try making up some scary war-paint designs of your own!

Roman conquerors built monuments to celebrate their victories. Trajan, who ruled from AD 98–117, was a famous soldier who became emperor of Rome. He led Roman armies on one of their most successful conquests, in Dacia (Romania) in AD 106. To record this achievement, he gave orders for a tall stone pillar (now known as Trajan's Column) to be built in the Forum in Rome. It was almost 30 metres high, and was decorated with carvings of 2500 Roman soldiers winning wars.

▲ A carving from Trajan's column of Roman soldiers building the walls of a new fort.

The farming life

Rome relied on farmers. Most people in Roman times lived in the countryside and worked on farms. Farmers produced food for city-dwellers. Without them, the citizens would not have survived. Food was grown on big estates by teams of slaves, and on small peasant farms where single families worked together.

Farm produce was imported from all over the empire. Wool and honey came from Britain, wine came from Greece, and 400,000 tonnes of wheat were shipped across the Mediterranean Sea from Egypt every year. It was ground into flour, which was used to make bread, the Romans' staple, or basic, food.

Farmers had no big machines to help them. Heavy work was done by animals, or by human muscle-power. Ploughs were pulled by oxen. Ripe crops were harvested by men and women with curved knives called sickles, and loaded by hand onto farm carts. Donkeys turned mill wheels to crush olives and grind grain, and to raise drinking water from wells.

Beehives for honey

Treading grapes for wine

Owner of the farm

▲ A large Roman farm estate with slaves working the land.

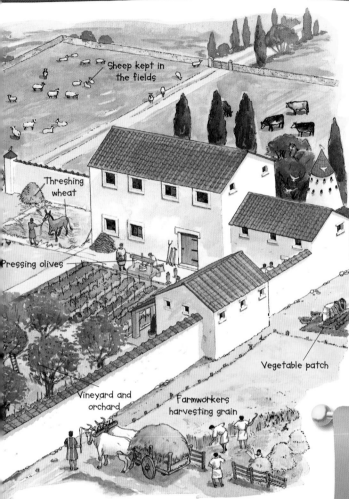

Sheep kept in the fields

Threshing wheat

Pressing olives

Vegetable patch

Vineyard and orchard

Farmworkers harvesting grain

The most valuable fruit was small, hard, green and bitter! It came from olive trees. Olives could be pickled in salty water to eat with bread and cheese, or crushed to provide oil. The Romans used olive oil as a medicine, for cooking and preserving food, for cleaning and softening the skin, and even for burning in lamps.

Roman grapes grew on trees! Vines, climbing plants that produce grapes, were planted among fruit trees in Roman orchards. They provided support for the vine stems, and welcome shade to stop the grapes getting scorched by the sun. Grapes were one of the most important crops on Roman farms. The ripe fruits were picked and dried to become raisins, or pulped and made into wine.

QUIZ

Imagine that you are a Roman farmer, talking to a visitor from the city. How would you answer their questions:

What crops do you grow?
Why do you keep oxen?
Who will harvest that grain?
How do you grind grain into flour?
Why are you growing olives?

Work like a slave!

Roman people were not all equal. There were different classes within Roman society. Throughout the Roman Empire, the biggest difference between people was whether they were slaves or free. Free-born men and women had rights that were guaranteed by law, for example, to find their own work, or travel from one place to another. In Rome, citizens also had the right to vote for government officials, and to receive free hand-outs of food. But slaves had hardly any rights at all. They belonged to their owners just like dogs or horses.

Slaves were trained to do all sorts of tasks. Slaves did everything their owners demanded, from babycare to hard labour on farms. Many slaves were trusted by their owners, who valued their skills. A few slaves became respected chefs or doctors.

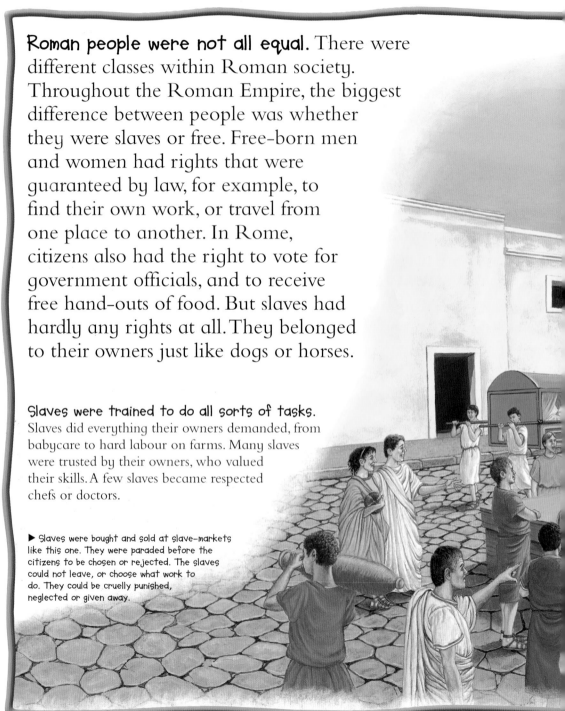

▶ Slaves were bought and sold at slave-markets like this one. They were paraded before the citizens to be chosen or rejected. The slaves could not leave, or choose what work to do. They could be cruelly punished, neglected or given away.

There were many different ways of becoming a slave. Slaves might be captured in war, purchased from a slave-trader or born to slave parents. They could also be people condemned to slavery as punishment for a serious crime.

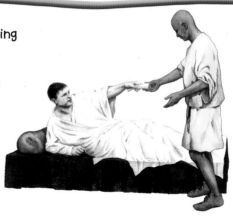

Slaves were sometimes set free by their owners. Freedom could be a reward for loyalty or long service. Some sick or dying slave-owners gave orders that their slaves should be freed. They did not want their slaves to pass to a new owner who might treat them badly.

I DON'T BELIEVE IT!

From 73 BC to 71 BC a slave called Spartacus led a revolt in southern Italy. He ran away to a hideout in the hills where 90,000 other slaves joined him.

Some slaves did very well after they were freed. Former slaves used the skills they had learned to set up businesses of their own. Many were successful, and a few became very rich.

Roman know-how

The Romans pioneered many new building materials and designs. They discovered concrete, which was much cheaper and easier to use than solid building stone. They made bricks of clay baked at high temperatures, which lasted much longer than unbaked ones. They found out how to use arches to create tall, strong walls and doorways. They designed massive domes for buildings that were too big to be roofed with wooden beams.

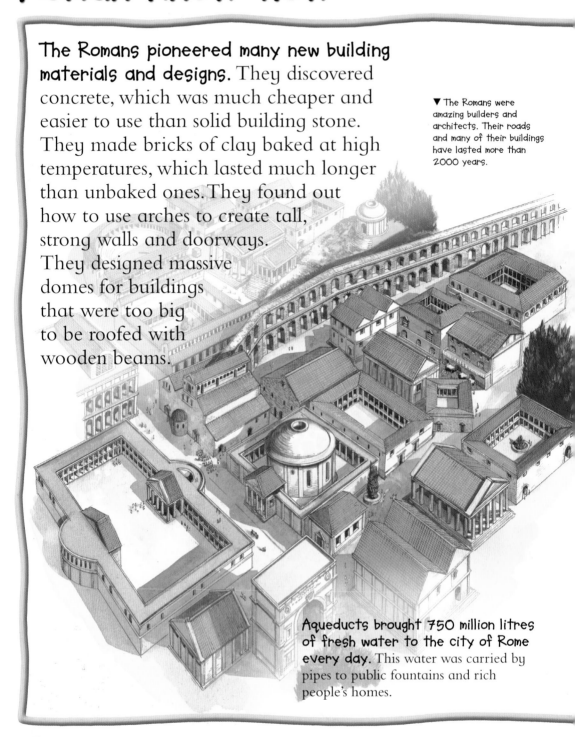

▼ The Romans were amazing builders and architects. Their roads and many of their buildings have lasted more than 2000 years.

Aqueducts brought 750 million litres of fresh water to the city of Rome every day. This water was carried by pipes to public fountains and rich people's homes.

◀▲ This is a Roman valve that allowed water to be pumped uphill. Water would then come out of fountains such as the one shown here.

The Roman's water supplies were so advanced that no one had anything better until the 1800s! They invented pumps with valves to pump water uphill. This went into high tanks above fountains. Gravity pulled the water out of the fountain's spout.

Even the best doctors often failed to cure their patients. But Roman doctors were skilled at sewing up cuts and joining broken bones. They also used herbs for medicines and painkillers.

▼ Romans believed in the ability of doctors to cure illnesses, but also thought witchcraft was the cause of ill health.

Despite their advanced technology, Romans believed that illness was caused by witchcraft. To find a cure, they gave presents to the witch, begging her to remove the spell, or made a special visit to a temple, to ask the gods to make them better.

Prayers and sacrifices

The Romans worshipped many different gods.
Jupiter, the king of the gods, protected
Roman lands. His wife Juno was worshipped
by married women. Mars was the god of
war, Venus was the goddess of love. Diana,
the moon goddess, guarded young girls
and wild animals; Neptune, god of the
sea, sent earthquakes and terrible storms.
Vesta was the goddess of Roman homes.
Her priestesses tended a holy flame in
a temple in the Forum in Rome.

Jupiter, king
of the gods

Juno, queen
of the gods

Mercury, the
messenger of
the gods

Neptune, god
of the sea

Mars,
god of
war

Minerva,
goddess of war

Venus, goddess of love

Diana, goddess
of the moon and
hunting

Pan, god of the
mountainside, pastures,
sheep and goats

Dis (Pluto),
god of the
underworld

The Roman emperor was also chief priest. As part
of his government duties he said prayers and offered
sacrifices to the gods who protected Rome. He was
given a special name 'pontifex maximus', which meant
chief bridge-builder, because people believed he acted
as a bridge between the gods and ordinary people.

Families made offerings to the gods every day. They left food, wine and incense in front of a shrine in their house. A shrine is like a mini temple. It contained statues of ancient gods called the 'lares' and 'penates'. The lares were ancestor spirits, who looked after living family members. The penates guarded the family's food.

Roman men and women could ask the gods to curse their enemies. They wrote their enemies' names, plus curse words, on metal or pottery scraps and left them at temples. They hoped that the gods would see them and harm the people they named in them.

Shrine

Statues of the lares and penates

▲ A Roman house shrine where families made offering to the gods.

▲ A Christian in Roman times praying in a catacomb.

Some of the world's first Christians lived in Rome. But until AD 313 Christianity was banned in the Roman Empire. Christians met secretly, in underground passages called catacombs, to say prayers and hold services. They also used the catacombs as a burial place.

Roman people were very superstitious. They decorated their homes with magic symbols, and hung good luck charms round children's necks. They believed that they could foretell the future by observing animals, birds, insects and even the weather! For example, bees were a sign of riches and happiness but a hooting owl foretold danger.

I DON'T BELIEVE IT!

After an animal had been sacrificed to the gods, a priest, called a 'haruspex', examined its liver. If it was diseased, bad luck was on the way!

On the move

All roads led to Rome.
The city was at the hub of a network of roads that stretched for more than 85,000 kilometres. They had been built to link outlying parts of the empire to the capital, so that Roman armies or government officials could travel quickly. To make travel as quick as possible, roads were built in straight lines, taking the shortest route.

▲ This map shows the Roman Empire in brown, and the roads that they built in black.

Rome's first main road was built in 312 BC. Its name was the Via Appia ('via' is the Latin word for road), and it ran from the city of Rome to the port of Brundisium on the south-east coast of Italy. Many travellers from Greece arrived there, and the new road made their journey to Rome quicker and easier.

Some Roman roads have survived for over 2000 years! Each road was made of layers of earth and stones on top of a firm, flat foundation. It was surfaced with stone slabs or gravel. The centre had a camber, a curved surface, so that rainwater drained away into ditches on either side.

Large surface slabs

Drainage ditch

Solid foundations

Route accurately marked out

Roman engineers used tools to help them to make accurate surveys.
They made careful plans and took measurements before starting any big building project, such as a new road or city walls.

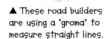

▲ These road builders are using a 'groma' to measure straight lines.

Poor people had to walk everywhere.
They could not afford to hire a horse or a donkey, or a cushioned carriage, pulled by oxen. If they were lucky, they might manage to hitch a lift in a lumbering farm wagon – but this would not give them a comfortable ride!

▲ Town streets were crowded and very dirty. Rich people travelled in curtained beds called litters, carried shoulder-high by slaves. Ordinary people used stepping-stones to avoid the mud and rubbish underfoot.

Heavy loads often travelled by water.
There were no big lorries in Roman times! Ships powered by sails and by slaves rowing carried people and cargo across the sea and along rivers. But water-transport was slow, and could be dangerous. Roman ships were often attacked by pirates, and shipwrecks were common.

▲ The Romans' knowledge of ship-building came from the Greeks. The Romans, though, were not really sailors, and they did not improve the designs.

Gladiators

Prepare to do battle with the finest
warriors of ancient Rome!

The Colosseum • Caesar • Schools • Training
Armour • Prisoners • Shields • Politics • Helmets
Spartacus • Games • Animals • Arenas
Daily life • Slaves

The great games

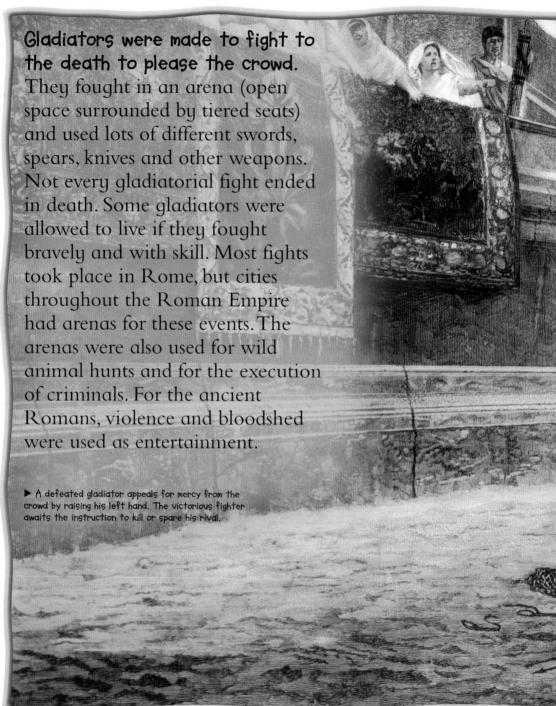

Gladiators were made to fight to the death to please the crowd. They fought in an arena (open space surrounded by tiered seats) and used lots of different swords, spears, knives and other weapons. Not every gladiatorial fight ended in death. Some gladiators were allowed to live if they fought bravely and with skill. Most fights took place in Rome, but cities throughout the Roman Empire had arenas for these events. The arenas were also used for wild animal hunts and for the execution of criminals. For the ancient Romans, violence and bloodshed were used as entertainment.

▶ A defeated gladiator appeals for mercy from the crowd by raising his left hand. The victorious fighter awaits the instruction to kill or spare his rival.

The first gladiators

The first gladiators were not from Rome. The Romans did not invent the idea of gladiators. They believed the idea of men fighting in an arena probably came to Rome from the region of Etruria. But the first proper gladiators probably came from Campania, an area of Italy south of Rome.

▲ The city of Rome began as a small town between Etruria and Campania in central Italy.

QUIZ

1. What were the gladiators named after?
2. Did the Romans invent the idea of gladiators?
3. What word did the Romans use to describe a gladiator show?

Answers:
1. Gladiators were named after the gladius, a type of short sword. 2. No. The idea came from the people of Campania, an area to the south of Rome. 3. The Romans called a gladiator show a munus.

The first Roman gladiators fought in 264 BC. Six slaves were set to fight each other with swords, but they were not allowed to wear any armour. The fights did not last long before one of the slaves in each pair was killed.

▶ The gladius was the standard weapon used by early gladiators.

The first gladiatorial fights were always part of a funeral. The name for a gladiatorial show, a munus, means a duty owed to the dead. The first fights were held at the funerals of politicians and noblemen, who ordered the games in their wills.

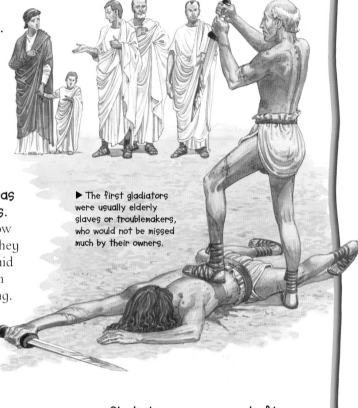

▶ The first gladiators were usually elderly slaves or troublemakers, who would not be missed much by their owners.

In early funeral games, food was more important than gladiators. The Romans used funerals to show off how wealthy and important they were. Free food and drink were laid out at the funeral for any Roman citizen who wanted to come along. Gifts of money, jewellery and clothing were also handed out. The family of the person being buried would wear their finest clothes. The first gladiator fights were just one part of the whole funeral.

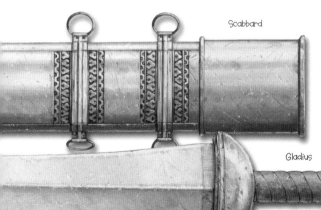

Scabbard

Gladius

Gladiators were named after their weapons. The word gladiator means 'a man who uses a gladius'. The gladius was a type of short, stabbing sword that was used by Roman soldiers. It was about 40 centimetres long and had a very sharp point. It was generally used for slashing, not for cutting. Not all gladiators used the gladius, but the name was used for all fighters in the arena.

Prisoners of war

Prisoners of war fought in the arena.
Between 250 BC and 100 BC the Romans fought many wars against foreign enemies. Prisoners captured in these wars were sold as slaves in Rome. Captured soldiers were made to fight in the arena, with weapons and armour from their own country.

▼ A Thracian armed with a square shield and curved sword faces a Samnite equipped with a larger shield and longer, straight sword.

Samnite

Thracian

The Samnites had the best weapons. The Romans fought a long series of wars against the Samnites between 343 BC and 290 BC. These men each carried a large, oval shield and wore a helmet with cheek guards (flaps that protected their cheeks). Samnite gladiators were famous for the quality of their swords and spears.

The Thracians had the strangest weapons. The men from the kingdom of Thrace carried small shields and wore helmets with crests. They were famous for being able to hit any target with their spears and carried short, curved swords. This mix of weapons proved very popular and many gladiators adopted them. They became known as Thracian gladiators, even if they were not from Thrace.

▶ The tall, fair-skinned Celts decorated their bodies and shields with bright colours.

Celts painted their bodies before going into battle. The Celts were the only people to have captured Rome, in 390 BC. They lived in northern Italy and across Europe. The Romans forced many Celtic prisoners to fight in their native clothes and with native weapons.

◀ The Numidians from North Africa were famous for their skill on horseback. They often fought in the arena using light javelins.

The Numidians fought on horseback. Numidia was an area of northern Africa in what is now Algeria. The area was famous for breeding quality horses and its army included large numbers of cavalry (soldiers on horseback). Prisoners of war from Numidia rode horses when they appeared in the arena.

Gladiators and politics

▲ A person's ashes were stored in a pot or urn until the funeral.

Funerals were delayed for years. Gladiatorial shows were organized as part of the funerals of rich and powerful noblemen. However, the heir of the man who had died would want to hold the show when he was standing for election so that he could impress the voters.

A good gladiator show could win an election. In ancient Rome, votes were not cast in secret. Each voter had to give his name to an official called a censor and then declare how he was voting. The men standing for election stood near the censor to see how people voted. Putting on an impressive gladiator show could gain votes.

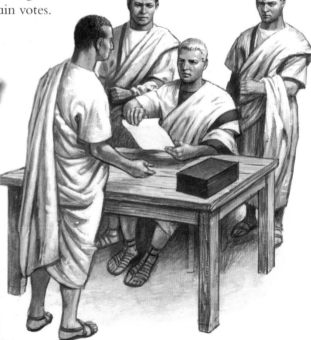

▼ A citizen waiting to vote at an election. The censor kept a list of everyone entitled to vote and people had to prove who they were before voting.

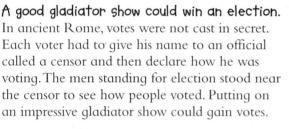

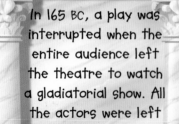

I DON'T BELIEVE IT!

In 165 BC, a play was interrupted when the entire audience left the theatre to watch a gladiatorial show. All the actors were left alone in the theatre!

Some politicians hired gangs of gladiators to beat up their opponents. If a citizen could not be persuaded, by gladiator shows or the payment of money, to vote for a certain candidate, the candidate might use gladiators to bully him. Gladiators were armed with clubs and given the names of citizens who should be threatened. Every election was accompanied by this sort of violence.

▲ Men were posted at the entrance to the arena to ensure that only voters entered.

Only voters could watch the games. The purpose of holding spectacular gladiatorial shows was to influence voters. Only citizens of Rome could vote, so only they were allowed to attend the shows. Citizens who were known to be voting for an opponent were turned away, as were slaves and foreigners who could not vote.

The best seats went to men who donated money to the election campaign. Standing for an election cost a lot of money in ancient Rome. Rich men would give or lend money to the candidate they preferred. In return they would get the best seats in a gladiatorial show and would expect to receive titles or government money if their candidate won.

◀ Roman coins were made of gold, silver or bronze and carried a portrait of the emperor on one side.

Caesar's games

Julius Caesar borrowed money to buy his gladiators. Julius Caesar rose to become the ruler of the Roman Empire. Early in his career he staged spectacular games to win votes in elections. But Caesar was too poor to afford to pay the bills, so he borrowed money from richer men. When he won the elections, Caesar repaid the men with favours and titles.

▲ Julius Caesar (102–44 BC) was a politician who won several elections after staging magnificent games to entertain the voters.

▲ War elephants were popular attractions, and gladiators were specially trained in how to fight against them.

Caesar's gladiators fought in silver armour. In 65 BC, Julius Caesar staged the funeral games for his father, who had died 20 years earlier. Caesar was standing for election to be chief priest of Rome. To make his games even more special, Caesar dressed his 640 gladiators in armour made of solid silver.

Caesar brought war elephants to Rome. In 46 BC Julius Caesar celebrated a victory in North Africa by staging gladiatorial games in Rome. Among the prisoners of war forced to fight in the arena were 40 war elephants, together with the men trained to fight them.

Caesar turned senators (governors of Rome) into gladiators. On one occasion Caesar forced two rich noblemen to fight in the arena. They had been sentenced to death by a court, but Caesar ordered that the man who killed the other in the arena could go free.

Caesar's final show was too big for the arena. The games staged by Julius Caesar when he wanted to become dictator of Rome were the grandest ever held. After weeks of shows and feasts, the final day saw a fight between two armies of 500 infantry (foot soldiers) and 30 cavalry. The battle was so large it had to be held in the enormous chariot race course, Circus Maximus.

QUIZ

1. Did Caesar's gladiators wear armour made of silver, gold or bronze?
2. Was Caesar's final show a big or small show?
3. Where did Caesar get the money to buy gladiators?

Answers:
1. Silver. 2. It was a big show.
3. He borrowed money from richer men.

▼ Chariot racing was a hugely popular sport that thrilled the crowds in ancient Rome.

143

The mob

The Roman mob could overpower emperors. Over a million people lived in ancient Rome. Many were voting citizens who did not have regular jobs. Even the most powerful emperors had to keep this vast mob of Romans happy. If an emperor did not put on impressive gladiatorial shows he could be booed, attacked or even be killed.

▲ Emperor Vitellius (AD 69) was murdered by a mob of Romans after failing to put on any impressive games.

▼ The seats in the arena were numbered and cushions were sometimes provided for extra comfort.

Each seat was saved for a particular person. People attending the gladiator games had their own seats. The row and seat number were written on small clay tablets that were handed out by the organizer of the games. Some seats were given to whoever queued up outside the arena.

Women in ancient Rome could not vote, so they were given seats at the back of the crowd. The best seats were reserved for the men who could vote and had money to help the editor (the man who staged gladiatorial games).

◀ A wounded gladiator pleads for his life by raising the first finger of his left hand. The thumbs downward signal from the mob indicates that he should die.

The mob decided which gladiators lived, and which died. A wounded gladiator could appeal for mercy by holding up the first finger of his left hand. The mob gave a thumbs down gesture if they thought the gladiator should die, or hid their thumbs in clenched fists if they thought he should live. The editor usually did what the mob wanted because he wanted them to vote for him.

I DON'T BELIEVE IT!

Poor Roman citizens were given free bread by the government. In one month in 44 BC, more than 330,000 men queued up to receive this free handout of food.

145

Amazing arenas

The first gladiator fights took place in the cattle market. The cattle market, or Forum Boarium, was a large open space by the river Tiber. Cattle pens were cleared away to make space for fighting, while the audience watched from shops and temples.

◀ The crowd watched early gladiatorial fights in the cattle market from shops and pavements.

Most fights took place in the Forum. This was the largest open square in the centre of Rome. The most important temples and government buildings stood around the Forum. After about 150 BC, gladiatorial games were held in the Forum and temporary wooden stands were erected in which spectators could sit.

One fight took place in a swivelling arena. In 53 BC, the politician Gaius Scribonius Curio put on a gladiator show and impressed the crowd by staging two plays in back-to-back theatres. The theatres swivelled around to form an arena for a small gladiator show. The crowd loved the new idea and Curio went on to win several elections.

The first purpose-built arena had the wrong name carved on it. In 29 BC an amphitheatre (an open-air building with rows of seats, one above the other) was built to the north of Rome by the politician Titus Statilius Taurus. The amphitheatre was built of stone and timber to replace temporary wooden stands in the Forum. Taurus wanted to impress Emperor Augustus so he carved the name 'Augustus' over the entrance.

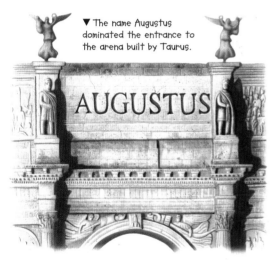

▼ The name Augustus dominated the entrance to the arena built by Taurus.

Every arena had the same layout.
Arenas were oval with an entrance at each end. The gladiators came into the arena through one entrance, and the other was reserved for servants and for carrying out any dead gladiators. The editor sat in a special section of the seating called the tribunal editoris, which was on the north side in the shade.

TRUE OR FALSE?
1. The cattle market was the largest open space in Rome.
2. At first spectators watched from shops and temples.
3. Some arenas were round, some oval and some square.

Answers:
1. FALSE The Forum was the largest open space in Rome.
2. TRUE Early gladiatorial fights took place in the cattle market and spectators watched from nearby buildings. 3. FALSE All arenas were oval.

▼ All gladiatorial stadiums were oval in shape, with blocks of seating rising from the central arena.

Seating for less important citizens

Seating for senators and important people

Seating for the editor

Gladiators' exit

Arena

Gladiators' entrance

Seating for women, slaves and unimportant people

The mighty Colosseum

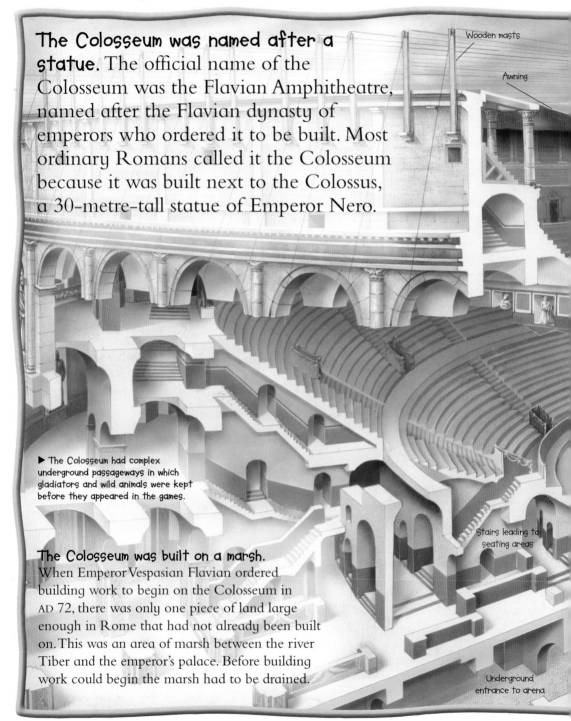

The Colosseum was named after a statue. The official name of the Colosseum was the Flavian Amphitheatre, named after the Flavian dynasty of emperors who ordered it to be built. Most ordinary Romans called it the Colosseum because it was built next to the Colossus, a 30-metre-tall statue of Emperor Nero.

Wooden masts

Awning

▶ The Colosseum had complex underground passageways in which gladiators and wild animals were kept before they appeared in the games.

Stairs leading to seating areas

The Colosseum was built on a marsh. When Emperor Vespasian Flavian ordered building work to begin on the Colosseum in AD 72, there was only one piece of land large enough in Rome that had not already been built on. This was an area of marsh between the river Tiber and the emperor's palace. Before building work could begin the marsh had to be drained.

Underground entrance to arena

The Colosseum could seat 50,000 spectators. The huge seating area was divided into more than 80 sections. Each section had a separate door and flight of steps that led to the outside of the Colosseum. It is thought that the entire audience could have left in less than 15 minutes of the end of the show. The standing room at the top was reserved for slaves and may have held another 4000 people.

The Colosseum was probably the largest building in the world. It was finished in AD 80 and the outer walls stood over 46 metres tall and covered an area 194 metres long by 160 metres wide. The walls were covered in stone, but most of the structure was made of brick or concrete.

The first games in the Colosseum lasted 100 days. The Colosseum was finished during the reign of Emperor Titus. He wanted to show that he was the most generous man ever to live in Rome, so he organized gladiatorial games to last for 100 days. Thousands of gladiators and animals fought in these games, which some people thought were the finest ever staged in Rome.

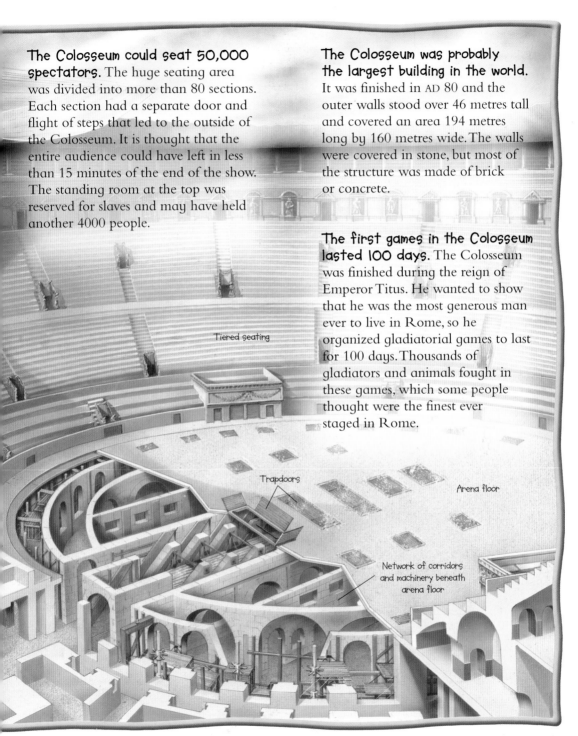

Tiered seating

Trapdoors

Arena floor

Network of corridors and machinery beneath arena floor

Who were the gladiators?

Gladiators were divided into types based on their weapons. Not all gladiators used the same weapons or fought in the same way. Some gladiators fought with weapons that had been popular in other countries or were used by different types of soldiers. Others used weapons and armour that were made especially for the arena.

Murmillo gladiators used army weapons and military armour. These gladiators used shields and swords similar to those used by infantry in the Roman army. The shield was one metre long and 65 centimetres wide. The sword was used for stabbing, not cutting.

Thracian gladiators used lightweight armour. The weapons of the Thracians were based on those used by soldiers from the kingdom of Thrace. The shield was small and square and the leg armour had long metal guards. The sword had a curved blade and the helmets were decorated with a griffin's head (a griffin was an imaginary bird).

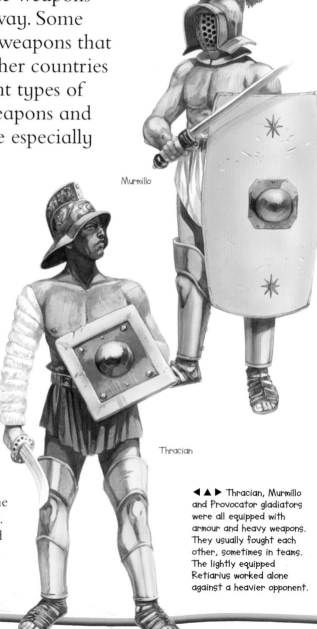

Murmillo

Thracian

◀ ▲ ▶ Thracian, Murmillo and Provocator gladiators were all equipped with armour and heavy weapons. They usually fought each other, sometimes in teams. The lightly equipped Retiarius worked alone against a heavier opponent.

Provocator gladiators wore the heaviest armour of all gladiators. They had a breastplate that protected the chest, a round helmet and leg armour that reached above the knees. The shield was about 80 centimetres long and 60 centimetres wide. They used a short, stabbing sword with a straight blade.

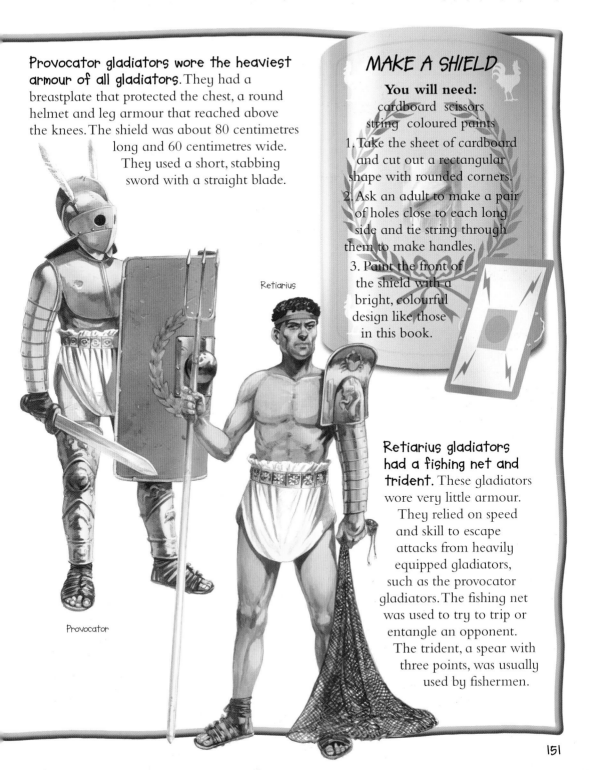

Retiarius

Provocator

MAKE A SHIELD

You will need:
cardboard scissors
string coloured paints

1. Take the sheet of cardboard and cut out a rectangular shape with rounded corners.

2. Ask an adult to make a pair of holes close to each long side and tie string through them to make handles.

3. Paint the front of the shield with a bright, colourful design like those in this book.

Retiarius gladiators had a fishing net and trident. These gladiators wore very little armour. They relied on speed and skill to escape attacks from heavily equipped gladiators, such as the provocator gladiators. The fishing net was used to try to trip or entangle an opponent. The trident, a spear with three points, was usually used by fishermen.

151

Special fighters

◀ The equite gladiators began their combat on horseback, but if one fell off his horse, the other had to fight on foot as well.

Equite gladiators were equipped in the same way as the cavalry in the Roman army. They used a small leather shield, a medium-length sword and a lance about 2.5 metres long. Only the helmet was different from that of the army. The army helmet had an open face and no brim. Whenever these gladiators appeared in a show they were the first to fight.

Female gladiators were rare. They first appeared around AD 55 in Rome as a novelty act. They fought only against other women or animals. Female gladiators were banned in AD 200.

▲ Female gladiators fought in the same style as the male gladiators.

The andabatae (an-dab-AH-tie) fought blindfolded.
The Romans loved anything new or unusual. Andabatae gladiators wore helmets with no eye-holes. They listened carefully for sounds of their opponent, then attacked with two swords. Sometimes the andabatae fought on horseback.

British gladiators fought from chariots. Known as the essedarii (ess-e-DAH-ree-ee), meaning chariot-man, these gladiators first appeared after Julius Caesar invaded Britain in 55 BC. The first chariot gladiators were prisoners of war.

▲ Andabatae helmets had no eye-holes – the gladiators had to rely on their hearing.

ANDABATAE FIGHT
Recreate the combat of the andabatae with this game

You will need:
blindfold   four or more players

1. One player is the andabatae. Tie on the blindfold, making sure the player can see nothing.
2. Other players run around the andabatae calling out their name.
3. The andabatae tries to catch someone. When they catch a person, that person puts on the blindfold and becomes the andabatae. The game continues for as long as you like.

Special clowns who fought with wooden weapons were known as paegniarii (payeg-nee-AH-ree-ee). They appeared at shows during gaps between gladiator fights. They were skilled acrobats and would sometimes tell jokes or make fun of important people in the audience.

▶ The paegniarii used wooden weapons and put on comic displays to entertain the crowd between gladiator fights.

153

Recruiting gladiators

The first gladiators were household slaves. The will of the dead man who was being honoured by the games would name his slaves who were to fight. They were made to fight during the funeral. Those who were killed were then buried with their owner.

AUGUSTUS
JULIUS
SPARTACUS
CLAUDIUS

▲ Before a show, the names of the gladiators who were to fight were written on a scroll.

SPQR

CASSIUS SCRIBONIUS
CRIME
ROBBERY
SENTENCE
THREE YEARS
AS GLADIATOR

◄ When convicted, the name, crime and sentence of each criminal was inscribed on a tablet.

Criminals could be sent to the arena. The Romans did not have prisons so criminals were usually fined, flogged or executed. Men guilty of some crimes might be ordered to become gladiators for a set period of time – such as three years for robbery. These men would be given a tablet showing the details of their crime and sentence.

I DON'T BELIEVE IT!
When the lanista wanted to buy slaves to become gladiators, he would choose big, strong men. On average a gladiator was about 5 centimetres taller than an ordinary Roman.

154

Some gladiators were volunteers.
These volunteers had often been former soldiers who wanted to earn money for their retirement. They signed up for a period of time or for a set number of fights and received a large payment of money if they survived.

Gladiators were recruited by the lanista. Every gladiator school was run by the lanista, the owner and chief trainer. The lanista decided who to recruit and how to train them. He would choose the strongest men to fight in heavy armour and the quickest men to fight as retiarius gladiators.

◄ Slaves for sale were paraded in front of potential buyers. They were sold to the highest bidder.

Strong slaves were sold to become gladiators. In ancient Rome, slaves were treated as the property of their owners and had no human rights at all. If a man wanted to raise money, he might sell a slave. The lanista would pay a high price for strong male slaves. Many young slaves were also sold to become gladiators.

▶ The price of slaves varied, but a slave might cost about the same as an average workman's wages for a year.

Learning to fight

Gladiators lived in a special training school called a ludus.
Most early schools were located near Naples, but they later moved to Rome. Some schools specialized in a particular type of gladiator, but others trained all types. The school was run by the lanista, but some were owned by wealthy noblemen.

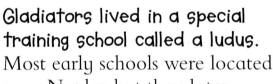

▲ Wooden training swords were the same size as real weapons.

Gladiators trained with wooden weapons.
The weapons made sure that gladiators were not seriously injured during training. It also made it more difficult for gladiators to organize a rebellion, as Spartacus had done. Some wooden weapons were bound with heavy lead weights so that when gladiators fought with normal weapons they could fight for longer.

A special oath was taken by trainee gladiators. The sacred oath (promise) was taken in front of a shrine to the gods. The oath made the gladiator obey the lanista without question or endure branding, flogging, chains or death. Gladiators were allowed to keep any prize money they won.

▲ Most arenas and gladiator schools had a small shrine dedicated to the war god Mars.

New trainees fought against a wooden post called a palus. A trainer known as a doctor taught the recruits how to use their weapons and shields to strike at the 2-metre-high wooden post. Only when the basic tactics had been learned did the recruits practise against other gladiators.

▲ Gladiators trained for several hours every day, being instructed on fighting techniques by retired gladiators and more experienced men.

The buildings of a gladiator school were constructed around a square training ground. This was where the gladiators did most of their training, exercises and other activities. Around the training ground were rooms where the gladiators lived. Recruits slept in dormitories, but fully trained gladiators had their own rooms.

157

Armour, shields and helmets

Gladiator helmets were decorated with colourful plumes and crests. These were made from coloured feathers or dyed horsehair and made the gladiators look taller and bigger. Sometimes gladiators fought in teams and wore colours to show which team they belonged to.

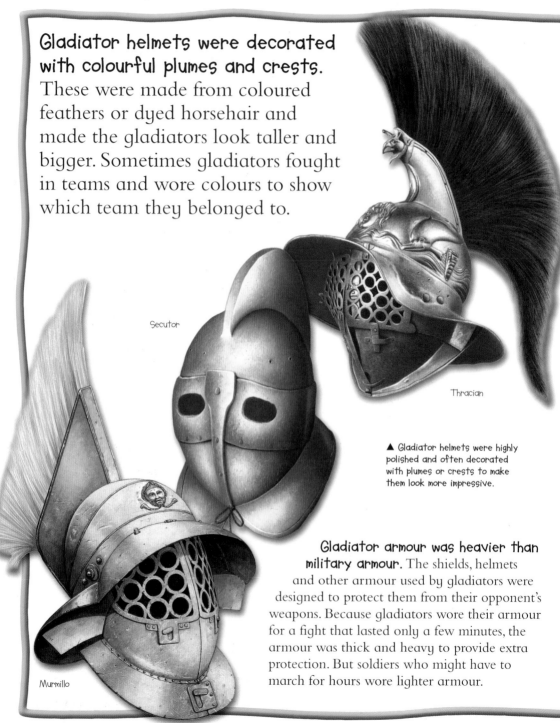

Secutor

Thracian

▲ Gladiator helmets were highly polished and often decorated with plumes or crests to make them look more impressive.

Murmillo

Gladiator armour was heavier than military armour. The shields, helmets and other armour used by gladiators were designed to protect them from their opponent's weapons. Because gladiators wore their armour for a fight that lasted only a few minutes, the armour was thick and heavy to provide extra protection. But soldiers who might have to march for hours wore lighter armour.

Some armour was covered with gold. Most gladiator armour was decorated with carvings and reliefs of gods such as Mars, god of war, or Victory, goddess of success. These decorations were often coated with thin sheets of pure gold.

Padded armour was worn on the arms and legs. Thick layers of cloth and padding gave protection from glancing blows from the weapons or from being hit by the shield of the opponent.

▲ Gladiator shields were painted and even decorated with gold to impress the audience.

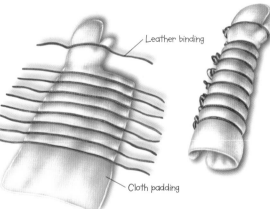

Leather binding

Cloth padding

▲ Arms and legs were often covered with layers of woollen cloth tied on with leather bindings.

The body was usually left without any armour at all. This meant that a single blow could kill them, or injure them so seriously that they had to ask for mercy. Gladiators needed to be skilful with both weapons and shields to survive.

I DON'T BELIEVE IT!

Gladiator helmets were very heavy — they weighed about 7 kilograms, twice as much as an army helmet!

A day in the life...

▲ A gladiator would be awoken at dawn by one of the slaves owned by the training school.

Gladiators were woken at dawn to begin training. They had several servants to look after them, usually boys or old men. A servant would wake the gladiator at sunrise to make sure he was ready to begin his training on time.

Training lasted for hours each day. Even the most experienced gladiator began his day practising weapon strokes at a wooden post. This allowed the fighter to warm up ready for the more serious training later in the day. Gladiators had special plain armour and blunt weapons to use when training.

GLADIATOR MEAL

Ask an adult to help you prepare this gladiator meal.

You will need:
60 g rolled porridge oats
400 ml water pinch of salt
50 g ham 5 dried figs
2 tbsp olive oil
1 tsp dried rosemary.

1. Chop the ham and figs. Fry in the olive oil and rosemary.
2. Place the oats, water and salt in a saucepan. Bring to the boil, then simmer for 5 minutes.
3. When the oats have thickened, scatter over the ham and figs.

◀ A stout wooden post about 2 metres tall was used for the more basic training exercises.

◀ Gladiators were given simple, but nutritious food such as porridge, carrots and sausages to keep them fit and healthy.

Barley porridge was the usual food of gladiators, but they also ate meats, fruits and vegetables. The Romans believed that barley was a highly nutritious food that helped to build up muscles. The owner of the gladiator school did not waste money on fancy foods, but provided plain and healthy meals.

▼ Gladiators were sometimes given treatment by masseurs, doctors and other specialists who looked after their health.

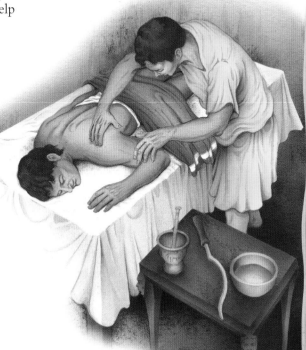

Gladiators received regular massages.
Romans knew that massages would help to ease stiff joints or relax muscles. Massages could be very helpful to old injuries. The gladiator school would employ at least one man who was an expert masseur to keep the gladiators in top condition.

Older, retired gladiators trained the new recruits.
Gladiators who survived long enough to win their freedom often found jobs at gladiator schools. They were expert fighters and knew many tricks and special moves. They trained the new recruits to be expert fighters. This would please the crowd, and give the gladiator a better chance of surviving.

Get ready for the games

The first decision was how much money to spend. The man who staged a munus, or gladiatorial games, was known as the editor. A munus was an expensive event but most editors wanted to put on the most impressive show possible. They would spend as much money as they could spare.

The editor would choose different features for his show. A lanista would be hired to organize the show. Together, they would decide how many gladiators would fight and how many musicians and other performers were needed. The lanista would make sure the event was a success.

▲ Musicians and dancers were popular at gladiator shows. Shows often included a parade of entertainers before the gladiators.

QUIZ

1. Who decided on the features for a gladiatorial show?
2. Did the editor of the games wear his everyday toga or expensive clothing?
3. Was a toga with purple edges worn by noblemen or ordinary citizens?

Answers:
1. The editor and lanista.
2. He hired special clothing to wear.
3. Noblemen.

A dead gladiator cost more than a wounded one. The editor would sign a contract with the lanista. This set down everything that would appear at the munus and the cost. If a gladiator was killed, a special payment was made so that the lanista could buy and train a replacement. Many editors granted mercy to a wounded man to avoid paying extra.

Everything was hired — even the clothes worn by the organizer.

The editor would hire expensive clothes and jewellery for himself and his family. He wanted to make sure that they looked their best when they appeared at the games. The editor wanted to impress his fellow citizens and make sure they would vote for him.

The star of the show was the editor.

Everything was arranged so that the editor of the games looked as important as possible. As well as wearing special clothes, he was given the most prominent seat in the amphitheatre and all the gladiators and other performers bowed to him. He was paying for the show and wanted to make sure he got all the credit.

▼ Smart clothes were hired for the editor and all his family so that they could show off to the audience.

A laurel wreath signified an honour granted by the Roman government

Gold jewellery indicated a family's wealth

Brightly coloured silk from China showed wealth and sophistication

A toga was a special item of clothing that indicated the rank within society of the man wearing it

Purple was the most expensive dye in ancient Rome

Showtime!

Advertising for the show began days beforehand. The lanista sent out slaves to paint signs on walls, while others shouted announcements on the street. The slaves told people when and where the show was and what it included. They also told them the name of the editor of the show.

The show began with a parade, which was led into the arena by the editor. He was dressed in beautiful clothes and often rode in a chariot. Behind him came the musicians playing lively tunes. Then came the gladiators, each followed by a slave who carried the gladiator's weapons and armour. Then came statues of the war god Mars and other gods. Finally the servants, referees and other officials entered the arena.

Gladiators were carefully paired against each other. Before the show began, the editor and lanista would decide which gladiators would fight each other. The show would start with beginners fighting each other, with the expert veterans appearing towards the end of the show. The results would be shouted out by a herald and written on a sign, or tabella, at one end of the arena.

The probatio was a crucial ceremony. Before the first fight of the show, the editor and lanista would enter the arena for the probatio. This ceremony involved the men testing the weapons and armour to be used in the show. Swords were tested by slicing up vegetables, and armour by being hit with clubs.

◀ Each gladiator show began with a grand parade of everyone involved in the show, led by the editor in a chariot.

Musicians performed first. The band included trumpets, curved horns and the hydraulis. This was a loud instrument like a modern church organ. The musicians entertained the crowd between fights and played music during the show ceremonies.

TRUE OR FALSE?

1. The hydraulis was an instrument like a modern trumpet.
2. Weapons were tested before the show to make sure they were sharp.
3. Gladiators wore their armour during the opening parade.

Answers:
1. FALSE The hydraulis was an instrument like a modern organ.
2. TRUE Weapons were tested during the probatio ceremony. 3. FALSE Slaves carried the armour behind the gladiators.

Water fights

Some gladiatorial shows took place on water. The most impressive of all were the naumachiae, or sea fights. For these shows, an artificial lake 557 metres long by 536 metres wide was dug beside the river Tiber. Small warships were brought up the river and launched on the lake when a sea fight was due to take place.

Naval fights were recreations of real battles. In 2 BC, Emperor Augustus staged a naumachia that recreated a battle fought 400 years earlier between the Greeks and the Persians. Emperor Titus staged a battle that originally started between the Greeks and Egyptians. These battles did not always end with the same winner as the real battle.

▼ Recreated naval battles were extremely expensive to stage, so didn't take place very often.

The first naval gladiators did not try to kill each other. The first of the sea battles were staged by Julius Caesar to celebrate a naval victory. The show was designed to impress the audience with the skills of the sailors and the way Caesar had won his victory.

One naval show involved 19,000 men. Emperor Claudius staged a sea battle on Lake Fucino. The men fighting were not sailors or gladiators but criminals condemned to death. Most of the men died and any survivors were sent to work as slaves.

The Colosseum in Rome could be flooded for naval fights. When the Colosseum was first built it had special pipes that could fill the arena with water and then drain it away again. The flooded arena was used for fights between special miniature warships crewed by gladiators. Later, the pipes were replaced by trapdoors and stage scenery.

I DON'T BELIEVE IT!

On one occasion, gladiators took one look at the poor condition of the warships and refused to board them.

Wild animal hunts

The first wild animal show was to celebrate a military victory. In 164 BC Rome defeated the powerful North African city of Carthage. The victorious general, Publius Cornelius Scipio, was given the nickname Africanus. He brought back to Rome hundreds of African wild animals, such as elephants, crocodiles and lions. After parading the animals through the streets, he included them in his gladiatorial games.

▲ This ancient mosaic shows the capture of wild animals, such as lions and gazelles. They were then shipped to Rome to fight in the arenas.

One elephant hunt went badly wrong. In 79 BC General Gnaeus Pompey staged a wild elephant hunt with 20 elephants in a temporary arena in Rome. The crowd was protected by a tall iron fence, but two of the elephants charged at the fence, smashing it down. The elephants were quickly killed by hunters, but several people were injured.

The design of the arena changed to make it safer for the crowds. As the wild animal shows became more popular the need to keep the watching crowd safe meant changes to the arena had to be made. The arena was sunk about 3 metres into the ground and surrounded by a vertical wall of smooth stone. No animal could leap up the wall or break it down, so the spectators were safe from attack.

Some animal shows were fantastic and strange. The Romans loved to see animals fighting each other. Sometimes a group of lions or wolves would be set to attack zebras or deer. At other times two hunting animals would be made to fight each other. They were often chained together to encourage them to fight. Some pairings were very odd. A snake was set against a lion, a seal set to fight a wolf or a bull against a bear.

Lions were set to fight tigers. One of the most popular animal fights was when a lion was set against a tiger. So many lions and tigers were sent to Rome to die in the fights that they became extinct in some areas of North Africa and the Middle East.

I DON'T BELIEVE IT!

The Romans loved watching animals that had been trained to perform tricks. One animal trainer put on shows in which an ape drove a chariot pulled by camels.

▼ A wild tiger attacks a gladiator, as seen in the 2000 movie *Gladiator*. Wild animals were part of most arena shows.

169

Outside Rome

More gladiators fought in southern Italy than in Rome. The idea of gladiatorial fights came from Campania, the area of Italy around Naples. For hundreds of years, the gladiator schools in Campania produced the best-trained gladiators and had more than anywhere else. One school had over 5000 gladiators training at one time.

The city of London had a small arena for gladiatorial games and other events. It stood inside the city walls beside the army fortress, near what is now St Paul's Cathedral. The 30-metre-long amphitheatre was built of stone and timber and could seat around 4000 spectators. St Albans, Chester and Caerleon also had amphitheatres.

▼ The arena at Pompeii. The oval shape, banked seating and two exits were the common design for all arenas.

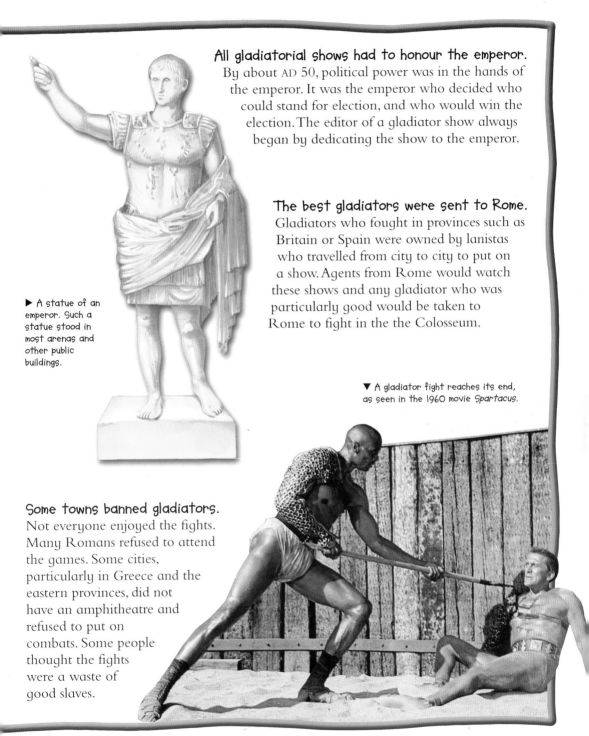

All gladiatorial shows had to honour the emperor.
By about AD 50, political power was in the hands of the emperor. It was the emperor who decided who could stand for election, and who would win the election. The editor of a gladiator show always began by dedicating the show to the emperor.

▶ A statue of an emperor. Such a statue stood in most arenas and other public buildings.

The best gladiators were sent to Rome.
Gladiators who fought in provinces such as Britain or Spain were owned by lanistas who travelled from city to city to put on a show. Agents from Rome would watch these shows and any gladiator who was particularly good would be taken to Rome to fight in the the Colosseum.

▼ A gladiator fight reaches its end, as seen in the 1960 movie *Spartacus*.

Some towns banned gladiators.
Not everyone enjoyed the fights. Many Romans refused to attend the games. Some cities, particularly in Greece and the eastern provinces, did not have an amphitheatre and refused to put on combats. Some people thought the fights were a waste of good slaves.

171

The last gladiators

▲ A scene from the 2000 movie *Gladiator*. The bloodshed in gladiator fights appalled some Romans.

Gladiatorial games became less and less popular. Seneca, a wise man and a great thinker, wrote that attending the games made Romans more cruel and inhuman than they had been before. The writer Artemidorus of Daldis said that the games were dishonourable, cruel and wicked. However most Romans approved of the games and enjoyed watching them.

In AD 324, Christian bishops tried to ban gladiatorial fights. After AD 250, Christianity became popular in the Roman Empire. Christians believed that the fights were sinful and they asked Emperor Constantine I to ban the fights. He banned private games, but allowed state games to continue.

In AD 366 Pope Damasus used gladiators to murder rival churchmen. When Pope Liberius died the cardinals of Rome could not agree on a successor. Followers who wanted Ursinus to be the next pope were meeting in the church of St Maria Trastevere when Damasus hired a gang of gladiators to attack them. The gladiators broke into the church and killed 137 people. Damasus then became pope.

The Christian monk Telemachus was the first to stop a gladiator fight. During a show in the Colosseum in AD 404, Telemachus forced apart two fighting gladiators. He made a speech asking for the shows to stop, but angry spectators killed him. Emperor Honorius then closed down all the gladiator schools in Rome.

▲ Heavily armed gladiators were sometimes hired by ambitious politicians and churchmen to murder their rivals.

The last gladiators fought in around AD 445. In AD 410, the city of Rome was captured by a tribe of barbarians. The Roman Empire was falling to pieces. People were too busy trying to escape invasions or to earn a living to organize gladiatorial fights.

◄ The monk Telemachus managed to stop a gladiator fight, but paid for his actions with his life.

Vikings

Discover the real facts about the Vikings and find out about their battles, religion and culture.

Kings • Weapons • Warriors • Clothes • Towns
Health • Food • Explorers • Raids • Legends
Law • Heroes • Gods • Traders • Music
Hunters • Jewellery • Sport

Who were the Vikings?

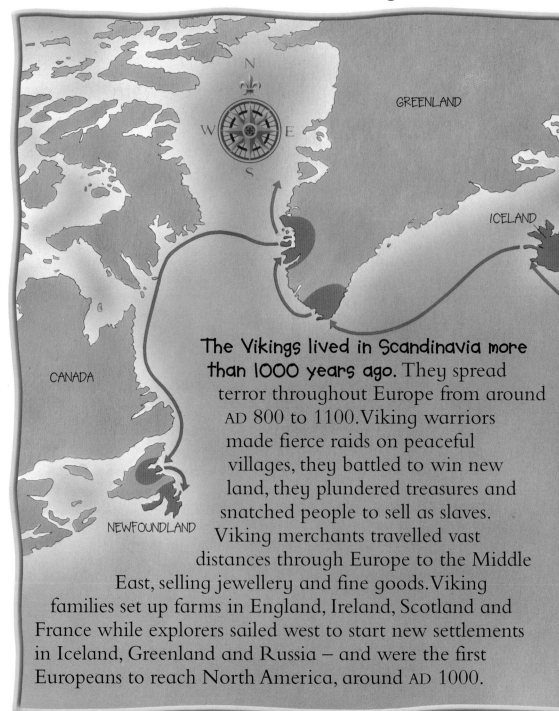

GREENLAND

ICELAND

CANADA

NEWFOUNDLAND

The Vikings lived in Scandinavia more than 1000 years ago. They spread terror throughout Europe from around AD 800 to 1100. Viking warriors made fierce raids on peaceful villages, they battled to win new land, they plundered treasures and snatched people to sell as slaves. Viking merchants travelled vast distances through Europe to the Middle East, selling jewellery and fine goods. Viking families set up farms in England, Ireland, Scotland and France while explorers sailed west to start new settlements in Iceland, Greenland and Russia – and were the first Europeans to reach North America, around AD 1000.

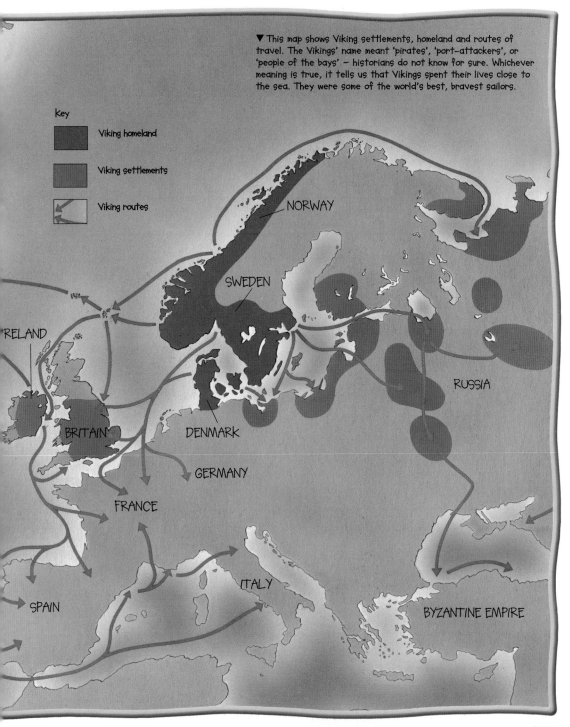

▼ This map shows Viking settlements, homeland and routes of travel. The Vikings' name meant 'pirates', 'port-attackers', or 'people of the bays' – historians do not know for sure. Whichever meaning is true, it tells us that Vikings spent their lives close to the sea. They were some of the world's best, bravest sailors.

Key

Viking homeland

Viking settlements

Viking routes

NORWAY

SWEDEN

RELAND

RUSSIA

BRITAIN

DENMARK

GERMANY

FRANCE

SPAIN

ITALY

BYZANTINE EMPIRE

Kings and people

Viking society had three classes. At the top were nobles (kings or chiefs). They were rich, owned land and had many servants. Freemen, the middle group, included farmers, traders, and craftworkers and their wives. Slaves were the lowest group. They worked hard for nobles and freemen and could not leave their owner.

Viking slave

Viking farmer

Viking noble warrior

▲ Slaves, farmers and warriors all worked hard to make Viking lands rich and powerful.

◄ Famous for his cruelty, Erik Bloodaxe was the last Viking to rule the kingdom of Northumbria, in north-east England.

Viking warlords turned into kings.
During early Viking times, local chiefs controlled large areas of land. They also had armies of freemen. Over the centuries, some nobles became richer and more powerful than the rest by raiding and conquering foreign lands. By AD 1050, just one noble controlled each Viking country, and called himself king.

King Erik Bloodaxe killed his brothers.
When a Viking king died, each of his sons had an equal right to inherit the throne. Members of Viking royal families often had to fight among themselves for the right to rule. In AD 930, King Erik of Norway killed his brothers so that he could rule alone.

King Harald Bluetooth left a magnificent memorial. King Harald ruled Denmark from around AD 935 to 985. He was one of the first Viking kings to become a Christian. He built a church at Jelling, the ancient Danish royal burial site, and had his parents' bodies dug up and re-buried inside. He also paid for a splendid pyramid-shaped monument to be built next to the church, in memory of them. This 'Jelling Stone' was decorated with carvings in Viking and Christian designs.

▶ The Jelling stone (far right of picture) has carvings of a snake and a lion-like monster, fighting together. They symbolize the forces of good and evil.

King Cnut ruled a European empire – but not the waves! King Cnut was one of the mightiest Viking kings. By 1028 he ruled England, Denmark and Norway. However he did not want to appear too proud. So, one day, he staged a strange event on an English beach and commanded the waves to obey him! When they did not he said, 'This proves that I am weak. Only God can control the sea.'

I DON'T BELIEVE IT!

Many Viking rulers had strange or violent names, such as Svein Forkbeard, Einar Falsemouth, Magnus Barelegs, Thorfinn Skullsplitter and Sigurd the Stout.

Sailors and raiders

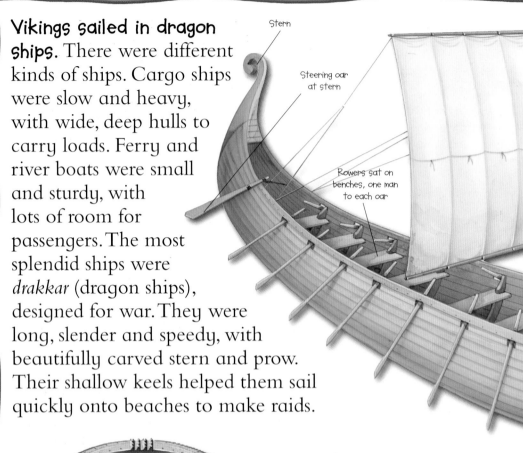

Vikings sailed in dragon ships. There were different kinds of ships. Cargo ships were slow and heavy, with wide, deep hulls to carry loads. Ferry and river boats were small and sturdy, with lots of room for passengers. The most splendid ships were *drakkar* (dragon ships), designed for war. They were long, slender and speedy, with beautifully carved stern and prow. Their shallow keels helped them sail quickly onto beaches to make raids.

Stern

Steering oar at stern

Rowers sat on benches, one man to each oar

QUIZ

1. What were *drakkar*?
2. When did Svein Forkbeard rule Denmark?
3. What kind of wood was used to make the keel of a boat?

Answers:
1. Viking ships 2. AD 987–1014
3. Oak

Sailors steered by the stars. The Vikings had no radio or satellite systems to help them navigate (steer a course) when they were out of sight of land. So they made careful observations of the Sun by day and the stars by night, to work out their position. They also studied the winds, waves and ocean currents, and the movements of fish and seabirds.

Square sail made of linen or wool

Carved, wooden prow

◀ A viking dragon ship that was built to be used in times of war.

Strong wooden keel (helped steer a swift, straight course through the waves)

Shipbuilders searched for tall trees. They used oak timbers to make the keel (backbone) of each vessel. The biggest keels came from trees at least 40 metres high. Builders added long overlapping planks of oak, ash or birch to make the hull. For masts, they used the trunks of very tall, straight trees, such as pine.

Pirates demanded gold to go away. Viking pirates such as King Svein Forkbeard of Denmark (ruled AD 985–1014) demanded money with menaces! He led Viking warships to England and promised to attack if he was not paid to sail away. Svein's tactics worked. Each time he returned, the English handed over 'Dane-geld' (gold for the Danes) – again and again – and again!

Raiders carried off treasure and slaves. Viking nobles recruited gangs of loyal warriors to go on raiding expeditions. They sailed away from Viking homelands to attack villages or defenceless monasteries. Their aim was to grab valuable treasure and healthy young men and women to sell as slaves.

▼ Families living in seaside villages lived in constant fear of a Viking pirate raid.

Warriors and weapons

Vikings valued glory more than long life.
They believed that a dead warrior's
fame lived on after him, and made
sure that his name would never die.
Myths and legends also told
how warriors who died in
battle would go to Valhalla,
where they feasted with
the gods.

Berserkirs were mad for battle. Berserkirs
('bear-shirts') were warriors who dressed in animal
skins and worked themselves into a trance before
battle. They charged at the enemy, howling and
growling like wolves and chewing at their shields.
In this state, they were wild and fearless and
dangerous to anyone who got in their way.
This is where the word 'beserk' comes from.

▲ Berserkir warriors
rushed madly into
battle, wearing
animal skins over
their mail armour.

Lords led followers into war.

There were no national armies in Viking times. Each king or lord led his followers into battle against a shared enemy. A lord's followers fought to win praise, plus rich rewards, such as arm rings of silver or a share of captured loot.

Warriors gave names to their swords.

A good sword was a Viking warrior's most treasured possession. He often asked to be buried with it and gave it a name such as 'Sharp Biter'. Viking swords were double-edged, with strong, flexible blades made by hammering layers of iron together. Their hilts (handles) were decorated with silver and gold patterns.

Viking soldiers lived in camps and forts.

Wars and raids took warriors far from home. Soldiers in places such as England built camps of wooden huts, surrounded by an earth bank topped by a wooden wall.

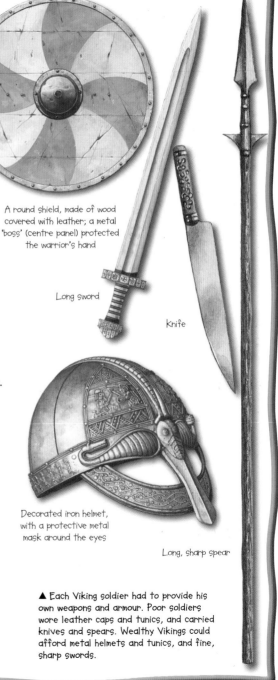

A round shield, made of wood covered with leather; a metal 'boss' (centre panel) protected the warrior's hand

Long sword

Knife

Decorated iron helmet, with a protective metal mask around the eyes

Long, sharp spear

▲ Each Viking soldier had to provide his own weapons and armour. Poor soldiers wore leather caps and tunics, and carried knives and spears. Wealthy Vikings could afford metal helmets and tunics, and fine, sharp swords.

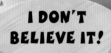

I DON'T BELIEVE IT!

Viking women went to war but they did not fight! Instead, they nursed wounded warriors and cooked meals for hungry soldiers.

Traders, explorers, settlers

Viking traders rode on camels and carried their ships! The Vikings were brave adventurers, keen to seek new land, slaves and treasures. Some traders travelled through Russia to Constantinople (now Istanbul in Turkey), and Jerusalem (in Israel). Each journey took several years. In Russia, they carried their ships over ground between rivers. In the desert near Jerusalem, they rode on camels, like local traders.

▼ Vikings made long overland journeys in winter. The frozen ground was easier to walk across – especially when carrying heavy loads.

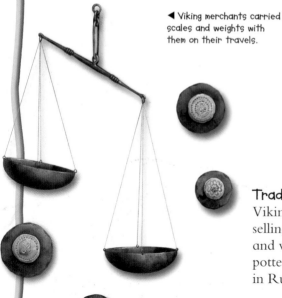

◀ Viking merchants carried scales and weights with them on their travels.

Traders carried scales and silver. Vikings traded with many different peoples. Some used coins for trading, others preferred to barter (swap). There were no banks in Viking times and traders could not be sure of having the right money for every business deal. So they bought and sold using pieces of silver, which they weighed out on delicate, portable scales.

Traders came home with lots of shopping! Viking merchants purchased goods, as well as selling them. They went to Britain to buy wheat and woollen cloth, and to France for wine and pottery. They bought glass in Germany, jewellery in Russia, and spices from the Middle East.

QUIZ

1. Where did the Vikings buy jewellery?
2. Who was the first Viking to see America?
3. When did Erik the Red reach Greenland?

Answers:
1. Russia 2. Bjarni Herjolfsson 3. Around AD 983

Vikings sailed to America – by mistake! In AD 986, Bjarni Herjolfsson was blown off course in a storm. He saw land, but did not stop to explore. A few years later, Greenland settler Lief Eriksson decided to look for the land Bjarni had seen. He landed in places he called Hellulland, Markland and Vinland. Today, we know that these are places on the east coast of North America.

Vikings settled from Scotland in the north of Europe to Sicily in the south. Everywhere they went, Vikings founded new villages and towns. Sometimes they fought for land from local peoples, and sometimes they lived peacefully alongside them.

Settlers were tricked into moving to Greenland. Erik the Red first reached the island of Greenland around AD 983. It was bleak and icy, with little pasture, and almost no land suitable for grain. But Erik wanted families to join his new settlement. So he called it 'Greenland'. In AD 986, Viking settlers sailed to join him. By the time they discovered what Greenland was really like, it was too late to turn back.

▶ The Vikings settled on Greenland's coastline as the inland areas were covered in ice. These settlements died out between 1480 and 1500 when the climate became even colder.

The Vikings at home

In the 700s and 800s, the Vikings were some of the best craftworkers in Europe. They lived in a harsh environment, with cold, long, dark winters. Buildings were needed to shelter livestock, as well as people. In towns, pigs, goats and horses were kept in sheds, but in parts of the countryside, farmers built longhouses, with rooms for the family at one end and for animals at the other.

Vikings built houses out of grass. In many lands where the Vikings settled, such as the Orkney Islands or Iceland, there were hardly any trees. So Viking families built homes out of slabs of turf (earth with grass growing in it), arranged on a low foundation of stone. If they could afford it, they lined the rooms with planks of wood imported from Scandinavia. Otherwise, they collected pieces of driftwood, washed up on shore.

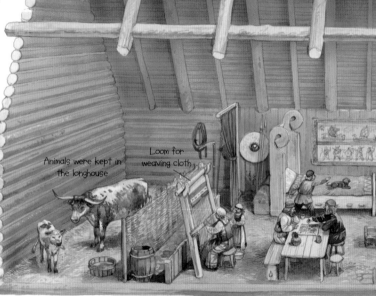

Animals were kept in the longhouse

Loom for weaving cloth

Walls made of logs

▶ Longhouses were usually built on sloping ground so that waste from the animals ran downhill, away from human living rooms.

Viking homes could be unhealthy.
Viking houses did not have windows – they would have let in too much cold. So homes were often damp, and full of smoke from the fire burning on the hearth. As a result, Viking people suffered from chest diseases. Some may also have been killed by a poisonous gas (called carbon monoxide) that is produced when a fire uses up all the oxygen in a room.

I DON'T BELIEVE IT!

Vikings liked living in longhouses, because heat from the animals provided a kind of central heating, keeping everyone warm.

Turf (earth with growing grass) roof

Wooden rafters

Meat was smoked to preserve it

Homeowners sat in the high seat.
Most Viking families had little furniture. Only the rich could afford beds, or tables with fixed legs. Most homes were simply furnished with trestle tables, wooden storage chests and wooden benches. The centre of one bench was marked off by two carved wooden pillars, and reserved as the 'high seat' (place of honour) for the house owner. Important guests sat facing him or her, on the bench opposite.

Outside lavatory

Farmers, fishers and hunters

Viking farmers prized pasture more than ploughed fields. In northern lands, the soil was too thin and stony for crops such as wheat and barley to grow well. Farmers relied on sheep and cattle to provide meat and milk. These animals needed fresh grass to eat so Viking farmers valued pasture land, where grass flourished, more than stony fields.

Flax and hay were the most important crops. They were needed to make clothes and feed cattle. Outer garments were made of wool, and could be very itchy, so women wove smoother, finer cloth to wear next to the skin. They used the stalks of a plant called flax, which farmers planted in damp ground. Farm animals needed hay (dried grass) to eat in winter, when pastures were covered by snow. Viking farmers grew grass in well-manured meadows, then cut it, dried it and stored it for winter.

Fish drying in the wind

Rack for drying grass to make hay

Ships anchored in
a safe harbour

**Hunters and fishermen found food around
the coast.** The Vikings lived close to some of
the world's richest fishing grounds. Fishermen
used nets and traps to catch sea fish such as cod
and herring, or river fish such as salmon, trout
and eels. They gathered mussels and oysters from
the seashore, and hunted whales, mostly for their
blubber. Young men climbed dangerous cliffs to
collect seabirds and their eggs or scrambled over
skerries – little rocky islands – to catch seals and
walruses basking there.

◄ The Vikings were not just interested in
raiding and stealing. They realized that the
British Isles provided good farmland and safe
areas for settlements.

Cutting
grass to
make hay

Ploughing with oxen

**Trappers tracked wild
animals.** In Norway and
Sweden, there were many
wild animals, such as bears,
wolves and foxes. These
were hunted for their furs,
which made warm clothes,
or were sold to rich customers.
Hunters also chased deer for their
meat, antlers and skins. Antlers were
used to make beads and combs.

Scattering grain to
feed chickens

189

Food and famine

Vikings ate two meals a day. First thing in the morning was the 'day meal' of barley bread or oatcakes, butter or cheese. The main meal – 'night meal' – was eaten in the early evening. It included meat or fish, plus wild berries in summer. Meals were served on wooden plates or soapstone bowls and eaten with metal knives and wood or horn spoons.

▼ Objects made from cattle horn were light but very strong – ideal for Viking traders or raiders to carry on their journeys.

Patterned silver cup used by the rich

Pottery beaker used by the poor

Drinking horn used by warriors

Warriors drank from hollow horns. Favourite Viking drinks were milk, whey (the liquid left over from cheese-making), ale (brewed from malted barley), and mead (honey wine). Rich people drank from glass or silver cups, but ordinary people had wooden or pottery beakers. On special occasions feasts were held, and Viking warriors drank from curved cattle horns.

Red-hot stones boiled water for cooking.

Few Viking homes had ovens. So women and their servants boiled meat in iron cauldrons, or in water-filled pits heated by stones that were made red-hot in a fire. This was a very efficient way of cooking.

The Vikings loved blood sausages.

Cooks made sausages by pouring fresh animal blood and offal (heart, liver and lungs) into cleaned sheep's intestines, then boiling them. Sometimes they added garlic, cumin seeds or juniper berries as flavouring. Vikings preferred these to vegetables such as cabbages, peas and beans.

▲ Viking vegetables included peas, beans, cabbages, onions – and garlic.

Cabbage

Beans

Garlic

Peas

Onion

Feasts went on for a week or more.

After winning a great victory, Vikings liked to celebrate. Kings and lords held feasts to reward their warriors, and families feasted at weddings. Guests dressed in their best clothes and hosts provided much food and drink. Everyone stayed in the feast hall until the food ran out, or they grew tired.

▼ Viking women and slaves cooked huge meals over open fires, and served them to feasting warriors.

Women and children

Viking women were independent.
They made important household
decisions, cooked, made clothes,
raised children, organized slaves
and managed farms and workshops
while their husbands were away.

▲ Women spun sheep's wool and wove it
into warm cloth on tall, upright looms.

MAKE A VIKING PENDANT

You will need:
String or cord 40 centimetres long
Modelling clay
White, yellow and brown paint
Paintbrush
Gold or silver paint

1. Shape some animal fangs
from modelling clay, about
4 centimetres long.

2. Make a hole through the widest
end of each fang. Leave to harden.

3. Paint the fangs with white,
brown or yellow paint. When
dry, decorate with gold and
silver paint.

4. Thread string through the fangs
and wear around your neck like a
Viking.

**Only widows could wed who they
wanted to.** If a Viking man wanted
to marry, he had to ask the young
woman's father for permission and
pay him a bride price. If the father
accepted this, the marriage went
ahead, even if the woman did not
agree. Widows had more
freedom. They did not need
anyone's permission to marry
again. Viking laws also gave all
women the right to ask for a
divorce if their husbands
treated them badly.

Old women won respect for wise advice. Many Viking women died young in childbirth or from infectious diseases. So older people, aged 50 or more, were a small minority in Viking society. While they were still fit, they were respected for their knowledge and experience. But if they grew sick or frail, their families saw them as a burden.

Viking fathers chose which children survived. Parents relied on children to care for them in old age so they wanted strong offspring. The father examined each baby after it was born. If it seemed healthy, he sprinkled it with water and named it to show it was part of his family. If the child looked sickly he told slaves to leave it outside to die.

◀ Feeding chickens and collecting eggs was work for Viking girls. They learned how to grow vegetables — and cook them — by helping their mothers.

Viking children did not go to school. Daughters helped their mothers with cooking and cleaning, fed farm animals, fetched water, gathered wood, nuts and berries and learned how to spin, weave and sew. Sons helped their fathers in the workshop or on the farm. They also learned how to ride horses and use weapons. Boys had to be ready to fight by the time they were 15 or 16 years old.

▲ Viking boys practised fighting with wooden swords and small, lightweight shields.

Clothes and jewellery

Vikings wore lots of layers to keep out the cold. Women wore a long dress of linen or wool with a woollen over-dress. Men wore wool tunics over linen undershirts and woollen trousers. Both men and women wore gloves, cloaks, socks, and leather boots or shoes. Men added fur or sheepskin caps while women wore headscarves and shawls.

▶ Viking men and women liked bright colours and patterns. They often decorated their clothes with strips of woven braid.

Furs, fleeces and feathers also helped Vikings keep warm. Vikings lined or trimmed their woollen cloaks with fur, or padded them, like quilts, with layers of goose-down. Some farmers used sheepskins to make cloaks that were hard-wearing, as well as very warm.

Brooches held Viking clothes in place. There were several different styles. Men wore big round brooches, pinned on their right shoulders, to hold their cloaks in place. Women wore pairs of brooches – one on each shoulder – to fasten the straps of their over-dresses. They might also wear another brooch at their throat, to fasten their cloak, plus a brooch with little hooks or chains, to carry their household keys.

▶ This beautiful brooch, decorated with real gold wire, was once worn by a very rich Viking nobleman.

Rings showed Vikings' wealth — and bravery.
Viking men, as well as women, liked to wear lots of jewellery. They thought it made them look good, but it also displayed their wealth, and sometimes, their achievements. Arm- and neck-rings, in particular, were often given to warriors as rewards for fighting bravely in battle.

Arm-ring of twisted gold

▼ Viking craftworkers used designs from many different lands to create beautiful jewellery.

Russian-style necklace of silver and rock crystal

Brooch with long pin — a typical British style

Small gold ring

Favourite Viking clothing colours were red and green. Archaeologists have found the remains of brightly coloured cloth at Viking sites. They have also found fragments of patterned braid, silk ribbon, and gold and silver thread. All were used to decorate Viking clothes.

I DON'T BELIEVE IT!
The Vikings imported boatloads of broken glass from Germany, to melt and recycle into beautiful glass beads.

Health and beauty

The English complained that Vikings were too clean! They said that the Vikings combed their hair too often, changed their clothes frequently and bathed once a week. Vikings bathed by pouring water over red-hot stones to create clouds of steam. They sat in the steam to sweat, then whipped their skin with birch twigs to help loosen the dirt. Then they jumped into a pool of cold water to rinse off.

▲ Vikings 'bathed' in clouds of steam. Similar steam baths, called saunas, are still popular in Scandinavia today.

Some Vikings took their swords to the lavatory. Most Viking homes had an outside lavatory, consisting of a bucket or a hole in the ground with a wooden seat on top. The lavatory walls were often made of wickerwork – panels of woven twigs. But Viking warriors in enemy lands made different arrangements. They went outside in groups of four, carrying swords to protect one another.

▲ Viking lavatories may have looked like this. Vikings used dried moss, grass or leaves as toilet paper.

Vikings used onions to diagnose illness. If a warrior was injured in the stomach during a battle, his comrades cooked a dish of porridge strongly flavoured with onion and gave it to him to eat. They waited, then sniffed the wound. If they could smell onions, they left the man to die. They knew that the injury had cut open the stomach, and the man would die of infection.

I DON'T BELIEVE IT!

Viking men wore make-up! They particularly liked eyeliner – probably made from soot, or crushed berries. They thought it made them look more handsome.

▲ Faith in the healing power of runes may have helped some Viking people feel better.

For painkilling power, the Vikings relied on runes. The Vikings made medicines from herbs and other plants, but they also believed that runes – their way of writing – had magic healing powers. They carved runic spells and charms on pieces of bone and left them under the heads of sleeping sick people. Runes were written on women's palms during childbirth to protect from pain.

Hair-care was very important. Viking women wore their hair long. They left it flowing loose until they married, then tied it in an elaborate knot at the nape of their neck. Viking men also liked fancy hairstyles. They cut their hair short at the back, but let their fringes grow very long. So that they could see where they were going, some Vikings plaited the strands that hung down either side of their face.

▲ Fashionable Viking hairstyles. Women also wove garlands of flowers to wear in their hear on special occasions.

Skilled craftworkers

Vikings made most of the things they needed.
Viking families had to make – and mend – almost everything they needed – from their houses and its furniture to farm carts, children's toys and clothes. They had no machines to help them, so most of this work was done slowly and carefully by hand.

Blacksmiths travelled from farm to farm.
Many Viking men had a simple smithy at home, where they could make and mend tools. For specialized work, they relied on skilled blacksmiths, who travelled the countryside, or they made a long journey to a workshop in a town.

▶ Blacksmiths heated iron over open fires until it was soft enough to hammer into shape to make tools and weapons.

Bones could be beautiful. Skilled craftworkers used deer antler to make fine combs. But these were too expensive for ordinary Vikings to buy. They carved bones left over from mealtimes into combs, beads and pins, as well as name tags and weaving tablets (used to make patterned braid).

Craftsmen carved cups from the cliff face. Deposits of soft soapstone were found in many Viking lands. It looked good, but it was very heavy. To save taking lumps of it to their workshops, stoneworkers carved rough shapes of cups and bowls into cliffs at soapstone quarries, then took them home to finish neatly.

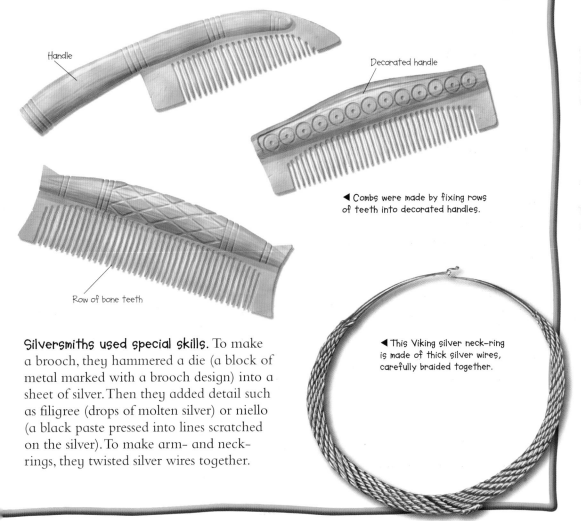

Handle

Decorated handle

◀ Combs were made by fixing rows of teeth into decorated handles.

Row of bone teeth

Silversmiths used special skills. To make a brooch, they hammered a die (a block of metal marked with a brooch design) into a sheet of silver. Then they added detail such as filigree (drops of molten silver) or niello (a black paste pressed into lines scratched on the silver). To make arm- and neck-rings, they twisted silver wires together.

◀ This Viking silver neck-ring is made of thick silver wires, carefully braided together.

Viking towns

Kings built towns to encourage trade. Before the Vikings grew so powerful, merchants traded at fairs held just once or twice a year. Viking kings decided to build towns so that trade could continue all year round. Taxes were collected from the people and merchants who traded there.

▶ Viking markets were often held on beaches. Farming families and travelling merchants met there to buy and sell.

Towns were tempting targets for attack. Pirates and raiders from Russia and north Germany sailed across the Baltic Sea to snatch valuable goods from Viking towns. So kings paid for towns to be defended with high banks of earth and strong wooden walls. They also sent troops of warriors to guard them.

Houses in towns were specially designed. Space was limited inside town walls so houses were built close together. They were smaller than country homes, as people needed less space to store crops or house animals. Most town houses were made of wood with thatched roofs. Many had craft workshops and showrooms inside.

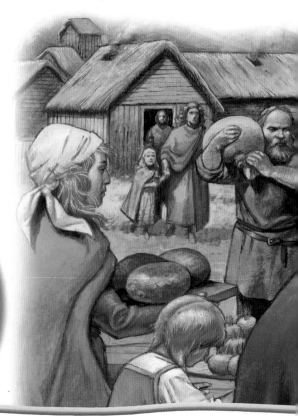

I DON'T BELIEVE IT!

The first Russians were Vikings! The name 'Russia' comes from the word, 'Rus', used by people living east of the Baltic Sea to describe Viking traders who settled there.

Towns made the first Viking coins.
As far as we know, there were no coins
in Scandinavia before the Viking age.
Traders bartered (swapped) goods, or
paid for them using bits of silver,
weighed out on tiny, portable scales.
But many foreign coins came to
Viking lands from overseas trading
and raiding. Around AD 825,
craftsmen in the Viking town
of Hedeby (now in north
Germany) began to copy them.
Later, other towns set up mints to
make coins of their own.

**Viking traders gave Russia its
name.** Adventurous Vikings visiting
the east shores of the Baltic set up
towns as bases for trade. Some of
the biggest were Staraja Ladoga
and Novgorod, in Russia, and
Kiev in the Ukraine.

◀ This Viking coin shows a
merchant ship. It comes from
the town of Hedeby.

Law and order

Vikings followed a strict code of honour. Men and women were proud and dignified and honour was important to them. It was a disgrace to be called a cheat or a coward, or to run away from a fight. Vikings also prized loyalty. They swore solemn promises to be faithful to lords and comrades and sealed bargains by shaking hands.

Many quarrels were settled by fighting. Quarrels between Viking families often led to feuds. If one family member was insulted or killed, all others had a duty to avenge him. Feuds could continue for months, with many people on both sides being killed, until each family was prepared to seek peace and pay compensation.

▲ Viking warriors challenged people who insulted them – or harmed their families – to a deadly duel.

Viking laws were not written down.
Instead, they were memorized by a man known as the law-speaker. He recited them out loud every year so that everyone else could hear and understand them. Because of their expert knowledge, law-speakers often became advisors to kings and lords.

Every year, Vikings met at the Thing. This was an open-air assembly of all free men in a district. It met to punish criminals and make new laws. The most usual punishments were heavy fines. Thing meetings were great social occasions where people from remote communities had the chance to meet and exchange news. Many traders also attended, setting up stalls with goods around the edge of a field.

▼ All free men – from noble chieftains to farmers – could speak and vote at a Viking Thing.

Ruthlessness was respected.
It was tough being a Viking. Everyone had to work hard to survive and there was no room in the community for people who were weak, lazy or troublesome. Thieves were often hanged and criminals who refused to pay compensation or fines were outlawed. This was a very harsh penalty. Without a home and family, it was hard for any individual to survive.

QUIZ

1. What were the two worst Viking punishments for crimes?

2. How did the Vikings settle family feuds?

3. Why did Vikings shake hands with each other?

Answers:
1. Hanging and outlaw
2. By fighting – a duel
3. To seal bargains

Gods and goddesses

Viking people honoured many gods.
The Aesir (sky gods) included Odin, Thor and Tyr, who were gods of war, and Loki, who was a trickster. The Vanir (gods of earth and water) included Njord (god of the sea) and Frey (the farmers' god). He and his sister Freyja brought pleasure and fertility.

▼ Odin, Viking god of war, rode an eight-legged horse. Two ravens, called Thought and Memory, flew by his side.

▼ Beautiful Viking goddess Freyja rode in a chariot pulled by cats.

Animals – and people – were killed as sacrifices.
The Vikings believed that they could win favours from the gods by offering them gifts. Since life was the most valuable gift, they gave the gods living sacrifices. Vikings also cooked meals of meat – called blood-offerings – to share with the gods.

Destiny controlled the Vikings.
According to legends, three sisters (Norns) decided what would happen in the world. They sat at the foot of Yggdrasil, the great tree that supported the universe, spinning 'the thread of destiny'. They also visited each newborn baby to decide its future. Once made, this decision could not be changed.

After death, Vikings went to Hel's kingdom. Warriors who died in battle went to Valhalla or to Freyja's peaceful home. Unmarried girls also joined Freyja, and good men went to live with gods in the sky. Most Vikings who lived ordinary lives and died of illness or old age could only look forward to a future in Niflheim. This was a gloomy place, shrouded in freezing fog, ruled by a fierce goddess called Hel.

Towards the end of the Viking age, many people became Christians. Missionaries from England, Germany and France visited Viking lands from around AD 725. The Vikings continued to worship their own gods for the next 300 years. Around AD 1000, Viking kings, such as Harald Bluetooth and Olaf Tryggvason decided to follow the Christian faith as it helped strengthen their power. They built churches and encouraged people to be Christians.

▶ Vikings asked fierce and furious god Tyr to help them win victories.

▼ Njord was god of the sea. He married the giantess Skadi, who watched over snowy mountains.

QUIZ

1. Who was Loki?
2. What tree supported the universe?
3. Where did warriors go when they died?

Answers:
1. A trickster god
2. Yggdrasil 3. Valhalla

Heroes, legends and sagas

◄ Vikings loved sagas – stories that recorded past events and famous peoples' lives.

Vikings honoured heroes who died in battle. They told stories, called 'sagas', about their adventures so that their name and fame never died. These stories were passed on by word of mouth for many years. After the end of the Viking Age, they were written down.

Skalds sang songs and told saga stories. Viking kings and lords employed their own personal poets, called skalds. A skald's job was to sing songs and recite poems praising his employer, and to entertain guests at feasts. Most skalds played music on harps or lyres to accompany their poems and songs.

Vikings feared that the world might end. There were many Viking stories foretelling Ragnarok – the Doom of the Gods. This would be a terrible time, when the forces of good clashed with the powers of evil. Viking gods would fight against giants and monsters – and lose. Then the world would come to an end.

▼ Viking legends told how the world would come to an end at the battle of Ragnarok. They also promised that a new world would be born from the ruins of the old.

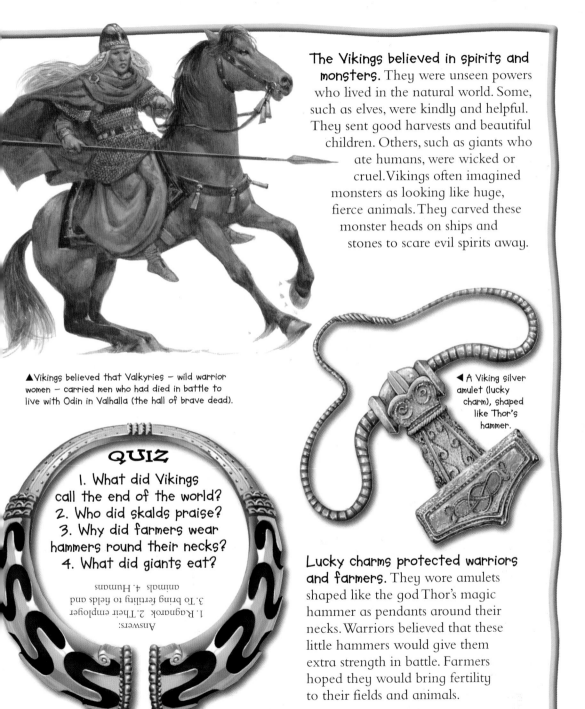

The Vikings believed in spirits and monsters. They were unseen powers who lived in the natural world. Some, such as elves, were kindly and helpful. They sent good harvests and beautiful children. Others, such as giants who ate humans, were wicked or cruel. Vikings often imagined monsters as looking like huge, fierce animals. They carved these monster heads on ships and stones to scare evil spirits away.

▲Vikings believed that Valkyries – wild warrior women – carried men who had died in battle to live with Odin in Valhalla (the hall of brave dead).

◄A Viking silver amulet (lucky charm), shaped like Thor's hammer.

QUIZ

1. What did Vikings call the end of the world?
2. Who did skalds praise?
3. Why did farmers wear hammers round their necks?
4. What did giants eat?

Answers:
1. Ragnarok 2. Their employer
3. To bring fertility to fields and animals 4. Humans

Lucky charms protected warriors and farmers. They wore amulets shaped like the god Thor's magic hammer as pendants around their necks. Warriors believed that these little hammers would give them extra strength in battle. Farmers hoped they would bring fertility to their fields and animals.

Death and burial

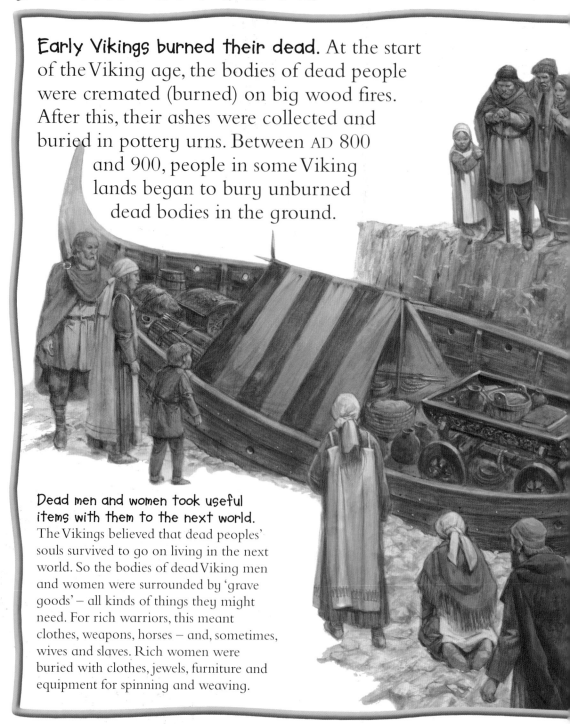

Early Vikings burned their dead. At the start of the Viking age, the bodies of dead people were cremated (burned) on big wood fires. After this, their ashes were collected and buried in pottery urns. Between AD 800 and 900, people in some Viking lands began to bury unburned dead bodies in the ground.

Dead men and women took useful items with them to the next world. The Vikings believed that dead peoples' souls survived to go on living in the next world. So the bodies of dead Viking men and women were surrounded by 'grave goods' – all kinds of things they might need. For rich warriors, this meant clothes, weapons, horses – and, sometimes, wives and slaves. Rich women were buried with clothes, jewels, furniture and equipment for spinning and weaving.

Viking graves have survived for hundreds of years. Archaeologists have discovered many collections of grave contents, in remarkably good condition. Some, such as jewellery, pottery and stone carvings, are made of materials that do not rot. Some, such as clothing, have survived by chance. Others, such as ship burials, have been preserved underwater. All have provided valuable evidence about life in Viking times.

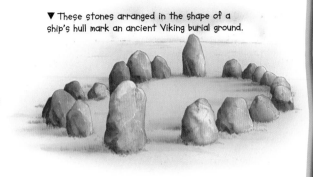

▼ These stones arranged in the shape of a ship's hull mark an ancient Viking burial ground.

◀ The dead were laid to rest in cloth–covered shelters on board real ships. Then the ships were set on fire so that their souls could 'sail away' to the next world.

Vikings hoped that ships might carry their souls away. So they surrounded buried cremation urns with ship-shaped enclosures of stones. Some enclosures were very large – up to 80 metres long – and were probably also used as places of worship. Very important Viking men and women were cremated or buried in real wooden ships, along with valuable grave-goods.

Vikings treated dead bodies with great respect. They washed them, dressed them and wrapped them in cloth or birch bark before burying them or cremating them. This was because the Vikings believed that dead people might come back to haunt them if they were not treated carefully.

I DON'T BELIEVE IT!

Some Viking skeletons and wooden ships that were buried in acid soils have been completely eaten away. But they have left 'shadows' in the ground, which archaeologists can use to find out more about them.

Writing and picture stories

Many ordinary Vikings could not read or write. They relied on the spoken word to communicate and on memory to preserve details of land, family histories and important events. At the beginning of the Viking age, all Vikings spoke the same language, the *donsk tunga* (Danish Tongue). But after AD 1000, different dialects developed.

▲ Viking runes. From top left, these symbols stand for the sounds:
F U Th A R K H N I A S T B M L R.

Viking scribes wrote in 'runes'. There were 16 letters, called runes, in the Viking alphabet. They were used for labelling valuable items with the owner's name, for recording accounts, keeping calendars and for sending messages. Runes were written in straight lines only. This made them easier to carve on wood and stone. The Vikings did not have paper!

▼ Vikings used sharp metal points to carve runes on useful or valuable items.

Viking calendar

Deer antler with runes carved on it

Comb with runes showing owner's name

Runes were used to cast magic spells. Sometimes, runes were used to write messages in secret code, or even magic spells. These supposedly gave the objects they were carved on special power. Some secret Viking writings in runes still have not been deciphered today.

▲ Rune stones were written records of Viking citizens.

Rune stones told stories. Wealthy families paid for expert rune masters to carve runic inscriptions on stones, praising and commemorating dead parents and children. Some boastful people also had stones carved with details of their own achievements. When the carvings were completed, the rune stones were raised up in public places where everyone could see them.

Picture stones told of great adventures. In some Viking lands, people carved memorial stones with pictures, instead of runes. These show scenes from the dead person's life and details of their adventures, together with pictures of gods, giants and monsters.

▲ Some picture stones told of people's achievements, others commemorated loved ones who had died.

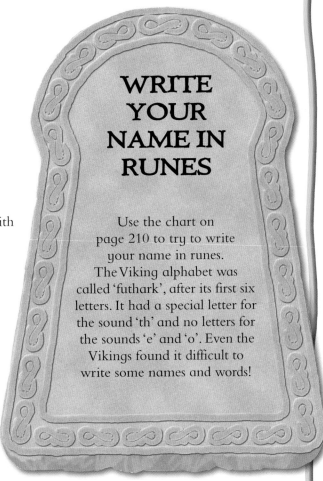

WRITE YOUR NAME IN RUNES

Use the chart on page 210 to try to write your name in runes. The Viking alphabet was called 'futhark', after its first six letters. It had a special letter for the sound 'th' and no letters for the sounds 'e' and 'o'. Even the Vikings found it difficult to write some names and words!

The end of the Vikings

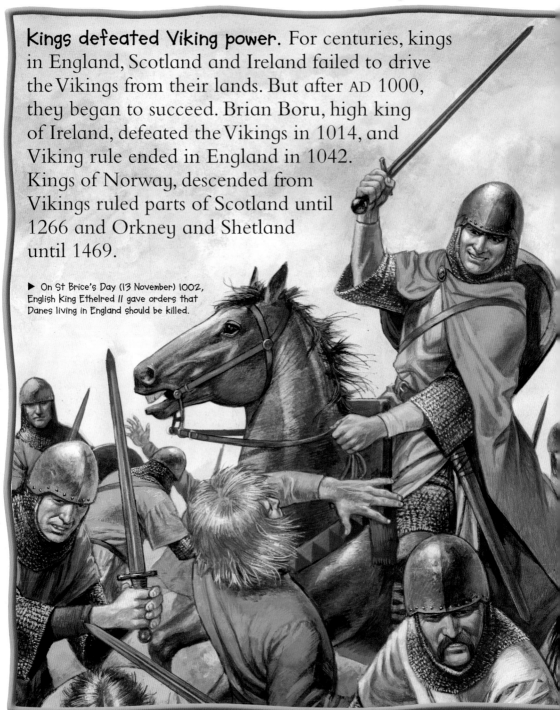

Kings defeated Viking power. For centuries, kings in England, Scotland and Ireland failed to drive the Vikings from their lands. But after AD 1000, they began to succeed. Brian Boru, high king of Ireland, defeated the Vikings in 1014, and Viking rule ended in England in 1042. Kings of Norway, descended from Vikings ruled parts of Scotland until 1266 and Orkney and Shetland until 1469.

▶ On St Brice's Day (13 November) 1002, English King Ethelred II gave orders that Danes living in England should be killed.

Vikings learned to live alongside other peoples. In most places where Vikings settled, they married local women and worked with local people. Some of their words and customs blended with local ones, but many disappeared. Viking traditions only survived if the place where they settled was uninhabited, such as Iceland, or the Orkney Islands, off the north of Scotland.

▲ In 1066, the Normans – descendants of Vikings who had settled in Normandy, France – invaded and conquered England. This scene from the huge Bayeux Tapestry (embroidered wall-hanging) shows their Viking-style ships.

Christianity destroyed faith in Viking gods. The Vikings believed their gods, such as Thor and Odin, would punish them if they did not worship them, and would kill Christian missionaries. But the missionaries survived. So did Vikings who became Christians. This made other Vikings wonder if their gods had any powers, at all.

◀ Christians living in Scandinavia after the end of the Viking age made statues of Jesus Christ to stand in their churches, as symbols of their faith.

Vikings set up new kingdoms outside Viking lands. In places far away from the Viking homelands, such as Novgorod in Russia, or Normandy, in northern France, Viking warlords set up kingdoms that developed independently. Over the years, they lost touch with their Viking origins, and created new customs, laws and lifestyles of their own.

Viking settlers abandoned America. Soon after AD 1000, Thorfinn Karlsefni, a Viking merchant from Iceland, led over 100 Viking men and women to settle at Vinland – the site in North America where Lief Eriksson landed. They stayed there for two years, but left because the Native North Americans attacked them and drove them away.

Knights and Castles

Sharpen your sword, pick up your shield
and prepare to do battle as a knight!

Castle life • Building a castle • Kings • Peasants
Knights • Battle • Coats of arms • Feasts • Songs
Poems • Dragons • Crusades • Famous castles
Eastern warriors • Minstrels • Training

Castle life

A castle was both a home and a fortress in the Middle Ages. It provided shelter for a king or a lord and his family, and it allowed him to defend his lands. Castles were also places where soldiers were stationed, wrong-doers were imprisoned, courts settled disputes, weapons and armour were made and great banquets and tournaments were held.

▶ In the castle grounds soldiers practised their fighting skills. Knights fought on horse back in tournaments, and peasants farmed the land.

In the beginning

The first castles were mostly built from wood on top of a hill. Sometimes castle builders piled up soil to make the hill artificially. On top of the hill, called a motte, stood a wooden tower, or keep. This was the central part of the castle and the easiest part to defend.

▶ This is a motte and bailey castle. The Normans from France introduced this kind of castle in the 1000s, and it soon became popular across Europe.

◀ Castles and forts have been built all over the world since the earliest times. This is the fortified town of Great Zimbabwe, in modern day Zimbabwe. The oldest part dates from the 700s.

▶ By the 1500s the Japanese were building strong, permanent castles of their own. Castles were often built with different layers to fire on the enemy from different heights.

At the bottom of the motte was a courtyard called a bailey. It was usually surrounded by a wooden fence. Castle builders dug a deep ditch, called a moat, all around the outside of the motte and bailey. They often filled the moat with water. Moats were designed to stop attackers reaching the castle walls.

◀ For extra protection, a wooden fence was often built around the top of the motte. The top of each wooden plank was shaped into a point to make it harder for the enemy to climb over.

Wooden castles were not very strong — and they caught fire easily. From around 1100 onwards, people began to build castles in stone. A stone castle gave better protection against attack, fire and cold rainy weather.

Gatehouse

Inner defensive wall

Outer defensive wall

Keep

Turret

▶ Sometimes an extra wall was built on the inside of the strong outer wall. Archers could stand on the inner wall and fire down onto the outer wall if it was captured.

Building a castle

The best place to build a castle was on top of a hill. A hilltop position gave good views over the surrounding countryside, and made it harder for an enemy to launch a surprise attack. Sometimes a castle was built on the banks of a river or lake, and its waters were used to create a moat.

▼ Building a castle took a lot of time and work. It could be a dangerous task.

The lord of the castle and his family lived in the safest part of the castle – the keep. The walls of the keep were built to be very strong, and at least 3.5 metres thick in some castles. Inside the keep were large rooms for receiving visitors and holding banquets, as well as smaller storerooms and guardrooms. The family's bedrooms were on the top floor of the keep. All these rooms and defences made building a castle very slow and expensive.

DESIGN YOUR OWN CASTLE

Imagine you have been asked to design a castle for your local lord. It is important that he can defend his castle and his family against attacks by his enemies.

Draw a plan of your ideal castle, making sure it has plenty of defences. And don't forget the drawbridge to let the lord and his family in and out of their castle.

Who's who in the castle

A castle was the home of an important and powerful person, such as a king, a lord or a knight. The lord of the castle controlled the castle itself, as well as the lands and people around it. The lady of the castle was in charge of the day-to-day running of the castle. She controlled the kitchens and gave the servants their orders for feasts and banquets.

▼ The lord and lady were the most important people in the castle.

The constable was in charge of defending the castle. He was usually a fierce and ruthless man. He trained his soldiers to guard the castle properly and organized the rota of guards and watchmen. The constable was in charge of the whole castle when the lord was away.

Many servants lived and worked inside the castle, looking after the lord and his family. They cooked, cleaned, served at table, worked as maids and servants and ran errands.

▼ A man called the steward was in charge of all the servants.

Servant   Steward   Cooks

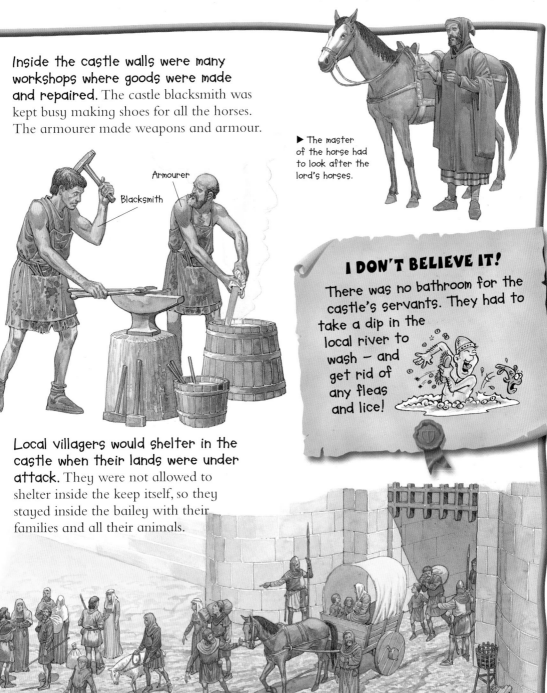

Inside the castle walls were many workshops where goods were made and repaired. The castle blacksmith was kept busy making shoes for all the horses. The armourer made weapons and armour.

▶ The master of the horse had to look after the lord's horses.

Armourer

Blacksmith

I DON'T BELIEVE IT!

There was no bathroom for the castle's servants. They had to take a dip in the local river to wash – and get rid of any fleas and lice!

Local villagers would shelter in the castle when their lands were under attack. They were not allowed to shelter inside the keep itself, so they stayed inside the bailey with their families and all their animals.

From kings to peasants

In medieval times, the king or queen was the most important person in the country.

The king gave land to his barons and other noblemen. In return, they supplied the king with soldiers, horses and weapons to fight wars. This system of giving away land in return for services was known as feudalism.

▶ In medieval times there was often conflict between the Church and the king. Both were very powerful, and they had to try to work together. The bishop had meetings, called an audience, with the king and queen.

The Church was very powerful in the Middle Ages. It controlled large areas of land, and grew rich from the taxes paid by the peasants who worked on these lands. Peasant farmers had to give the church a tithe, one-tenth of everything they produced.

The barons were the most powerful noblemen. A wealthy baron might supply the king with around 5000 fighting men. Some barons also had their own private army to keep control over their own lands.

Quiz

1. What is the name of the mound of soil on which early castles were built?
2. Which was the safest and best-protected part of the castle?
3. What is a moat?
4. Who was in charge of the castle guards?
5. What did the king give to his lords in return for their services?

Answers:
1. Motte 2. Keep 3. Water-filled ditch around the outside of the castle walls 4. Constable 5. Land

The wealthier lords and barons often gave away some of their lands to professional fighters called knights. Knights were skilled soldiers who rode into battle on horseback.

At the very bottom of the feudal system was the poor peasant. In the Middle Ages over 90 percent of people living in Europe worked on the land. Everything in their lives – their land, animals, food, even their clothes – belonged to the local lord.

How to be a good knight

It took about 14 years of training to become a knight. The son of a noble joined a lord's household aged seven. He learned how to ride, to shoot a bow and arrow and how to behave in front of nobles. He then became a squire, where he learned how to fight with a sword, and he looked after his master's armour and weapons. If he was successful, he became a knight at 21.

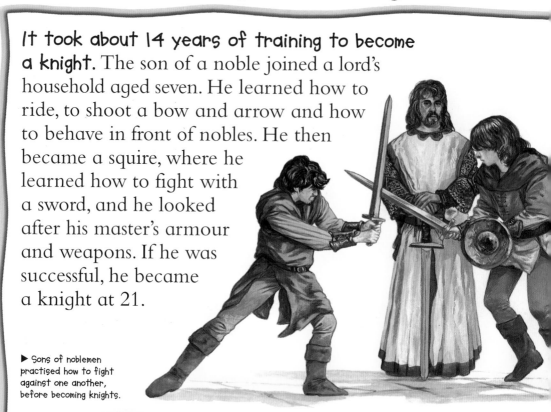

▶ Sons of noblemen practised how to fight against one another, before becoming knights.

The ceremony of making a new knight was known as dubbing. A knight had to spend a whole night in church before his dubbing ceremony took place. First, he had a cold bath and dressed in a plain white tunic. After this he went on to his vigil.

◀ Before dubbing a knight held an all-night watch called a vigil. He spent the night on his knees praying and confessing his sins.

The dubbing ceremony changed over time. In the beginning a knight was struck on the back of the neck. Later, dubbing involved a tap on the knight's shoulder with a sword.

I DON'T BELIEVE IT!

A French knight called Jaufré Rudel sent love poems to the Countess of Tripoli even though he had never met her. When he finally saw her beautiful face he fell into her arms and died.

Knights had to behave according to a set of rules, known as the 'code of chivalry'. The code involved being brave and honourable on the battlefield, and treating the enemy politely and fairly. It also instructed knights how to behave towards women.

A knight who behaved badly was disgraced and punished. A knight in disgrace had either behaved in a cowardly way on the battlefield, cheated in a tournament or treated another knight badly.

A rich knight would have three horses. He rode his heaviest horse for fighting and tournaments. He also had a horse for riding, and a baggage horse. The best horses were warhorses from Italy and Spain. They were quick but strong and sturdy.

Ready for battle

Knights wore a long-sleeved tunic made of linen or wool, with a cloak over the top. By the 1200s knights had started to wear long hooded coats called surcoats. Knights nearly always wore bright colours, and some even wore fancy items such as shoes with curled pointed toes, and hats decorated with sparkling jewels.

Gradually, knights began to wear more and more armour. They added solid metal plates shaped to fit their body. By the 1400s knights were wearing full suits of steel armour. They wore metal gloves, called gauntlets, and even metal shoes!

▲ A knight was dressed for battle from the feet upwards. The last item of armour to be put on him was his helmet.

Early knights wore a type of armour called chainmail. It was made of thousands of tiny iron rings joined onto each other. A piece of chainmail looked a bit like knitting, except it was made of metal, not wool. But a knight also wore a padded jacket under his chainmail to make sure he wasn't cut by his own armour!

A knight had two main weapons: his sword and his shield. The sword was double edged and was sharp enough to pierce chainmail. Knights also fought with lances, daggers and axes.

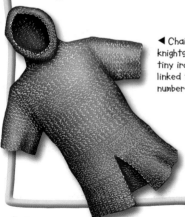

◀ Chainmail protected knights from injury. The tiny iron rings could be linked together in a number of different ways.

I DON'T BELIEVE IT!

Soldiers called 'retrievers' used to have to run into the middle of the battle and collect up all the spare arrows!

Between 1337 and 1453 England and France were almost continually at war with each other, what we now know as the Hundred Years War. The English armies won important battles against the French in 1356 and at Agincourt in 1415. The skilled English and Welsh longbowmen, who could fire as many as 12 arrows every minute, helped to stop the French knights.

A Swiss foot soldier's main weapon was a halberd. This was a combined spear and battleaxe, and was a particularly nasty, but very effective, way of a foot soldier getting a knight off his horse.

Halberd

Colours and coats of arms

When a knight went into battle in full armour wearing a helmet with a visor, no one could recognize him. This problem was solved by putting a different set of coloured symbols on each knight's shield. These sets of symbols became known as coats of arms, and each family had its own personal design. No other family was allowed to use that design.

◄ ▲ ► Coats of arms were displayed on a knight's shield. This system became known as heraldry. Many different symbols and signs were used, but only in a few colours.

Only certain colours and styles of design could be used to create a coat of arms. The colours allowed were red, blue, black, green, purple, silver and gold. The arms also indicated the wearer's position in his family. So, a second son showed a crescent symbol, and a seventh son displayed a rose.

On the battlefield, each nobleman had his own banner around which his knights and other soldiers could meet. The nobleman's colours and coat of arms were displayed on the banner. Banners decorated with coats of arms also made a colourful display at tournaments and parades.

◄ The banner of a nobleman was a very important symbol during battle. If the person holding the banner was killed in battle, someone had to pick the banner up and raise it straight away.

Messengers called heralds carried messages between knights during battle. They had to be able to recognize each individual knight quickly. After coats of arms were introduced, the heralds became experts at identifying them.

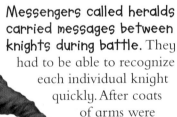

◄ After a battle, it was the sad job of a herald to walk around the battlefield and identify the dead by their coats of arms.

DESIGN YOUR OWN COAT OF ARMS

Would you like your own personal coat of arms? You can design one by following the basic rules of heraldry explained on these pages. You will need the seven paint colours listed opposite, a paintbrush, a fine-tipped black felt pen, a ruler and some thick white paper. Good luck!

Famous knights

Roland was a brave, loyal knight who died in the service of his master. Roland served King Charles the Great – Charlemagne – who ruled much of France and Germany in the 800s. Roland had to protect Charlemagne and his army from Muslim attackers as they crossed from Spain into France. But Roland was betrayed and died fighting for his king.

▲ Famous stories of old knights have been recorded in old books, like this one bound in leather.

The Spanish knight Rodrigo Díaz de Vivar had the nickname 'El Cid'. This comes from the Arabic for 'the Lord'. El Cid fought against the Moors from North Africa. He was exiled by his lord, King Alfonso VI, after the knight's enemies turned the king against him.

▼ Don Quixote charged at windmills because he thought they were giants.

Rodrigo Díaz de Vivar, 'El Cid'

The book 'Don Quixote' tells the story of an old man who dreams about past deeds of bravery and chivalry. It was written in the 1500s by a Spaniard called Miguel de Cervantes. After reading about the knights of old, Don Quixote dresses in armour and sets off on horseback to become famous. He takes a peasant called Sancho Panzo with him as his squire, and it is his squire who gets Don Quixote out of trouble during his travels.

Lancelot was the favourite knight of King Arthur.
Tales of Arthur and his Knights of the Round Table
were very popular in the 1200s. Lancelot fell in love
with Arthur's wife Guinevere. The struggle between
the two men, and the scandal caused by the
romance between Lancelot and Guinevere,
eventually destroyed Arthur's court.

▼ Lancelot was in love with
Guinevere. This greatly angered
her husband King Arthur.

**The Black Prince was the
nickname of Edward, the
oldest son of Edward III of
England.** The Black Prince was a
great warrior who captured the
French king, John II, at the battle
of Poitiers in 1356.

I DON'T BELIEVE IT!

During his travels,
Don Quixote
mistakes
flocks of
farmyard
animals
for enemy
armies!

A castle tour

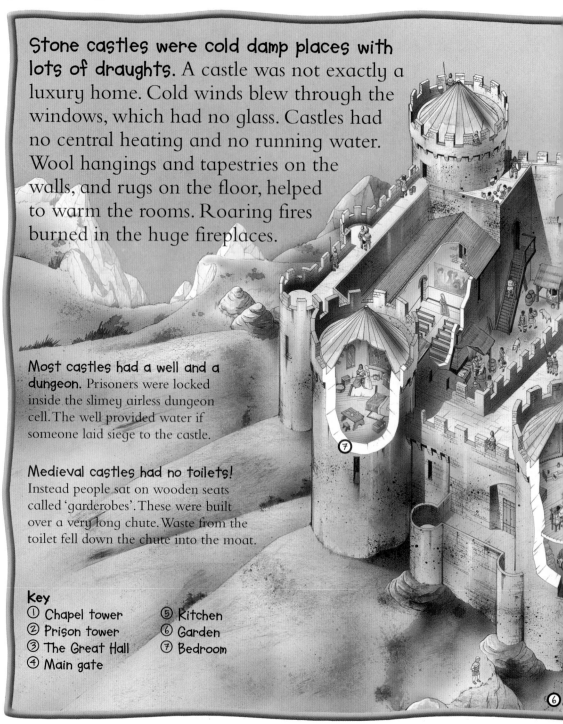

Stone castles were cold damp places with lots of draughts. A castle was not exactly a luxury home. Cold winds blew through the windows, which had no glass. Castles had no central heating and no running water. Wool hangings and tapestries on the walls, and rugs on the floor, helped to warm the rooms. Roaring fires burned in the huge fireplaces.

Most castles had a well and a dungeon. Prisoners were locked inside the slimey airless dungeon cell. The well provided water if someone laid siege to the castle.

Medieval castles had no toilets! Instead people sat on wooden seats called 'garderobes'. These were built over a very long chute. Waste from the toilet fell down the chute into the moat.

Key
① Chapel tower
② Prison tower
③ The Great Hall
④ Main gate
⑤ Kitchen
⑥ Garden
⑦ Bedroom

▼ A castle was a large building with many different rooms and sections. Each area had a different use.

Castle kitchens were built away from the keep in case they caught fire. Only the lord of the castle and his family slept in beds. Most people slept on wooden pallets covered with straw.

There were many workshops and other buildings inside the safety of the castle walls. They included an armoury, a smithy, stables, kennels, a mill for making flour and a chapel. There were sometimes even gardens and orchards!

235

Feasts and fun

The Great Hall was the centre of castle life. The lord and his family ate their meals here and carried out their daily business. Colourful banners, coats of arms and shiny pieces of armour hung from the walls of the Great Hall. The hall was sometimes turned into a courtroom to try local law-breakers.

Musicians entertained the lord and his guests at banquets in the Great Hall. They played instruments such as pipes, drums, fiddles and lutes.

▲ Jesters, jugglers and acrobats performed for the diners between courses. Sometimes a dancing bear might be brought in to entertain the guests.

BAKE A 'TARTE OF APPLES AND ORANGES'

You will need:

a packet of shortcrust pastry
4 eating apples
4 oranges
juice of ½ lemon
3 cups of water
1 cup of honey

½ cup of brown sugar
¼ tsp cinnamon
a pinch of dried ginger
a little milk
a little caster sugar

Ask an adult to help you. Line a pie dish with pastry and bake for 10 minutes in a medium-hot oven. Slice the oranges thinly. Boil the water, honey and lemon juice, then add the oranges. Cover and simmer for two hours, then drain. Peel, core and slice the apples and mix with the sugar, cinnamon and ginger. Place a layer of apples in the bottom of the dish followed by a layer of oranges, then alternate layers until the fruit is used up. Place a pastry lid over the top and brush with a little milk. Make small slits in the lid. Bake in a medium-hot oven for about 45 minutes. Enjoy!

Huge amounts of exotic-looking and delicious foods were served at banquets.
Roast meats included stuffed peacock and swan, as well as venison, beef, goose, duck and wild boar. Whole roasted fish were also served. These foods were followed by dishes made from spices brought from Asia, and then fruit and nuts.

The lord, his family and important guests sat at the high table on a platform called a dais.
From their raised position they could look down over the rest of the diners. The most important guests such as priests and noblemen sat next to the lord.

Important guests drank fine wine out of proper glasses. Cup-bearers poured the wine out of decorated pottery jugs. Less important diners drank ale or wine from mugs or tankards made of wood, pewter or leather.

Knights and dragons

The legend of St George tells how the brave knight killed a dragon. The dragon was terrorizing the people of Lydia (part of modern Turkey). The king offered his daughter to the dragon if the dragon left. St George said he would kill their dragon if they became Christians. Thousands accepted his offer, and George killed the dragon.

▶ St George fought dragons and was adopted as the patron saint of England.

Legend says that King Arthur became king after pulling a magic sword called Excalibur out of a stone. This act proved that he was the right person to rule Britain. People have written stories about Arthur and his followers, the Knights of the Round Table, for more than 1000 years.

◀ No one really knows who the real Arthur was, but he may have been a Celtic warrior who lived about 1400 years ago.

In the 1300s an Englishman called Geoffrey Chaucer wrote 'The Canterbury Tales'. These stories were about a group of pilgrims travelling from a London inn to a religious site in Canterbury.

Ivanhoe was a medieval knight who lived in the time of Richard the Lionheart. He is the hero of a historical book called 'Ivanhoe', written by the Scottish novelist Sir Walter Scott in the 1800s. 'Ivanhoe' describes the conflict between the Saxon people and their Norman conquerors at a time when the Normans had ruled England for at least 100 years.

King Arthur had many castle homes but his favourite was Camelot. Historians think that Camelot was really an English castle called Tintagel. When Arthur heard that his best friend and favourite knight, Sir Lancelot, had fallen in love with Arthur's wife, Queen Guinevere, Arthur banished Lancelot from his court at Camelot.

Practice for battle

In a tournament, knights divided into two sides and fought each other as if in a proper battle. Tournaments were good practice for the real thing – war. The idea for these mock battles, called tourneys, probably started in France in the 12th century.

▼ Jousting knights charged at each other at top speed. Each one tried to knock his opponent off his horse with a blow from a long wooden lance.

▲ Edward I of England was a keen supporter of tournaments and jousts. He banned spectators from carrying weapons themselves because this caused too much trouble among the watching crowds.

Tournaments took place under strict rules. There were safe areas where knights could rest without being attacked by the other side. Knights were not meant to kill their opponents but they often did. Several kings became so angry at losing their best knights that all tournaments were banned unless the king had given his permission.

I DON'T BELIEVE IT!

Some knights cheated in jousts by wearing special armour that was fixed onto the horse's saddle!

Sometimes the knights carried on fighting on the ground with their swords. The problem was that this was as dangerous as a tourney!

Jousts were very social events watched by ladies of the court as well as ordinary people. Knights could show off their skills and bravery to impress the spectators.

Jousting was introduced because so many knights were being killed or wounded during tournaments. More than 60 knights were killed in a single tourney in Cologne, Germany. Jousting was a fight between two knights on horseback. Each knight tried to win by knocking the other off his horse. Knights were protected by armour, and their lances were not sharp.

▼ A joust gave a knight the chance to prove himself in front of the woman he loved.

A knight's code of chivalry did not allow him to win a tournament by cheating. It was better to lose with honour than to win in disgrace.

Friend or enemy?

When Edward the Confessor died in 1066, Duke William of Normandy, his cousin, claimed that he had been promised the throne of England. William and his knights invaded England and defeated Harold, the English king, at the Battle of Hastings.

▲ The Bayeux Tapestry records the story of the Norman invasion of England. It shows William and his knights landing along the English coast, and also shows the moment when England's King Harold was killed at the Battle of Hastings.

One of the major battles of the Hundred Years War was fought at Crécy in 1346. English soldiers defeated a much larger French army, killing almost half the French soldiers. During the battle, the English army used gunpowder and cannons for possibly the first time.

On and off between 1337 and 1453 the neighbouring countries of England and France were at war. The Hundred Years War, as it was called, carried on through the reigns of five English kings and five French ones. The two countries fought each other to decide who should control France. In the end the French were victorious, and England lost control of all her lands in France apart from the port of Calais.

◄ The use of cannons and gun powder during the Hundred Years War changed warfare forever.

Deadly weapons called caltrops were used in the Hundred Years War. A caltrop was a star-shaped piece of metal. These were scattered along the ground in front of an attacking army. They stopped both horses and footsoldiers in their tracks.

A young French girl called Joan of Arc led the French army against the English, who had surrounded the city of Orléans. After 10 days the English were defeated. Joan was later captured, accused of being a witch, and burned to death.

I DON'T BELIEVE IT!

If you captured a knight alive during battle, you could offer him back to his family in return for a generous ransom!

Under attack

An attacking enemy had to break through a castle's defences to get inside its walls. One method was to break down the castle gates with giant battering rams. Attackers and defenders also used siege engines to hurl boulders at each other.

A siege is when an enemy surrounds a castle and stops all supplies from reaching the people inside. The idea is to starve the castle occupants until they surrender or die.

▼ Attackers used many different machines to invade the castle. Siege engines and wooden ladders were just some of these.

▼ Battering rams were used to bash down castles defences. A roof over the battering ram stopped attackers from being hit by arrows or spears.

A riskier way of trying to get inside a castle was to climb over the walls. Attackers either used ladders or moved wooden towers with men hidden inside them into position beside the walls.

Giant catapults were sometimes uses to fire stones or burning pieces of wood inside the castle. The Romans were some of the first people to use catapults in warfare.

▶ Attackers could also dig a tunnel under a wall or a tower. They would then light a fire that burnt away the tunnel's supports. The tunnel collapsed, and brought down the building above.

▲ This siege engine was called a trebuchet. It had a long wooden arm with a heavy weight at one end and a sling at the other. A heavy stone was placed inside the sling. As the weight dropped, the stone was hurled towards the castle walls, sometimes travelling as far as 300 metres.

The enemy sometimes succeeded in tunnelling beneath the castle walls. They surprised the defenders when they appeared inside the castle itself.

I DON'T BELIEVE IT!

The ropes used to wind up siege catapults were made from plaits of human hair!

▼ Cannons were first used to attack castles and fortified towns and cities in the 1300s. Early cannons, called bombards, were made of bronze or iron and they were not very accurate.

The invention of cannons and gunpowder brought the building of castle strongholds almost to an end. It marked the end of warrior knights, too. Castle walls could not stand up to the powerful cannonballs that exploded against them. Guns and cannons were now used on the battlefield, so armies no longer needed the services of brave armoured knights on horseback.

Defending a castle

When the enemy was first spotted approaching a castle, its defenders first pulled up the castle drawbridge. They also lowered an iron grate, called a portcullis, to form an extra barrier behind the drawbridge.

The castle archers fired their arrows through narrow slits in the thick castle walls. They also fired through the gaps in the battlements.

▶ Crossbows were far slower to aim and fire than longbows.

In the middle of the night, a raiding party might leave a besieged castle to surprise the enemy camped outside. The raiders would move along secret passages and climb out through hidden gates or doorways.

◀ Soldiers in the raiding party snuck out of the castle when the enemy was unprepared.

Defenders poured boiling-hot water onto the heads of the enemy as they tried to climb the castle walls. Quicklime was also poured over the enemy soldiers, making their skin burn.

▶ Soldiers threw boulders and poured water onto the enemy's heads through holes in the stonework of the castle's battlements.

Heavy stones and other missiles often rained down from the battlements onto the enemy below. Hidden from view by the high battlements, the defenders stood on wooden platforms to throw the missiles.

Quiz

1. What is the name of the mock battles held between large numbers of knights?

2. Which weapon did jousting knights use when on horseback?

3. Which two countries fought a war that lasted 100 years?

4. In what year was the Battle of Agincourt?

5. Which machine was used to break down castle walls and gates?

Answers:
1. Tourneys 2. Lance
3. England and France 4. 1415
5. Battering ram

247

Off to the crusades

The crusades were military expeditions from Europe to Palestine. The aim for European Christians was to recapture Palestine, at the eastern end of the Mediterranean Sea, from the Muslim Turks who had seized control of it. The First Crusade set off from Europe in 1096. Between 1096 and 1204 there were four separate crusades.

The crusaders built huge castles to defend their lands against the much larger Muslim armies. Many of these castles were big enough to house thousands of soldiers as well as their servants and horses. In the port of Acre the crusaders had constructed a vast underground fortress.

Thousands of young boys and girls set off for the Holy Land in 1212 in one of the strangest crusades – the Children's Crusade. Many died of cold or hunger while marching to the Mediterranean ports. Others drowned during the sea crossing, and some were sold as slaves along the way.

The Muslim leader Saladin fought against the knights of the Third Crusade. Saladin had already defeated the Christian armies and seized the city of Jerusalem. The Third Crusade was meant to recapture Jerusalem. It was led by an emperor and two kings – Emperor Frederick I of Germany, and Richard the Lionheart of England and Philip II of France – but the crusaders failed to regain Jerusalem.

I DON'T BELIEVE IT!

A crusader knight would share his tent with his beloved horse – it must have been a bit of a squeeze!

Many crusaders fought in these religious wars for personal riches. They came from all over western Europe. This was a time when European countries were trying to become more powerful – and wealthier, too. Merchants from Italy wanted to increase their trade, knights from France wanted to grow richer, and priests from England wanted to collect religious treasures.

249

Garters and elephants

A group of Christian knights living in the Holy Land were in charge of protecting pilgrims on their way to and from Palestine. They were the Templar knights, or Templars. Their headquarters were in the Aqsa Mosque in the city of Jerusalem. The Templars grew very rich during their time in the Holy Land, but their organization was eventually broken up.

The Knights of St John looked after the safety and health of pilgrims while they were in the Holy Land. The knights lived like monks and followed strict rules, but they also continued to provide soldiers to fight the Muslims.

▶ The Knights of St John had been monks who cared for sick people before becoming religious knights. They were often referred to as the Hospitallers.

Medieval knights began to band together to form special groups called orders. Each order had its own badge showing the symbol chosen by the order. It was considered an honour to be asked to join an order. New orders began to appear in many countries across Europe. The Order of the Golden Fleece, for example, was started in France by Philip the Good.

▼ Knights wore the badge of their order on a chain around the neck. Knights from the Order of the Golden Fleece wore a badge depicting a golden sheep.

The Order of the Bath was founded in Britain in the early 1400s. Knights who belonged to an order swore loyalty to their king or queen, and promised to fight against their enemies.

The Order of the Garter is the oldest and most important order in Britain. According to the story, Edward III was dancing with a countess when she lost her garter. As the king gave it back to her, he heard the people near him laughing and joking about what they had seen. Angry, the king said that anyone who had evil thoughts should be ashamed. This is still the motto of the order.

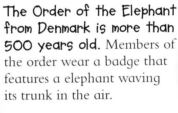

▼ Edward III handed back the lost garter to the countess he had been dancing with.

Quiz

1. Which Muslim warrior fought against the knights of the Third Crusade?

2. By what other name is Richard I of England known?

3. In which city can you find important Muslim and Christian sites?

4. What do knights of the Order of the Golden Fleece wear around their necks?

Answers:
1. Saladin
2. Richard the Lionheart
3. Jerusalem 4. a golden sheep

The Order of the Elephant from Denmark is more than 500 years old. Members of the order wear a badge that features a elephant waving its trunk in the air.

Warriors from the East

Warrior knights in Japan in the Middle Ages were known as samurai. People in Japan were also divided into different feudal groups, where people in each group served someone in a higher-ranking group. The samurai, like European knights, served a lord. They usually fought on horseback but later on they began to fight more on foot.

▲ Early samurai fought on horseback carrying a bow and arrow, and a samurai sword.

▼ The Seljuk Turks were named after their first leader, Seljuk.

A long curving sword was a samurai warrior's most treasured possession. Samurai warriors wore armour on the bodies, arms and legs, a helmet and often a crest made up of a pair of horns.

Samurai sword

The fierce Seljuk Turks fought against Christian knights during the crusades. The Seljuks swept across southwest Asia in the 1000s and 1100s. They conquered many lands, including Syria, Palestine, Asia Minor (modern Turkey) and Persia (modern Iran).

Fierce Mongol warriors from the East terrified the enemy in battle. The Mongols were expert horsemen who controlled their horses with their feet while standing up in their stirrups. This way of riding left both hands free to shoot a bow and arrow.

▼ Each Mongol warrior had a team of five horses ready for battle. As well as being skilled archers, the Mongols were highly trained spear-throwers.

Genghis Khan was the greatest of the Mongol leaders. He became leader of his tribe when he was just 13 years old. He united all the Mongol tribes, and went on to conquer northern China, Korea, northern India, Afghanistan, Persia and parts of Russia.

I DON'T BELIEVE IT!

The Turks fought with gold pieces in their mouths — to stop the crusader knights from stealing them. If a Turkish warrior thought he was going to die, he swallowed the gold.

253

Pirates

From buried treasure to battles at sea,
learn about the exciting world of pirates.

Pirate rivals • Sea dogs • Desert islands • Gallows
Junks • Thieves • Treasure • Shipwrecks • Myths
Attacks • Women pirates • Storms • Corsairs
Outriggers • The Spanish Main

The world of pirates

A pirate is a robber on the sea. Pirates attack ships and ports, stealing treasure and other goods. As soon as the first ships began to carry cargo, pirates began to plunder them – and they are still a threat today. About 500 years ago some areas became special pirate strongholds. The 'corsairs' swooped on vessels in the Mediterranean. The 'buccaneers' of the Caribbean attacked treasure galleons on their way to Europe. The Indian Ocean and the South China Seas were also dangerous places for merchant ships to sail.

Terror from the sea

The Greek islands were home to some of the earliest known pirates. In around 500 BC, there were many cargo ships trading along the Mediterranean coasts. They were easy prey for the pirates, who stole their loads of silver, copper and amber (a precious fossilized resin) before disappearing to their hideouts among the islands.

In 67 BC, the Roman leader Pompey sent a huge fleet to wipe out the pirates of the Mediterranean. They had become a threat to the city of Rome itself by stealing grain supplies. For several years, the Roman campaign got rid of the pirate menace.

▼ Pirates attacked Mediterranean cargo ships and often stole the goods they carried.

Pirates in ancient times used small, fast ships with shallow bottoms. They could steer them easily, and escape into small bays and channels where bigger boats could not go.

This Greek ship called a trireme was used to fight pirates. It had three banks of rowers on each side. Count them up and see how many were needed to push the trireme along.

Answer:
60 rowers powered this ship.

Julius Caesar was captured by pirates when he was 25. While still a prisoner, he joked that he would come back and kill them all. In the end, he was released – and kept his promise. Caesar's troops seized and executed the pirates a few months later.

Viking ships crossed the North Sea to raid settlements on the British coast. Bands of up to 50 Vikings terrified Britons with their battle axes and wide two-edged swords. Their speedy flat-bottomed 'longships' could even carry them up rivers to attack villages inland.

▶ Vikings attacked towns and villages on the coast. They stole treasures and kidnapped people to sell as slaves.

259

Rivals at sea

Pirates of the Mediterranean were known as 'corsairs'.
The most famous corsairs were Muslims from the Barbary Coast of North Africa. They plundered Christian ships – especially when the two sides were at war after the crusades began in about 1100.

The corsairs wanted people, not treasure. They sold their ordinary captives as slaves, or forced them to work in their galleys. Richer people were more valuable. The corsairs demanded ransoms for their release.

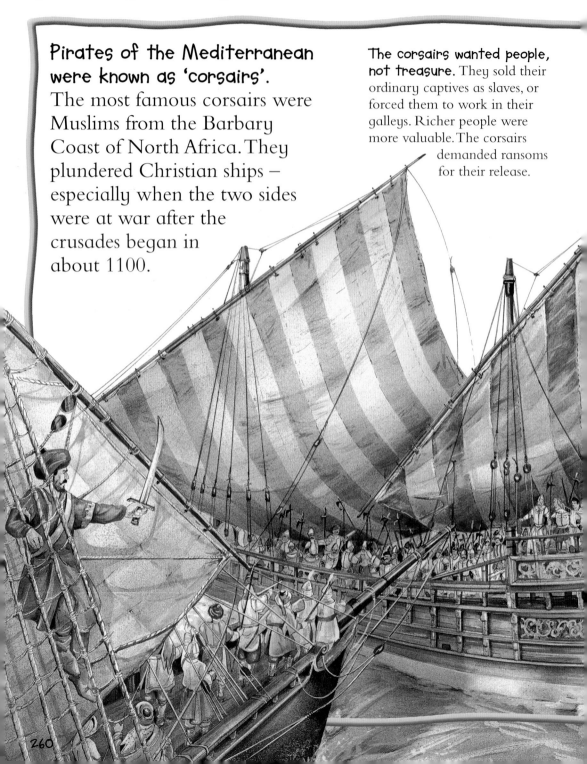

A pirate blunderbuss had a wider end, or muzzle, designed to spread the shot widely before boarding a ship.

Early grenade

Dagger sheath

Cannon ball

Dagger

At the front of the ship a corsair galley had a massive ram. The galley was rammed into the side of the Christian vessel. Then soldiers called janissaries jumped aboard and quickly overpowered the enemy.

Corsairs fought with curved swords called scimitars. Muslim craftsmen made the sharpest and most beautiful swords and daggers in the world. Some corsairs also carried muskets, while the galleys were armed with small brass cannons.

The two most feared corsairs were the Barbarossa brothers. One attacked ships belonging to the Pope and even captured the town of Algiers in north Africa, but he was killed there in 1518. The other Barbarossa became an ally of the Turkish emperor.

◄ Corsairs rammed Christian ships before kidnapping those on board.

I DON'T BELIEVE IT!
'Barbarossa' was not the brothers' real name. It was a nickname given to them by their enemies because of the colour of their beards. Barba rossa means 'Redbeard' in Latin.

Captured by corsairs

The life of a galley slave was horrible. The oars were so big and heavy that they needed as many as six men to pull them. The slaves were chained to rows of benches. In between the rows strode the overseer, or officer in charge. He would drive the men to work harder, either by shouting or by lashing them with his whip.

▼ Going to sea in a stolen, or even a hand-made boat, was the only way for slaves to escape.

Many slaves tried to escape. Some went inland, but found only desert regions short of food and water. The only other way was to escape by sea, making or stealing a boat. Very few got away.

▲ Galley slaves were forced to break rocks and dig.

On land, the slaves lived in a prison, or bagnio. Each slave had a heavy ring and chain riveted to his ankle, and was given a blanket to sleep on. When he was not rowing in the galleys, he spent his time digging or breaking rocks. There was little food apart from bread, and many slaves died in the bagnio.

There were Christian corsairs, too.
Many were based on the island of Malta,
where they were supported by Christian
knights on the island who wanted to see
the Muslims defeated. Maltese corsairs
also used galleys rowed by men captured
and forced to work, and were just as
brutal as their enemies in North Africa.

▼ The English and Dutch fleet bombarded
Algiers with cannon to stop the corsairs
and free their slaves.

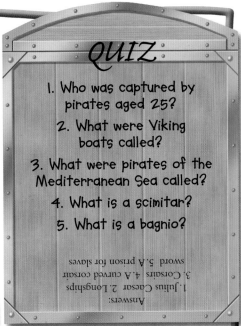

QUIZ

1. Who was captured by
pirates aged 25?

2. What were Viking
boats called?

3. What were pirates of the
Mediterranean Sea called?

4. What is a scimitar?

5. What is a bagnio?

Answers:
1. Julius Caesar 2. Longships
3. Corsairs 4. A curved corsair
sword 5. A prison for slaves

In 1816 a fleet of English
and Dutch ships
bombarded Algiers. They
forced the corsairs to release
over 3000 slaves. A few years
later French troops invaded
Algiers, and brought the
ravages of the corsair bands
to an end.

Some corsairs attacked
countries far from the
Mediterranean. Murad
Rais sailed all the way to
Iceland in 1627. His
plundered treasure included
salted fish and leather!

The Spanish Main

From the early 1500s, Spanish galleons carried vast amounts of treasure across the Atlantic. Loaded with American gold, silver, jewels and other riches, these big vessels were heavily armed. But they were also slow and heavy, and attracted pirates.

Francis le Clerc was one of the first and fiercest pirates on the Spanish Main. Known as 'Peg Leg' because of his wooden leg, le Clerc raided towns on the coasts of Hispaniola, what we now call Cuba. He even captured the port of Havana and demanded a huge ransom for it. No money was paid, and so Peg Leg burned the town and all the ships in its harbour. Then he set fire to the countryside around it.

▼ The soldiers guarding the treasure were called 'Conquistadores', who were the first of the Spanish soldiers to invade South America. They often travelled with the treasure ships, but were no match for the pirates.

Soon the Spaniards began to assemble their galleons into fleets. They realized that groups of ships would be safer from pirates than single ones. Two big fleets arrived in the Spanish Main each year. One loaded up with treasure from Mexico. The other went to Panama, where it took on silver brought overland from mines in Peru, and treasures ferried across the Pacific from the Philippines. Small and heavily armed warships protected the treasure fleets as they made their way back home to Spain.

PICTURE PUZZLE

Can you spot the different kinds of treasure hidden aboard this galleon?

Answer: You should be able to spot gold, jewels and 'pieces of eight'.

Sea dogs

John Hawkins made many raids on treasure ships in the Spanish Main. But he did not call himself a pirate. He carried a letter from his Queen, Elizabeth I of England, which allowed him to attack ships from an enemy nation. England and Spain were not at war, but they were enemies. Hawkins, and many like him, were called 'privateers'.

▲ This letter of marque was issued by King George III of England. Genuine letters contained restrictions on which ships they could attack.

▲ The slave trade lasted for hundreds of years. Up to 70,000 slaves were transported in horrible conditions every year. Some people say that a total of 15 million slaves were delivered, but many millions died on the way.

Hawkins' voyages made him very rich. He sailed first to West Africa where he rounded up 400 slaves and loaded them on board. Next he sailed to the Caribbean where he sold the slaves in exchange for gold, silver and pearls.

Walter Raleigh never found any gold in South America. He made two voyages in search of the fabulous gold-encrusted man – El Dorado. Both voyages were failures, and when he returned, Raleigh was beheaded.

Francis Drake was the greatest of the Elizabethan 'sea dogs'. He first went to sea at 14, and later joined his cousin John Hawkins on his expeditions. Like Hawkins, he became a privateer, and carried on an unofficial war against Spain.

▲ A privateer called Francis Drake attacked a mule train and stole their riches.

▲ The route of Drake's three-year voyage round the world.

In 1572 Drake attacked Spanish settlements in Panama. He ambushed a mule train laden with silver at Nombre de Dios. He became the first Englishman to see the Pacific Ocean. He vowed that one day he would sail there.

Drake's most amazing exploit was his voyage around the world. He set out in 1577 and found his way to the Pacific. Here he captured the giant Spanish treasure ship 'Cacafuego', which was carrying a cargo worth over £12 million in today's money. By the time Drake got back to England in 1580, his two remaining ships were crammed with riches as well.

I DON'T BELIEVE IT!
When Drake raided the treasure store at Nombre de Dios, he landed at night, captured the guns and fought off the guards. But when the store was opened, it was empty!

Pig hunters

The original buccaneers were drifters and criminals on the island of Hispaniola, modern Cuba. They wandered about, hunting the wild pigs for food. They cooked them over wood fires.

▼ Buccaneers of Hispaniola enjoyed eating wild pigs.

During the 1630s, the Spanish drove out these 'buccaneers' and killed all the wild pigs. So the buccaneer bands, who had to find food somewhere, became pirates instead. They began to attack and loot passing Spanish merchant ships.

The first buccaneer stronghold was a small rocky island called Tortuga. It had a sheltered harbour, and was close to the main shipping route. Buccaneers built a fort at Tortuga and placed 24 cannons there, pointing out to sea.

Henry Morgan started out as a privateer, but soon became a famous buccaneer leader. In 1668 he led an army overland to sack the city of Portobello in Cuba. Two years later, Morgan conquered Panama City, and opened the way for pirates into the Pacific.

Henry Morgan

▼ Fear caused many ship's crew to quickly surrender.

PICTURE PUZZLE

There are six pirate weapons hidden in this picture. Can you find a scimitar, a dagger, a pistol, a musket, an axe and a firebomb?

The name of Francis L'Ollonais struck terror into Spanish hearts. This buccaneer became famous for his cruel and heartless deeds. This meant that people were more likely to surrender straight away when they knew it was him.

The buccaneers even invented a special kind of sword – the cutlass. This began as a knife that they used for cutting up the wild pigs. It soon became a broad, short sword that many pirates and other sailors carried as their main weapon in battle.

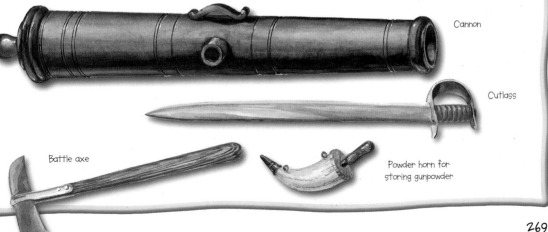

Cannon

Cutlass

Battle axe

Powder horn for storing gunpowder

Pirate stronghold

In the 1650s, most buccaneers moved to a new hideout on Jamaica. This was Port Royal, set at the end of a narrow spit of land. There was a fort to guard the harbour entrance, and docks where pirates could repair their ships. The British, who ruled Jamaica, did not try to interfere with the buccaneers. Port Royal was a pirate paradise!

Port Royal was a wild and wealthy place. The buccaneers brought their plunder to the docks to sell to merchants. With the money they roamed the streets looking for a good time. The town had 44 taverns, crowded with drunkards, pickpockets and runaway slaves as well as pirates. The money disappeared fast. Buccaneers were known to spend as much as 3000 pieces of eight (silver coins) in one night. That is £45,000 in today's money.

Port Royal was destroyed by a monster earthquake in 1692. Buildings collapsed, and two whole streets were swallowed up by the sea. A giant wave followed the earthquake, washing right over the town. Altogether, 4000 people died in the disaster. Some saw it as God's punishment for their wicked ways.

QUIZ

1. What kind of meat did the first buccaneers eat?
2. Which island did they live on?
3. What kind of sword did the buccaneers invent?
4. Where were the treasure galleons going?
5. What were pieces of eight?

Answers:
1. wild pig 2. Hispaniola 3. the cutlass 4. Spain 5. silver coins

Island of thieves

Pirates had prowled the Indian Ocean for many centuries.
From bases on the Indian coast, more than 100 pirate ships put to sea. They scoured the ocean all summer, seizing the cargoes of lone merchant ships.

The exotic treasures of the East quickly attracted many buccaneers. They moved from the Caribbean to the Indian Ocean, many settling on the island of Madagascar, off the east coast of Africa. This was a wild and unexplored land, where it was easy to hide.

◄ The large island of Madagascar lies at the southeast corner of Africa. Its remote and forested coast made a perfect stronghold for pirates.

When Portuguese sailors reached the Indian Ocean, they soon became pirates, too. From about 1500, Portuguese traders began sailing from Africa to India, and then on to the Far East. They stole silks, spices, jewels and gold from the Arab merchants.

William Kidd started out as a pirate-hunter, but became a pirate! He was sent to chase pirates in the Indian Ocean in 1696. Within a few months, Kidd was attacking ordinary trading ship. When he returned home he was arrested and hanged for piracy. His body was displayed in a cage for several years.

▼ The Arch Pirate's crew boarding the Indian Emperor's ship.

Henry Avery was feared as 'The Arch Pirate'. His most ferocious deed was the capture of the Indian Emperor's treasure ship in the Red Sea. He tortured many passengers, and terrified the women so much that they jumped overboard.

Kanhoji Angria was the greatest of the Indian Ocean pirates. Setting sail from India's west coast, he led his ships against any merchant ships that passed. He also built a series of forts along the coast, and defied the strength of the British navy. His followers were called 'Angrians'.

PIRATE SEARCH

The surnames of seven pirates and privateers are hidden in this letter square. Can you find them all?

B	R	N	A	D	C	X	M
D	R	A	K	E	B	N	O
L	E	C	L	E	R	C	R
K	R	K	S	E	S	W	G
L	O	I	A	A	I	G	A
D	S	D	N	L	S	G	N
C	Y	D	T	E	A	C	H

Answers :
Drake, Raleigh, Morgan, Le Clerc, Read, Kidd, Teach

Junks and outriggers

The South China Seas were a perfect place for pirates. There was a maze of small islands, mangrove swamps and narrow channels to hide in, and many merchant ships to ambush. Chinese pirates became famous for their violence and brutal methods.

▲ A map showing the popular pirate islands.

Ching–Chi–Ling was the first great Chinese pirate leader. With his fleet of more than 1000 junks, he brought terror to the coast of China.

Chinese pirates sailed in ships called junks. These were often captured trading vessels, with three masts carrying square bamboo sails. The pirate captain lived in the stern cabin with his family, while his men often slept on the open deck. Junks were armed with cannons, while sailors had muskets and pistols.

The Balanini pirates came from the islands of Sulu. They sailed in small, speedy canoes with extra beams called outriggers. In these, the Balanini swooped down on the nearby islands, kidnapping hundreds of slaves to sell in the mainland markets.

▲ With their huge fleets of pirate junks, Chinese pirates like Ching-Chi-Ling and Shap-'ng-tsai wielded huge power in the South China Sea and through to the Indian Ocean.

South Seas pirates used many fearsome weapons. They shot poisoned arrows through a blowpipe called a sumpitan. They brandished a razor-sharp chopping sword called a parang, or a knife called a kris. Some knives were completely straight, others had a rippled effect. Some were straight near the handle, or hilt, but were curved at the end. Some weapons were decorated with tufts of human hair.

British ships were sent to wipe out the last great pirate fleet in 1849. They chased the junks, commanded by Shap-'ng-tsai, for more than 1600 kilometres before they caught them. Then they blew the junks to pieces and killed more than 1800 pirates. Shap-'ng-tsai escaped and lived to a ripe old age, but the pirate menace was ended – for the time being.

◄ A kris, or 'flashing blade', used by pirates from Borneo, with its wooden scabbard.

Women pirates

Mary Read dressed in men's clothing so that she could become a sailor. But her ship was captured by pirates on its way to the West Indies, and Mary was taken prisoner. She joined the pirates, and then became a privateer. Once again, her ship fell victim to rival sea robbers, this time to 'Calico Jack' Rackham and his wife Anne Bonny. The two women were soon close friends. In a battle against the British navy, they both fought while the rest of the crew (all men) hid below!

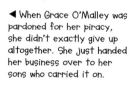

◄ When Grace O'Malley was pardoned for her piracy, she didn't exactly give up altogether. She just handed her business over to her sons who carried it on.

Grace O'Malley commanded a pirate fleet on Ireland's west coast. She went to sea as a young girl, and later moved into a massive stone castle right on the coast. Her fleet of twenty sailing ships and rowing boats attacked passing merchant vessels. In 1593 Grace gave up her piratical ways and begged Queen Elizabeth for a pardon. She lived to be more than 70 years old.

◀ Women pirates helping the other pirates to fight their enemy.

I DON'T BELIEVE IT!

While she was a pirate Grace O'Malley cut her hair short to look like her sailors. This earned her the nickname of 'Baldy'!

One of the greatest woman pirates was Ching Shih. When her husband died in 1807, she took over his raiding fleet on the Chinese coast. She was a brilliant leader, and forced her sailors to obey a strict set of rules. But life on her pirate junks was not pleasant. Prisoners told stories of how they lived for three weeks on caterpillars boiled in rice.

◀ Prisoners had to eat horrible food.

All aboard!

Most pirate ships had to be small and fast. On the Spanish Main, there were 'schooners', with two masts, and galleys with three masts. The captain's cabin was in the stern, while the crew slept in the middle of the ship. Treasure, gunpowder and food stores were kept in the hold.

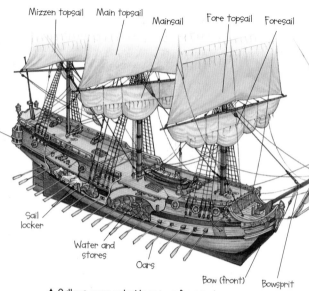

Mizzen topsail · Main topsail · Mainsail · Fore topsail · Foresail

Stern (back)

Sail locker

Water and stores

Oars

Bow (front) · Bowsprit

▲ Galleys were valuable prizes for pirates as they were powered by sail and oar and could reach high speeds.

Food was pretty horrible on board a pirate ship. The cook was often a pirate who had lost a leg or arm and couldn't do anything else. And he seldom had anything to serve except dry biscuits and pickled meat. Whenever the crew landed on a remote island, they hunted for fresh meat and – even more important – fresh water.

Below decks, it was very cramped and smelly. There was little space for the crew to sleep. Pirates barely had room to put up their hammocks, and spent most of their lives on deck, except in the worst weather.

In calm weather, there was little for the pirates to do. They would mend ropes and sails, or gamble with dice. In bad weather, or when they were chasing another ship, life was very busy. The crew might have to climb aloft in the rigging to alter the sails, keep lookout from high on the mainmast, or prepare the cannon for firing.

▼ Pirates had to clean their ships on land.

The hull of the ship had to be kept clean. Weeds and barnacles would slow it down, so pirates regularly dragged their vessel up onto a beach where they could scrape off any rubbish. This was also a chance to go hunting for food.

DRESS UP AS A PIRATE

Tie a red scarf round your head. Put on trousers, shirt and waistcoat – as brightly coloured as you can find. Earrings are easy, and it's not hard to make your own black moustache (out of wool) and eyepatch (cardboard and elastic bands). Now all you need is a bloodcurdling pirate yell!

Most pirates dressed just like other sailors of the time. They wore short blue jackets, checked shirts and baggy canvas trousers. But some showed off the finery they had stolen, such as velvet trousers, black felt hats, silk shirts and crimson waistcoats with gold buttons and gold lace.

▶ If a pirate had stolen clothing, they would often just sell it. But if they liked something, they may just wear it!

Attack!

When a pirate captain decided to attack, he raised a special flag. Not every pirate flag was the famous skull-and-crossbones. Nor were they always black. Most early pirates used a bright red flag to frighten their victims. Black flags became popular in the early 1700s, with pirates adding their own initials or symbols.

When they were near enough the attackers threw ropes with hooked grappling irons into the rigging. Then the pirates climbed up the sides and jumped aboard. Sometimes they had a bloody fight, but often the enemy crew were so terrified that they surrendered.

Pirates depended on speed to catch their prey. If they had cannons, they would try and hit the other ship's mast or rigging. Otherwise, they fired muskets at the helmsman and other men working in the sails. In this way they could slow the ship down. If they got near enough, they might even jam the rudder so that it would not steer properly.

A pirate bristled with weapons. His cutlass was in his hand, and a dagger was in his belt. He might carry as many as six loaded pistols tied to a sash which he wore over his shoulder.

Merchants often hid their cargo.
The pirates had to search everywhere and tear apart walls and doors to find it. They might even torture their captives until they told them where the treasure was.

DESIGN A PIRATE FLAG

You can have your very own personal pirate flag. On a black background, draw your own scary design using bones, skulls and anything else you fancy. No-one else is allowed to copy it!

Bartholomew Roberts was probably the most successful pirate ever.
Known as Black Bart, he captured as many as 400 ships in the 1720s. Handsome, bold, he was everyone's ideal buccaneer. Yet he never drank anything stronger than tea!

◀ One of the best ways to slow a ship was to fire at the sails and rigging.

Pirate plunder

All pirates dreamed of gold and silver. Some were lucky enough to capture ships packed with them – in the form of coins, gold bars or finely made ornaments. But most merchant ships carried humbler goods, such as cloth, coal or iron.

▲ After capturing a cargo vessel, the pirates transfer all the treasure and other valuables to their own ship.

The most famous coins of the Spanish Main were 'pieces of eight' or simply pesos. These were silver, and as big as a 50 pence piece. Each one was worth about £15 in today's money.

Silk and porcelain were the most precious goods from China. For centuries, no-one in Europe knew how silk or porcelain (fine earthenware) were made. They were very delicate, and pirates had to handle them carefully.

▼ People too could be valuable. Pirates might hold a rich captive and demand a ransom from their relatives. When this was paid, the prisoner was freed.

▼ Pirates got excited as their captain shared out the treasure.

Pirates also needed everyday things. If they had been away from land for several weeks, they would be glad to steal food, drink and other provisions. And fresh guns, cannon balls and gunpowder always came in useful.

Some treasure chests were full of jewels. There were diamonds from Africa, rubies and sapphires from Burma, emeralds from Colombia and pearls from the Persian Gulf. Many of these were made up into beautiful jewellery.

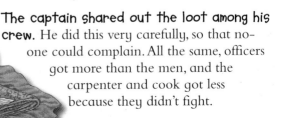

The captain shared out the loot among his crew. He did this very carefully, so that no-one could complain. All the same, officers got more than the men, and the carpenter and cook got less because they didn't fight.

Buried treasure

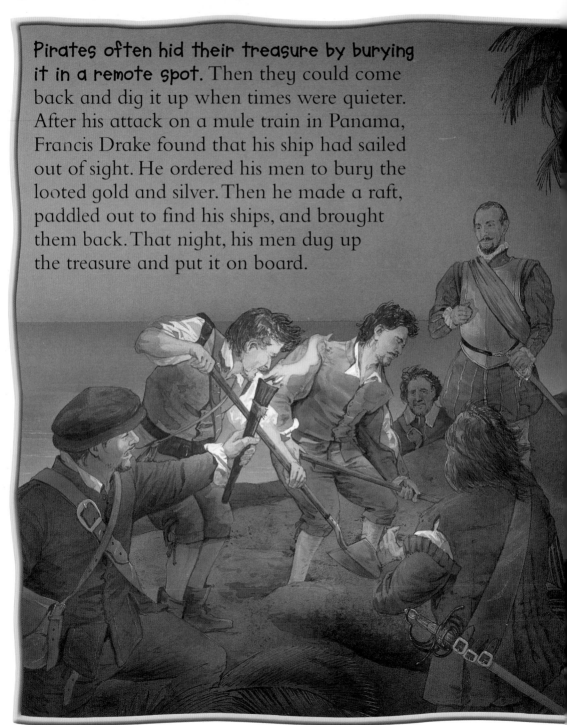

Pirates often hid their treasure by burying it in a remote spot. Then they could come back and dig it up when times were quieter. After his attack on a mule train in Panama, Francis Drake found that his ship had sailed out of sight. He ordered his men to bury the looted gold and silver. Then he made a raft, paddled out to find his ships, and brought them back. That night, his men dug up the treasure and put it on board.

Many believe that William Kidd buried a vast store of treasure before he was captured. His piracy had gained him a huge amount of cargo, most of which he sold off or gave to his crew. But when he was arrested in 1699 he claimed that he had hidden £100,000 of treasure. Since then, hundreds of people have looked for it all over the world – but no one has found a single coin.

▼ Pirates lived in a rough and dangerous world. There was no code of conduct between ships, so there was no reason for a pirate ship not to steal the treasure from another pirate ship.

BURIED TREASURE

Can you follow the trail and find the buried treasure?

Start on a crescent shape of sand. Go two squares northwest. Go three squares east. Follow the river right to the sea. Now go one square north, and two squares east. Finally, go two squares due north and get sight of the treasure!

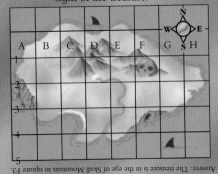

Answer: The treasure is in the eye of Skull Mountain in square F3.

The pirates of the ship 'Mary Dear' buried their loot in the Cocos Islands of the Pacific in 1820. It included over 12,000 gemstones and 9000 gold coins, as well as seven chests of gold ornaments. Then the pirates set the ship on fire and rowed off in the longboats. When they reached land, they were arrested. None of the pirates ever went back to dig up the treasure, and no one has discovered it since.

Desert islands

Some pirate captains had strict rules. 'Black Bart' Roberts made his crew promise to keep to a code of conduct. They must not gamble or fight on board ship, or keep lights and candles burning after 8 o'clock at night. Anyone who brought a woman on board, or who deserted the ship, would be put to death or marooned.

◀ Marooned pirates begged to be allowed back onto the main ship.

Marooning was a terrible fate. The pirate was left alone on a deserted island while his shipmates sailed away. He was given a few vital things – a pistol and ammunition, and a bottle of water. But it was almost impossible to escape, and food was hard to find. The only hope was to be picked up by another ship.

▼ The group of islands on which Selkirk was marooned were the Juan Fernandez islands. Selkirk's island was called Más á Tierra. He was very lucky that he had plenty of food and water.

Goat Rock

Goat Quarters

NORTH AMERICA
ASIA
AFRICA
SOUTH AMERICA
Más á Tierra

Open Bay

Sharpes Bay

Windy Bay

The most famous of all castaways was Alexander Selkirk. He was stranded on a desert island off the coast of Chile in 1704, and stayed there for five years. Selkirk was very lucky, for his island had plenty of fresh water, along with wild pigs and goats. At last, dressed in goat skins, he was rescued by a passing English ship. Writer Daniel Defoe based his story of 'Robinson Crusoe' on Selkirk's adventures.

The Pacific and the Caribbean were dotted with thousands of small islands. Very few had people living on them. Many were far away from the main shipping routes. The castaway had to hunt for fruit and small animals, or fish in the warm seas.

Sometimes the crew marooned their captain. This happened to Jeremy Rendell in 1684. After an argument with his crew, he was left on an island near Honduras with three other men, a gun, a canoe and a net for catching turtles. They were never heard from again.

PICTURE PUZZLE

You've been marooned on a desert island. Somewhere are hidden a water bottle, a pistol, a knife, a blanket, a kettle and an axe. Can you find them?

287

Storm and shipwreck

Shipwreck was a pirate's biggest nightmare. Violent storms could spring up suddenly, especially in the warm seas of the Caribbean. In 1712, a hurricane brought racing winds and giant waves into Port Royal harbour in Jamaica, smashing 38 ships.

Storms could drive helpless ships onto a rocky shore. In 1717 the pirate ship *Whydah* was heading for Cape Cod, off North America, loaded with booty. A storm sprang up, pushing the vessel onto rocks. The mainmast fell down, and the 'Whydah' started to break up. Only two of the crew reached land alive.

▲ Bad weather could lead to a shipwreck, one of pirates biggest fears.

A hole in the hull had to be patched — fast! The quickest way was to 'fother' it, by lowering a sail with ropes so that it fitted over the hole. But sails were not very watertight, and the patch did not last long.

There were few ways to cope with an emergency. If the ship was leaking, sailors could try pumping out the water. If the ship ran aground, they could throw heavy objects overboard, such as cannon or food barrels. This made the ship lighter, and ride higher in the water.

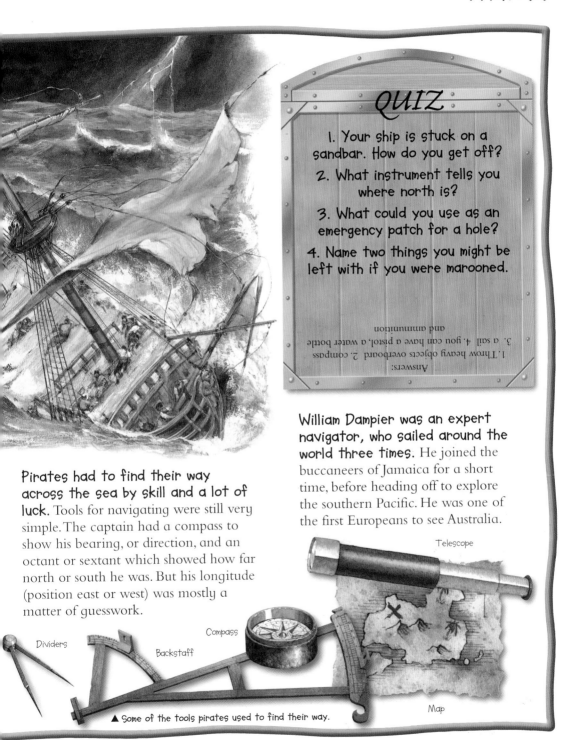

QUIZ

1. Your ship is stuck on a sandbar. How do you get off?

2. What instrument tells you where north is?

3. What could you use as an emergency patch for a hole?

4. Name two things you might be left with if you were marooned.

Answers:
1. Throw heavy objects overboard 2. compass 3. a sail 4. you can have a pistol, a water bottle and ammunition

William Dampier was an expert navigator, who sailed around the world three times. He joined the buccaneers of Jamaica for a short time, before heading off to explore the southern Pacific. He was one of the first Europeans to see Australia.

Pirates had to find their way across the sea by skill and a lot of luck. Tools for navigating were still very simple. The captain had a compass to show his bearing, or direction, and an octant or sextant which showed how far north or south he was. But his longitude (position east or west) was mostly a matter of guesswork.

Telescope

Dividers

Backstaff

Compass

Map

▲ Some of the tools pirates used to find their way.

Hunting the pirates

European countries began to build bigger and stronger navies. With these, they were able to begin sweeping the pirates from the seas. Well-armed navy fleets patrolled the trouble spots. Pirates were offered free pardons if they gave up their lives of crime. Large rewards were given to anyone who helped to capture pirate ships.

▶ Blackbeard was a fearsome pirate who attacked navy fleets.

Edward Teach was the most terrifying pirate on the high seas. Better known as 'Blackbeard', he made himself look as frightening as possible. He plaited ribbons into his long beard, carried six pistols slung over his shoulder, and stuck lighted matches under his hat. But one man was not afraid of Blackbeard – naval officer Robert Maynard. In 1718 he cornered the pirate, who shouted "Damnation seize my soul if I give you quarter!" Maynard leapt aboard his ship and fought him to the death. Then he cut off Blackbeard's hairy head and hung it in the bows of his vessel.

PICTURE PUZZLE

Which pirate names do these pictures make you think of?

A

B

C

D

E

Answers:
A. Barbarossa ('red beard') B. Francis Drake
C. Francois 'Peg-leg' Le Clerc D. Grace 'Baldy'
O'Malley E. Edward 'Blackbeard' Teach

Steam power spelled the end for most pirates. The navy built steam ships, which could travel much faster than the old sailing ships and did not depend on the wind. The pirates simply couldn't get away.

On the gallows

Many captured pirates were taken back to Britain in chains. But most never got that far. They were taken to the nearest American port and executed as quickly as possible. Only the younger criminals of 15 or 16 years old were pardoned and released.

▲ Captured prisoners were manacled together with long chains on the voyage to prison and trial.

Before and after trial, the pirates were kept in prison. In London, this would probably be the hated Newgate Prison, which was foul-smelling, dirty and overcrowded. Many prisoners died of disease or starvation before they ever came to be executed.

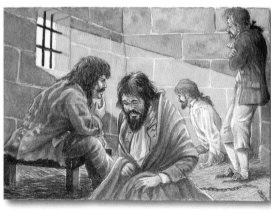

Trials in Britain lasted only one or two days. The judges were keen to condemn the pirates as quickly as possible, so that they would frighten those still at large. Anyone who was known to have fired a cannon, carried a gun or taken part in looting was found guilty.

▲ Newgate Prison in London was a brutal, unhealthy place.

◀ This is one of the dreaded 'hulks'. These were naval ships that had got too old to be used for sailing, so were converted and used as floating prisons for the worst criminals.

The bodies were left on the gallows until the tide came in and covered them. After three tides, they were either taken down and buried or left hanging in a cage as a lesson for others. Some bodies were coated in tar so that they would last longer.

Pirates that had been found guilty were hanged at Execution Dock in London. They sometimes took a long time to die. William Kidd had to be hanged a second time after the rope broke. As a deterrent, a warning to other people who might become pirates, their bodies were displayed in cages.

▶ An iron cage, used to display the bodies of executed pirates.

I DON'T BELIEVE IT!

After William Duell was hanged his body was taken down and washed. Then someone saw that he was still breathing! The courts did not have the heart to hang him again, so he was sent to Australia instead.

The British navy destroyed many pirate ships. An entire fleet of Chinese junks was sunk or set on fire near Hong Kong in 1849, and 400 pirates were killed. The naval commander went on to smash up the pirate dockyards and confiscate all the weapons.

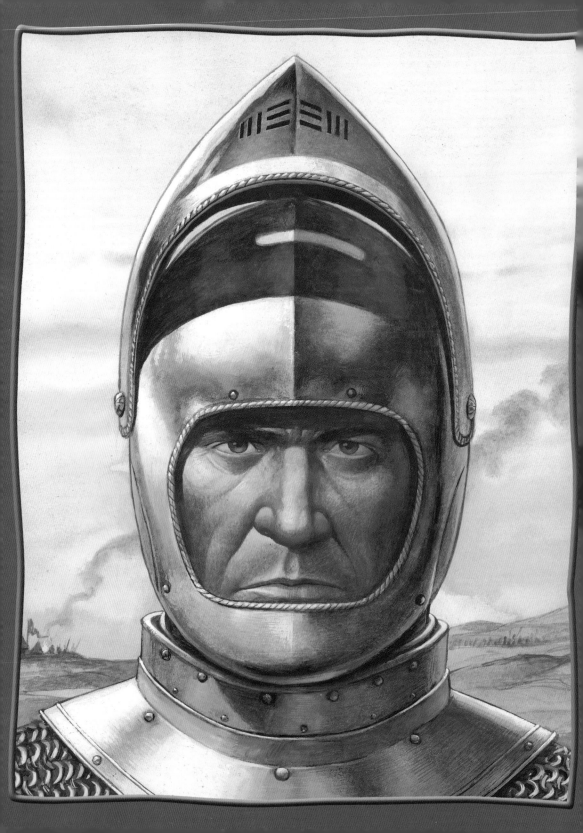

Arms and Armour

Journey through history and discover how warfare has developed. Find out how weapons were made and about the soldiers who used them.

Shields • Chainmail • Bushido • Crossbows
Hoplites • Barbarians • Roman legions • Archers
Swords • Arrows • Guns • Boomerangs

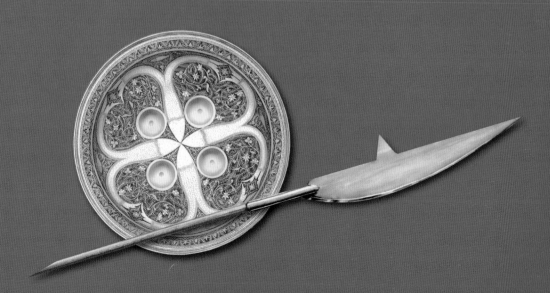

Weapons of war

People have used arms and armour to hunt, defend themselves and attack other people for thousands of years. Arms are weapons that are carried by a single person. Armour is something that is worn or carried to protect against injury. Early armour was made from wood or leather, and the first arms were made from wood or stone.

▼ At the battle of Lechfeld in AD 955 the Germans crushed the much larger army of Magyars. The Germans succeeded because they were wearing suits of mail armour and carrying new weapons.

The first arms

Some of the first arms were made from
stone. The earliest humans lived hundreds
of thousands of years ago. Archaeologists
(scientists who study the remains of
ancient humans) have found weapons
made of sharpened stone that were made
by these ancient people.

▲ This handaxe is made
from a single piece of
stone. It was held in
the hand and used with
a chopping motion.

Early weapons were used for both
hunting and fighting. Archaeologists
have found bones from cattle, deer
and mammoths, and discovered
that these animals were hunted
and killed by ancient people
using stone weapons.

▶ Around 75,000 years ago, spears were
made from a stone point, which was attached
to a wooden handle with leather straps.

The first warriors did not
use armour. It is thought that
early tribes of people fought
each other to get control of the
best hunting grounds or sources
of water. These men may not
have used armour, relying
instead on dodging out of
the way of enemy weapons.

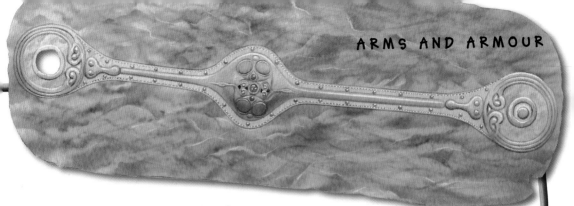

Shields were an early form of defence.

A thrust from a spear could be stopped by holding a piece of wood in the way. People soon began to produce shields made of flat pieces of wood with a handle on the back. Over the years, shields came to be produced in many different shapes, and from a wide range of materials including metal, wood and leather.

▲ By about 300 BC, the Celts of Europe were producing beautiful shields decorated with bronze and colourful enamel. Some, like this one found in London, may have been used in ceremonies.

▶ Flint is a hard stone that can be chipped and flaked into a wide variety of shapes to produce different types of weapons, such as these points or tips for arrows.

Spears were the first effective
weapons. Many early spears consisted of a stone point mounted on the end of a wooden pole. With a spear, a man could reach his enemy while still out of reach of the opponent's hand-held weapons. The earliest known spears are 400,000 years old and were found in Germany.

I DON'T BELIEVE IT!

The oldest signs of warfare come from Krapina, Croatia. Human bones more than 120,000 years old have been found there that show marks caused by stone spearheads.

Ancient civilizations

Early Egyptians may have used their hair as armour. Some ancient Egyptians grew their hair very long, then plaited it thickly and wrapped it around their heads when going into battle. It is thought that this may have helped to protect their heads.

▲ The Egyptian pharaoh Tutankhamun is shown firing a bow while riding in a chariot to attack the enemies of Egypt.

Some Egyptian soldiers had shields that were as big as themselves. Around 1800 BC, soldiers carried shields that were the height of a man. They hid behind their shields as the enemy attacked, then leapt out to use their spears.

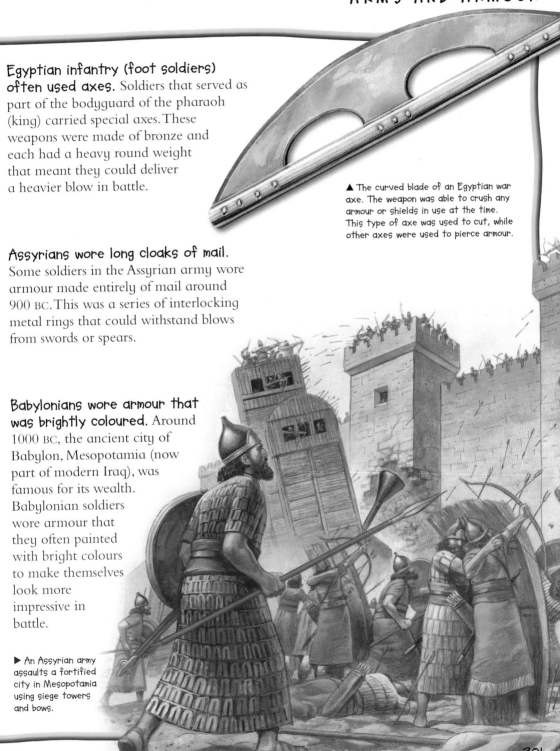

Egyptian infantry (foot soldiers) often used axes. Soldiers that served as part of the bodyguard of the pharaoh (king) carried special axes. These weapons were made of bronze and each had a heavy round weight that meant they could deliver a heavier blow in battle.

▲ The curved blade of an Egyptian war axe. The weapon was able to crush any armour or shields in use at the time. This type of axe was used to cut, while other axes were used to pierce armour.

Assyrians wore long cloaks of mail. Some soldiers in the Assyrian army wore armour made entirely of mail around 900 BC. This was a series of interlocking metal rings that could withstand blows from swords or spears.

Babylonians wore armour that was brightly coloured. Around 1000 BC, the ancient city of Babylon, Mesopotamia (now part of modern Iraq), was famous for its wealth. Babylonian soldiers wore armour that they often painted with bright colours to make themselves look more impressive in battle.

▶ An Assyrian army assaults a fortified city in Mesopotamia using siege towers and bows.

301

Hoplites and phalanxes

Hoplites were armoured infantry. From about 700 BC Greek infantry (foot soldiers) were equipped with a shield, helmet, spear and sword. They were called 'hoplites' (armoured men). Each hoplite used his own weapons and armour.

A Greek who lost his shield was a coward. The shield carried by hoplites was over one metre across and made of wood and bronze. It was very heavy, and anyone trying to run away from an enemy would throw it away, so men who lost their shields in battle were often accused of cowardice.

Hoplites fought in formations called phalanxes. When going into battle, hoplites stood shoulder to shoulder so that their shields overlapped, and pointed their spears forwards over the shields. A phalanx was made up of six or more ranks of hoplites, one behind the other.

▶ The success of Greek soldiers in battle depended on them keeping tightly in formation so that enemy soldiers could not get past the line of shields.

I DON'T BELIEVE IT!

Spartan hoplites were so tough that they reckoned they could easily win any battle, even if they were outnumbered by as many as five to one!

Greek spears had a 'lizard stabber'.
Hoplite spears had a bronze spike at the
bottom end. This was used to stick the
spear upright into the ground and was
called a 'sauroter', meaning 'lizard stabber'.

**The best helmets were made from
a single sheet of metal.** Skilled
metalworkers in the Greek city of
Corinth invented a way to make a
helmet by beating a single sheet of
bronze into shape. This produced a
helmet that was much stronger than
one made of several pieces of metal.
The helmets were called 'Corinthian'.

303

Roman legions

▲ A Roman legion marches out of a border fortress supervised by the legate, who commands the legion.

Armoured infantry formed the legions. The main fighting formation of the Roman army was the legion, a force of about 6000 men. Most were equipped with body armour, a helmet, a large rectangular shield, a sword and a throwing spear.

Roman armour was made of metal strips. At the height of the Roman Empire, around AD 50 to AD 250, legionaries wore armour called *lorica segmentata*. It was made up of strips of metal that were bent to fit the body, and held together by straps and buckles.

▶ The armour of a legionary was made up of several pieces, each of which could be replaced if it was damaged.

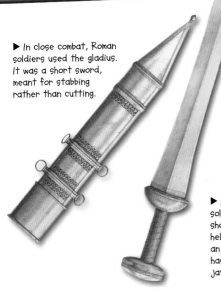

▶ In close combat, Roman soldiers used the gladius. It was a short sword, meant for stabbing rather than cutting.

Roman swords were copied from the Spanish. After 200 BC, Roman soldiers carried swords with straight blades and sharp points. They were copied from swords used by Spanish soldiers who defeated the Romans in battle.

▶ An auxiliary soldier wearing a short mail tunic and helmet, and carrying an oval shield. He has a gladius and javelin as weapons.

Roman auxiliaries wore cheaper armour.
Every Roman legion included soldiers called auxiliaries (soldiers from places other than Rome). These units had to provide their own armour, often wearing tunics covered with mail or scale armour, which was made up of lots of small metal plates.

Roman shields could form a 'tortoise'.
One tactic used by the Romans was called the 'testudo', or 'tortoise'. Soldiers formed short lines close together, holding their shields so they interlocked on all sides and overhead, just like the shell of a tortoise. In this formation they could advance on an enemy, safe from spears or arrows.

The fall of Rome

Later Roman infantry abandoned armour. By around AD 350, Roman legions preferred to fight by moving quickly around the battlefield. They stopped wearing heavy armour and relied upon large shields and metal helmets for protection.

Later Roman armies used mercenary archers. Roman commanders found that archers were useful for attacking barbarian tribesmen. Few Romans were skilled at archery, so the Romans hired soldiers (mercenaries) from other countries to fight as archers in the Roman army.

Roman shields were brightly coloured. Each unit in the late Roman army had its own design of shield. Some were decorated with pictures of eagles, scorpions or dolphins, while others had lightning bolts or spirals.

◀ Late Roman shields were brightly decorated. Each unit in the army had its own design.

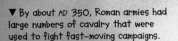
▼ By about AD 350, Roman armies had large numbers of cavalry that were used to fight fast-moving campaigns.

The eagle was a sacred standard. Each Roman legion had an eagle standard, the *aquila* – a bronze eagle covered in gold leaf mounted on top of a pole about 3 metres long. The *aquila* was thought to be sacred to the gods and it was a great humiliation if it was captured by the enemy.

▶ A Roman *aquilifer* (standard bearer) carrying an eagle standard. Each legion had an eagle standard that was sacred to the gods. Units of cavalry and auxiliaries carried standards of other animals instead of an eagle.

Later Roman cavalry had enormous shields. One later group of Roman mounted soldiers was the *scutati*. These men wore coats of mail, and carried enormous shields with which they were expected to defend themselves and their horses. They would gallop towards the enemy army, throw javelins and then ride away before the enemy could strike back.

I DON'T BELIEVE IT!

Alaric the Goth and his men looted Rome in AD 410. Alaric was famously known to carry a sword with a handle made of solid gold.

The Barbarians

Celts used chariots to intimidate the enemy. Battles between rival Celt tribes often began with famous warriors riding in chariots and performing tricks to show how skilled they were.

The Huns were lightly equipped. Around the year AD 370 the Huns swept into Europe from Asia. They fought on horseback with bows and spears, but wore no armour. They moved quickly, and showed no mercy.

The Dacian falx was a terrible weapon. The Dacians lived in what is now Romania around AD 400–600 and fought mostly on foot. Some Dacian warriors carried a long, curved sword with a broad blade that was called a falx. This weapon was so sharp and heavy that it could slice a person in half.

▶ The speed and accuracy of mounted Hun archers terrified the Romans.

The Franks were named after their favourite weapon. One tribe of Germans who lived around AD 300–600 were famous for using small throwing axes. These weapons had a short haft and a small, square-shaped head and were called 'francisca'. The men who used them were called franks, and soon the entire tribe took the name. They later gave the name to the country France.

◀ A Dacian warrior carrying a falx. Dacians were a people who lived outside the Roman Empire and often fought the Romans.

QUIZ

1. Did Hun warriors wear armour?
2. What was a 'francisca'?
3. Who did the Romans call 'barbarians'?

Answers:
1. No 2. A small throwing axe
3. Any uncivilized people who lived outside the Roman Empire

▼ A helmet belonging to an Anglo-Saxon king who ruled in East Anglia, England, about AD 625. It was made of iron and decorated with gold and silver.

Many barbarians wore armour decorated with gold, silver and precious stones. 'Barbarian' was the Roman name for uncivilized peoples outside the Roman Empire. They loved to show how rich they were and did this to emphasize their status within their tribe.

The Heavenly Kingdom

Chinese troops wore armour made of dozens of metal plates. The plates were about 8 centimetres by 6 centimetres and were sewn onto a leather garment or held together by leather thongs. Around 221 BC the various Chinese states were united. The Chinese believed this unity was the basis of their power and wealth.

Silk shirts helped to protect against arrows. Many Chinese soldiers wore silk shirts under their armour. If an arrow pierced the armour it would drag the silk shirt into the wound without tearing it. By gently pulling on the shirt, the arrow could be extracted cleanly.

▼ A patrol of Chinese soldiers guarding the Great Wall around AD 200.

Crossbows were first used in China. They were more powerful than the bows used by nomadic tribesmen living north of China, so they were often used by troops manning the northern frontier. Crossbows consist of a short, powerful bow mounted on a wooden shaft and operated by a trigger.

Infantry used pole weapons. Chinese infantry often carried spears around 2 metres in length. Often an axelike chopping weapon, a slicing blade or a side spike replaced the spearhead. These weapons allowed the infantry to attack their enemies with a variety of actions to get around shields.

Chinese cavalry were heavily armed. When patrolling border regions, the Chinese cavalry operated in large formations that could defeat any tribal force causing trouble. The men were equipped with iron helmets and body armour, together with wooden shields and long lances tipped with iron.

QUIZ

1. In what year was China first united?
2. What did Chinese soldiers wear as protection against arrows?
3. Did the nomadic tribesmen live north or south of China?

Answers:
1. 221 BC 2. Silk shirts 3. North of China

The Dark Ages

The Dark Ages followed the fall of Rome in AD 410.
Barbarian peoples took over the Western Roman Empire, and ancient culture and skills were lost. The Eastern Roman Empire lost power and lands to barbarians, but survived to become the Byzantine Empire. The Byzantines continued to use Roman-style arms and armour.

▲ English warriors patrol the great dyke built by King Offa of Mercia to define the border with Wales in AD 784.

QUIZ

1. Which warriors wore animal skins?
2. Who won the Battle of Lechfeld?
3. Who built a dyke between England and Wales?

Answers:
1. Berserkers
2. The Germans 3. Offa

English cavalry were lightly armed.
Britain was invaded and settled by Germanic tribes from around AD 450, and by around AD 700 they ruled most of the island. Only the richest Englishmen wore body armour. Most went into battle armed with a spear and sword and carrying a round shield and a helmet as armour.

Berserkers wore animal skins instead of armour. Some Viking warriors were known as 'berserkers', meaning 'bear-shirts', from their habit of wearing bear or wolf skins in battle.

The battleaxe was a terrible weapon. Many Scandinavian peoples used a battleaxe that had a haft up to 2 metres long and a blade more than 30 centimetres across. It was used with both hands. In the hands of a master, it could kill a horse and rider with a single blow.

◄ A Viking raiding party wielding battleaxes attacks a group of Englishmen.

The heavy cavalrymen ruled the battlefield.

In AD 955 a small army of German knights destroyed the larger Magyar cavalry at the Battle of Lechfeld, in Germany. Knights (mounted men in armour carrying a spear and sword) were recognized as the most effective type of soldier.

Early knights

The first knights wore mail armour. Around the year 1000, most body armour in Europe was made of mail. This was flexible to wear and could stop a sword blow with ease. Such armour was expensive to make so only richer men could afford to wear it.

1. Iron ring

2. Holes pierced in ends

3. Ends joined with a rivet

▲ Mail armour was made by linking together hundreds of small iron rings. The rings could be linked in a number of different ways, just like knitting a sweater.

Shields were decorated to identify their owners. From about 1150, knights wore helmets that covered their faces for extra protection. Around the same time, they began to paint heraldic designs (coats of arms) on their shields so that they could recognize each other in battle.

Early knights sometimes used leather armour. Mail armour was effective, but heavy and expensive, so some knights wore armour made of boiled, hardened leather. This was lighter and easier to wear, and was still some defence against attack.

◄ A knight in about 1100. He wears a shirt and trousers made of mail and a helmet shaped from a sheet of steel. His shield is made of wood.

Plate armour gave better protection than mail.
By about 1300, new types of arrow and swords had developed to pierce mail armour. This led to the development of plate armour, made of sheets of steel shaped to fit the body, which arrows and swords could not easily penetrate.

The mace could smash armour to pieces.
The most effective of the crushing weapons developed to destroy plate armour, the mace had a big metal head on a long shaft. A blow from a mace crushed plate armour, breaking the bones of the person wearing it.

The armour around the stomach and groin had to be flexible enough to allow bending and twisting movements

The most complicated section of plate armour was the gauntlet that covered the hands. It might contain 30 pieces of metal

The legs and feet were protected by armour that covered the limbs entirely

▶ A suit of plate armour made in Europe in the early 14th century.

QUIZ

1. Why did knights paint coats of arms on their shields?
2. How was leather armour treated to make it tough?
3. Which was the most effective crushing weapon?

Answers:
1. So that they could recognize each other in battle 2. It was boiled 3. The mace

315

Archers and peasants

Infantry were usually poorly armed. Around 1000 years ago, ordinary farmers or craftsmen would turn out to protect their homes against an enemy army. Such men could not afford armour and usually carried just a spear and a large knife or an axe. Normally they guarded castles and towns.

▼ A Welsh spearman in about 1350. He carries a spear and sword, but has no armour at all.

◄ An English archer in about 1400. He wears a metal helmet and has quilted body armour.

The longbow was a deadly weapon. From about 1320 the English included thousands of archers in their armies. The archers were trained to shoot up to eight arrows each minute, producing a deadly rain of arrows that could slaughter an enemy force at a distance.

Some weapons were based on farming tools. Many soldiers used weapons that were simply specialized forms of farming tools. The bill was based on a hedge-trimmer but could be used to pull a knight from his horse, and then smash through his plate armour.

▲ The heads of an English bill (left) and Dutch godendag (right). Both were pole weapons used by infantrymen.

Crossbows were used in some countries. Soldiers from Italy, the Low Countries (now Belgium and the Netherlands) and some other areas of Europe preferred to use the crossbow instead of the bow. It could not shoot as quickly, but was easier to learn how to use and much more powerful.

Some foot soldiers wore armour. Infantrymen sent to war by wealthy towns or cities were often equipped with armour. They usually formed solid formations with their long spears pointing forward, and could be highly effective in battle.

◄ A crossbowman would hide behind a large shield called a pavise while reloading his weapon.

Make a castle bookmark

You will need:
card   scissors   crayons   sticky tape

1. Draw a tower 12 centimetres tall on card and cut it out.

2. Draw the top half of a soldier holding a shield on card and cut it out.

3. Colour in the tower and soldier.

4. Place the soldier so that his body is behind the tower and his shield in front.

5. Tape the soldier's body to the back of the tower to hold it in place.

Your bookmark is ready to use!

Later knights

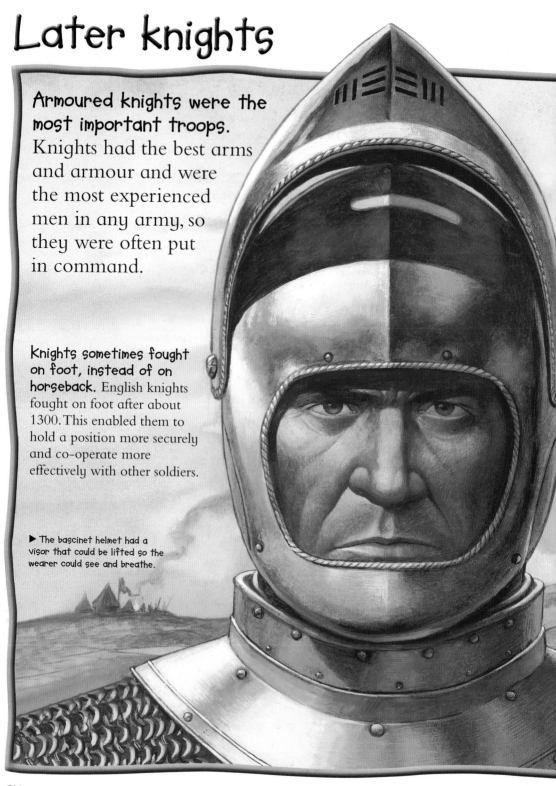

Armoured knights were the most important troops. Knights had the best arms and armour and were the most experienced men in any army, so they were often put in command.

Knights sometimes fought on foot, instead of on horseback. English knights fought on foot after about 1300. This enabled them to hold a position more securely and co-operate more effectively with other soldiers.

▶ The bascinet helmet had a visor that could be lifted so the wearer could see and breathe.

Horse armour made of metal and leather was introduced to protect horses. By about 1300, knights began to dress their horses in various sorts of armour. Horses without armour could be killed or injured by enemy arrows or spears, leaving the knight open to attack. Men with armoured horses were put in the front rank during battle.

▶ Horse armour was shaped to fit the horse's head and neck, then was left loose to dangle down over the legs.

The flail was a difficult weapon to use. It consisted of a big metal ball studded with spikes and attached to a chain on a wooden handle. It could inflict terrible injuries, but also swing back unexpectedly, so only men who practised with it for hours each day could use it properly.

I DON'T BELIEVE IT!

At the Battle of Agincourt in France in 1415, the English killed 10,000 Frenchmen, but only about 100 Englishmen lost their lives.

Each man had his place in battle. Before each battle, the commander would position his men to ensure that the abilities of each were put to best use. The men with the best armour were placed where the enemy was expected to attack, while archers were positioned on the flank (left or right side) where they could shoot across the battlefield. Lightly armoured men were held in the rear, ready to chase enemy soldiers if they began to retreat.

Desert warfare

Bows were made of many materials. In the desert areas of the Middle East, soldiers used bows made from layers of animal horn, bone and sinew that were stuck tightly together and then carved into shape. These were called 'composite bows', and fired arrows with much greater force than longbows.

▲ The recurved bow was short, but powerful.

The Mongols wore light armour. A tribe from central Asia called the Mongols were led by Genghis Khan (1162–1227). Their armour was light because there was a lack of iron in Central Asia. As a result, they developed tactics based on fast-moving cavalry attacks.

Curved swords were known as scimitars.
Armourers working in the city of Damascus,
Syria, invented a new way to make swords
around the year 1100. This involved folding
the steel over on itself several times while the
metal was white hot. The new type of steel
was used to make curved swords that were
both light in weight and incredibly sharp,
called scimitars.

**Teneke armour was made up of a
mail coat onto which were fixed
overlapping pieces of flat metal.**
These pieces were about 6 centimetres
by 2 centimetres. The plates were loosely
hinged so that air could pass through
easily but blows from a sword could not.
The armour was light, comfortable and
effective, but it was also expensive.

▲ A Saracen wearing teneke armour and wielding a scimitar.
The Saracens wore flowing cloaks and turbans to help
combat the heat of the desert.

◄ A Mongol army attacks men from the city
of Kiev, Ukraine. Although designed for
grasslands and deserts, Mongol weaponry
was effective in cold forests as well.

**Armour was light because of the desert
heat.** The plate armour in use in Europe was
not worn in the deserts of the Middle East.
The plates of metal stopped air circulating
around the body and were very
uncomfortable to wear. Instead
desert fighters in the 13th
to 15th centuries wore
loose robes and
light pieces
of armour.

Indian arms

► Indian shields often had intricate designs to make them look more impressive.

India had a unique tradition of arms manufacture. Between 1650 and 1800 the vast lands south of the Himalayas, modern India, Pakistan and Bangladesh, were divided into lots of small states. Each state had its own army, and made great efforts to have impressive weapons.

The khanda was a sword with a long, straight blade. These swords had heavy, double-edged blades that often had handles big enough to allow them to be held in both hands. Larger khanda were slung from a belt over the shoulder so that they hung down the user's back.

Indian soldiers used the pata. This was an iron glove (gauntlet) that extended almost to the elbow, attached to a sword blade. It was very useful for thrusting, especially when attacking infantry from horseback, but was less effective at cutting.

Talwars were curved swords with a single, sharp cutting edge. The handles were often rounded, rather like the butt of a pistol. They were highly decorated with silver, gold and semi-precious stones.

▲ The talwar sword was invented around AD 1000 and was used in battle for over 900 years.

Elephants were used in warfare. A small platform, ('howdah'), was strapped to the back of the elephant. Men armed with bows, or later with guns, sat in the howdah and shot at the enemy over the elephant's head.

▶ War elephants were often covered in armour, while the howdah, in which the soldiers sat, could be covered with iron.

Island wars

Polynesians fought without armour or shields. The islands in the Pacific Ocean were home to people of the Polynesian culture. Before contact with Europeans around 1750, the Polynesians made their weapons from natural materials. They preferred to rely on skill and movement in battle rather than armour, though some men wore thick shirts of plaited coconut fibres as protection.

Shark teeth were made into swords. In western Polynesia, shark teeth were added to the sides of long clubs to produce a weapon called the tebutje. This was used to cut as well as smash and was a vicious close-combat weapon.

▼ A Polynesian war canoe on its way to a raid on another island. The warriors paddling the canoe kept their weapons beside them.

▲ Boomerangs often had decorative carvings or were brightly painted.

The boomerang didn't always come back. Native Australian people used spears and bows and arrows, as well as the boomerang. This heavy throwing stick was shaped so that it spun round in the air and could be thrown with accuracy. Only the lighter boomerangs, used for hunting birds, were designed to come back to the thrower.

War clubs were favoured weapons. Wooden clubs were carved from single pieces of wood and were over one metre in length. They had wide, heavy heads that were often elaborately carved with shapes and patterns.

▶ A Maori mere, or short club. These weapons were made from very hard woods.

The Maori used wooden weapons. The Polynesian people who live in New Zealand are known as the Maori. They produced unique types of club. One type was the mere, which had a short handle and a wide curved blade that could be used for slashing at the enemy.

I DON'T BELIEVE IT!

In the Fiji islands warriors would often use a wooden club shaped like a pineapple to attack their victims.

African arms

The iklwa was a deadly weapon. The Zulu nation of southern Africa was ruled by King Shaka from 1816–28, who built up an empire covering thousands of square kilometres. Shaka introduced a new weapon, the iklwa, a short spear with a broad blade used for stabbing. It proved more deadly than the traditional throwing spears used by other peoples in the area.

Assegai were throwing spears. They had smaller and lighter heads than the iklwa. Zulu warriors would begin a battle by throwing their two or three assegai. Then they would run quickly forward to attack with their iklwa.

Helmets were for show, not defence. Zulu warriors wore headdresses to make them look tall and impressive. They were made of wickerwork with tall ostrich feathers, flowing crane feathers and strips of coloured fur or woollen tufts attached.

Knobkerries could crush skulls. Many Zulu warriors carried a heavy wooden club, or knobkerrie, as well as the iklwa. If the iklwa was lost, the knobkerrie could be used for close fighting.

Shields were made of cowhide. Zulu shields were nearly 2 metres in length, and were cut from cowhide, which was laced onto a central wooden pole with strips of leather.

Make Zulu puppets

You will need:
card   ice-lolly sticks
crayons   glue

1. Draw some Zulu warriors onto card.

2. Cut out each of the warriors and colour them in.

3. Glue an ice-lolly stick to the back of each warrior.

4. If you make enough Zulus, glue the lolly sticks to a straight piece of wood so that the warriors form a rank.

◄ A Zulu impi, or army, on the march. Boys followed the warriors carrying bedding, food and spare weapons.

The Americas

In South America, spears were thrown at the start of a battle. The Aztec people built up a large empire in what is now Mexico between 1400 and 1510. Their warriors won a series of battles against other American peoples. Each battle began with men on both sides throwing light javelins at the enemy. Then the men would charge at each other to fight at close quarters.

◀ In battle, some Aztec warriors dressed as eagles, jaguars and other fierce animals.

Obsidian stone was razor sharp. The Aztec, Maya and other peoples of South America did not know how to make iron or bronze, so they made their weapons from natural materials. The most effective weapons were edged with slivers of obsidian, a hard, glasslike stone that has a very sharp edge when first broken.

Clubs were used to knock enemies unconscious. One of the main purposes of warfare among the Maya and Aztec people was to capture prisoners. The prisoners were then taken to temples to be sacrificed to gods such as Huitzilopochtli, the god of war, by having their hearts cut out while still beating.

Shields were highly decorated. The shields used by Aztec and Maya warriors were made of wood, and covered with brightly coloured animal skins and feathers. They often had strings of feathers or fur dangling down underneath to deflect javelins.

◄ The Maya tried to capture enemy noblemen and rulers to use as sacrifices to the gods.

The tomahawk was a famous weapon of the North American tribes. This was a short-handled axe with a heavy head. The first tomahawks were made with stone heads, but after Europeans reached North America, the tribes began buying steel-headed tomahawks.

► The native peoples of the eastern areas of North America used spears and special axes, known as tomahawks.

The code of Bushido

Samurai wore elaborate armour. From around 800–1860, warriors known as the samurai ruled the islands of Japan. Samurai wore suits of armour made from hundreds of small plates of metal laced together with silk. Each group of samurai had a badge, or sashimono, which was often a picture of a plant or animal.

Bushido was the way of the warrior. By around 1500 the samurai were expected to follow a code of behaviour known as Bushido, which demanded loyalty and honour as well as bravery and skill with weapons.

The swords of the samurai took weeks to make. The samurai sword was produced by blending strips of different types of steel, and shaping them to produce a smooth blade. Each sword was made by a master craftsman in a process that involved prayers and religious rituals as well as metalwork.

▲ The samurai practised with weapons and armour for long periods. They sometimes exercised with elaborate displays.

Make Sashimono flags

You will need:

rectangles of A4 coloured paper
scissors   string   crayons

1. Fold each piece of paper in half.

2. On both sides of each piece of paper draw an animal or plant.

3. Hang each piece of paper over the string at the fold to make a line of flags.

4. Hang the flags up in your room.

▲ All samurai were trained in mounted combat and were expected to use their bows as well as their swords when riding at a gallop.

Archery was a great skill. Around AD 800, the earliest samurai called their profession 'the path of the arrow'. This was because skill at archery was thought to be the most important for a warrior. Swords later became more important, but archery remained a key skill until the end of the samurai period in the 1860s.

Most samurai carried two swords. The katana was most often used in combat, while the shorter wakizashi was used in an emergency or for ritual suicide. Some samurai preferred the much longer two-handed nodachi sword when going into battle.

▶ A print of a samurai warrior showing the brightly patterned clothes that the warriors liked to wear.

331

The end of an era

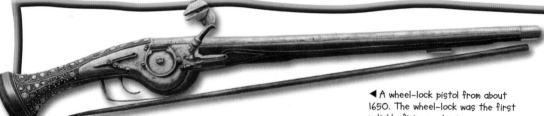

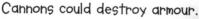

◄ A wheel-lock pistol from about 1650. The wheel-lock was the first reliable firing mechanism.

The first guns could not penetrate heavy armour. Early forms of gunpowder were not powerful enough to shoot a bullet from a hand-held gun with much force. By 1600, armourers were producing helmets and breastplates that were bulletproof.

Cavalry continued to wear body armour. Until 1914, cavalry engaged in fast-moving fights could often not reload their guns once they had been fired. As a result cavalrymen often fought using swords and lances, so armour was still useful.

Cannons could destroy armour. Large cannons fired iron or stone balls that weighed up to 25 kilograms. They were designed to knock down stone walls, but were also used in battle. No armour could survive being hit by such a weapon.

◄ A musketeer in about 1660. Each cartridge on his belt holds a bullet and powder to fire it.

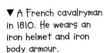

▼ A French cavalryman in 1810. He wears an iron helmet and iron body armour.

Infantry officers wore gorget armour. This was one of the last kinds of armour to be worn. It was a small piece of armour that fitted under the front of the helmet and protected the neck. Gorgets were often used to show the rank of the man wearing them, so they continued to be worn long after helmets were abandoned. They were used until 1914 in some countries.

▶ A musketeer in about 1770. He is using a ramrod to push the bullet and gunpowder down the barrel of a gun before firing it.

By 1850 most soldiers no longer wore armour. As guns became more effective, they were able to fire bullets with greater accuracy over longer distances and with more power. By 1850 most infantry were armed with guns that could shoot through any type of armour, so most soldiers stopped wearing armour.

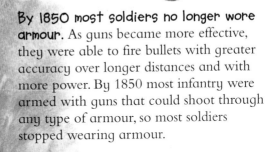

I DON'T BELIEVE IT!

As late as 1914 some French cavalry went to war wearing armour, despite the fact that they had to face artillery and machine guns.

Modern arms and armour

The first modern use of chemical weapons was in World War I. In April 1915, the Germans used poison gas against French soldiers. It worked by irritating the lining of the lungs and throat. Soldiers then began to wear anti-gas uniforms as protection.

▲ A British cavalryman charges in 1916. Both the man and horse wear gasmasks to protect them against poisoned gas.

▶ A British infantryman in 1944. He wears a steel helmet and carries a Sten gun — a light machine gun.

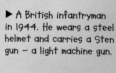

QUIZ

1. Was poisoned gas first used in World War II?
2. What does APC stand for?
3. Do bomb disposal men wear special anti-blast armour?

Answers:
1. No. It was first used in World War I 2. Armoured Personnel Carrier 3. Yes

Modern soldiers always wear helmets. Exploding shells and rockets often throw out sharp splinters of metal called shrapnel. Soldiers take cover in trenches or holes. Metal helmets protect the head, the most likely part of the body to be hit by shrapnel.

▶ A Main Battle Tank (MBT) advances through the desert. The arrival of tanks and other armoured vehicles has transformed modern warfare.

Modern armoured warfare involves tanks. The armour needed to stop modern shells and rockets is too heavy for a person to carry, but it can be mounted on a vehicle, such as a tank or an armoured personnel carrier (APC). These vehicles are the key feature of a modern army, as the armoured knights were in the middle ages.

The best armour makes you disappear. Camouflage conceals soldiers by using colours that blend into the background of plants, sky or sand. Helmets often have a strap that can be used to attach vegetation for extra camouflage.

▼ An American soldier in Iraq. He wears bulletproof body armour as well as a helmet.

Bomb disposal soldiers use special armour. Designed to give protection against blast waves, the armour covers as much of the body as possible while still allowing the soldier to use his hands to defuse the bomb.

Explorers

Begin a voyage around the world with famous
explorers and learn about the lands they visited.

Marco Polo • The Nile • Charles Darwin • Petra
Ibn Battuta • Conquistadors • Polar lands • Space
Africa • Captain Cook • America • Mount Everest
Vasco da Gama • Ferdinand Magellan

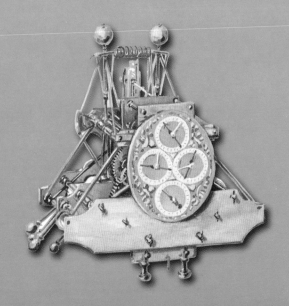

The first explorers

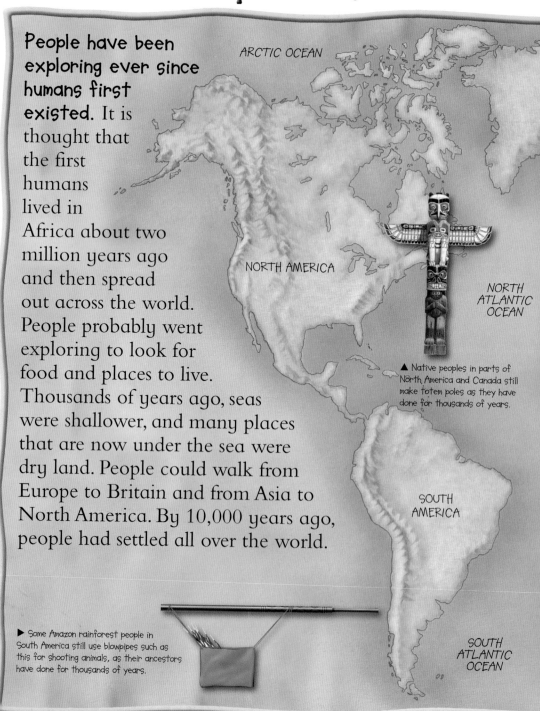

People have been exploring ever since humans first existed. It is thought that the first humans lived in Africa about two million years ago and then spread out across the world. People probably went exploring to look for food and places to live. Thousands of years ago, seas were shallower, and many places that are now under the sea were dry land. People could walk from Europe to Britain and from Asia to North America. By 10,000 years ago, people had settled all over the world.

ARCTIC OCEAN

NORTH AMERICA

NORTH ATLANTIC OCEAN

▲ Native peoples in parts of North America and Canada still make totem poles as they have done for thousands of years.

SOUTH AMERICA

SOUTH ATLANTIC OCEAN

▶ Some Amazon rainforest people in South America still use blowpipes such as this for shooting animals, as their ancestors have done for thousands of years.

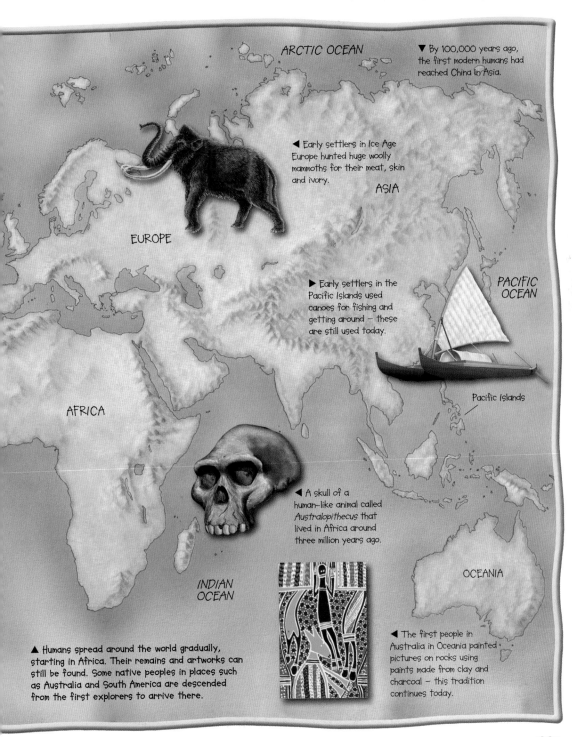

ARCTIC OCEAN

▼ By 100,000 years ago, the first modern humans had reached China in Asia.

◀ Early settlers in Ice Age Europe hunted huge woolly mammoths for their meat, skin and ivory.

ASIA

EUROPE

▶ Early settlers in the Pacific Islands used canoes for fishing and getting around — these are still used today.

PACIFIC OCEAN

Pacific Islands

AFRICA

◀ A skull of a human-like animal called *Australopithecus* that lived in Africa around three million years ago.

INDIAN OCEAN

OCEANIA

▲ Humans spread around the world gradually, starting in Africa. Their remains and artworks can still be found. Some native peoples in places such as Australia and South America are descended from the first explorers to arrive there.

◀ The first people in Australia in Oceania painted pictures on rocks using paints made from clay and charcoal — this tradition continues today.

339

Ancient adventurers

The ancient Greeks and Egyptians were great explorers, building boats to sail the oceans. Their kings and queens had enough money to pay for big exploring trips. They sent explorers to look for new lands, collect treasure and meet peoples from other parts of the world.

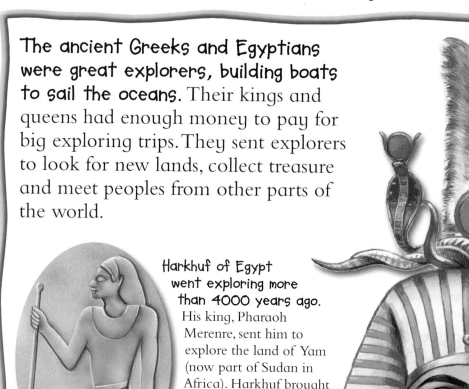

Harkhuf of Egypt went exploring more than 4000 years ago. His king, Pharaoh Merenre, sent him to explore the land of Yam (now part of Sudan in Africa). Harkhuf brought back gifts of precious ivory, spices and wild animals such as leopards.

◀ An ancient Egyptian carving of Harkhuf.

Egyptian Queen Hatshepsut sent explorers to look for a magical land she had heard about. The land, called Punt, was said to be full of treasure and beautiful animals. It was probably part of present-day Somalia, in Africa. Hatshepsut's sailors set off to find Punt. They brought back gold, ivory, monkeys, perfumes and special oils and resins, from which the Egyptians made make-up for their faces.

In ancient times, the best sailors of all were the Phoenicians (say 'fuh-nee-shuns'). They came from what is now Syria and Lebanon and sailed all over the Mediterranean Sea. In 600 BC, an Egyptian king, Pharaoh Necho II, asked a crew of Phoenicians to see if they could sail all the way around Africa. The trip took them three years. It was 2000 years before anyone sailed around Africa again. The Phoenicians used the stars to help them to navigate (find their way).

▼ For long-distance journeys, the Phoenicians used ships with both sails and oars.

Pytheas was an ancient Greek who explored the icy north between 380 and 310 BC. He sailed out of the Mediterranean Sea, past Spain and Britain, and discovered a cold land he named Thule. This might have been Iceland, or part of Norway. Pytheas was the first Greek to see icebergs, the northern lights, and the Sun shining at midnight. However, when he returned to Greece, few people believed his stories.

◄ Hatshepsut stayed at home attending to her duties as queen, while her sailors set off to look for Punt.

I DON'T BELIEVE IT!

When Pytheas sailed past Scotland, he was amazed to see fish the size of boats. In fact they weren't fish at all – they were whales!

Marco Polo

Marco Polo is one of the most famous explorers of all time. Marco lived in Venice in Italy in the 1200s and travelled to Asia at a time when most people in Europe never ventured far from their home village. Altogether, Marco travelled more than 40,000 kilometres.

◄ When Marco Polo visited Far Eastern lands such as China, hardly anyone in Europe had ever been there.

◄ This map shows Marco Polo's route across Asia. The journey home took three years.

Venice

CHINA

INDIA

INDIAN OCEAN

Marco Polo started exploring when he was just 17 years old. His father and uncle were merchants who went to the Far East on business. When Marco was old enough, they took him with them. In 1271, they all set off for China – a journey that took them three years.

In China, the Polos stayed with a mighty emperor called Kublai Khan. He had enormous palaces, rooms full of treasure, and many wives and servants. Kublai Khan gave Marco the job of travelling around his lands to bring him news. Marco went all over China and Southeast Asia.

◀ Coal, fireworks, eyeglasses, ice cream, pasta and paper money were some of the things Marco saw for the first time on his travels.

After 20 years away, the Polos were ready to go home. They sailed most of the way in a junk – a Chinese sailing ship. More than 600 passengers and crew died of diseases on the way, but the Polos got home to Venice safely in 1295.

Later, there was a war in Italy and Marco Polo was captured. He ended up sharing a prison cell with a writer, and told him his life story. The writer wrote down Marco's travel tales to make a book called *The Travels of Marco Polo*. It became a bestseller!

On his travels through Asia, Marco Polo discovered all kinds of amazing inventions. He saw fireworks, coal, paper money, pasta, ice-cream and eyeglasses for the first time. He was also impressed to find that the Chinese had a postage system and could post each other letters.

TRUE OR FALSE?

1. In Indonesia, Marco met human beings with tails.
2. A junk is a type of carriage.
3. Christopher Columbus loved reading Marco Polo's book.
4. Marco discovered pizza in China.

Answers:
1. FALSE In his book, Marco said men with tails existed, but he never saw them himself. Now we know it was just an old wives' tale.
2. FALSE It is a type of ship.
3. TRUE Reading Marco Polo's book inspired Columbus to become an explorer.
4. FALSE He discovered pasta, not pizza.

Ibn Battuta

Ibn Battuta became an explorer because of a dream. Battuta was visiting Mecca, the Muslim holy city, in 1325. There he dreamed that a giant bird picked him up and carried him away. Battuta thought the dream was a message from God, telling him to go exploring. Since he was a Muslim, he decided to visit every Muslim country in the world.

Ibn Battuta set off on his travels, and kept going for nearly 30 years! He visited more than 40 countries, including present-day Kenya, Iran, Turkey, India and China. Just as he had planned, he visited every Muslim land that existed at the time. Altogether, he travelled more than 120,000 kilometres.

▶ India's Sultan, Muhammad Tughluq, was violent and cruel.

Ibn Battuta stayed in India for seven years, working for the Sultan. Battuta's job was to be a judge, deciding whether people charged with crimes were innocent or guilty. Battuta was afraid of the Sultan, who was cruel. If anyone disagreed with him, he would have them boiled, beheaded or skinned alive. Once, he nearly beheaded Battuta for being friends with a man he didn't like.

▼ Ibn Battuta's travels began after he dreamed of setting off to the East, carried by a giant bird.

Ibn Battuta was lucky to finish his travels alive. During his journey, Battuta was attacked by robbers in India, kept prisoner in the Maldives, chased by pirates in Sri Lanka and shipwrecked several times. At the end of his journey, he saw people suffering from the Black Death, a terrible and deadly disease. Fortunately Battuta managed to avoid catching it.

At last, Ibn Battuta went home to Morocco, his own country. When the Sultan heard about his adventures, he asked Battuta to write them all down for him. Battuta didn't have to do the writing himself, though. Instead, he told his story to a scribe (writer) who wrote it all down for him. The finished book was called the *Rihala*, meaning the travels.

I DON'T BELIEVE IT!

In many of the places he visited, Ibn Battuta got married. He had several wives and children in different parts of the world.

Chinese explorers

▲ The Silk Road reached across Asia, from Europe to China.

Some of the greatest ever explorers came from China. The first was a soldier, Zhang Qian, who lived around 114 BC. The Chinese emporer sent him to find a tribe called the Yueh-Chih, who they hoped would help them fight their enemies, the Huns. On their journey, the Huns captured Zhang Qian and put him in prison for ten years. When he finally escaped and found the Yueh-Chih, they said they didn't want to help!

The explorer Xuan-Zang was banned from going exploring, but he went anyway. The Chinese emperor wanted him to work in a temple but Xuan-Zang wanted to go to India to learn about his religion, Buddhism. In the year 629, he sneaked out of China and followed the Silk Road to Afghanistan. Then he went south to India. Xuan-Zang returned 16 years later, with a collection of Buddhist holy books and statues. The emperor was so pleased, he forgave Xuan-Zang and gave him a royal welcome.

MAKE A COMPASS

On his travels, Zheng He used a compass to find his way about.

You will need:

magnet   water   large bowl   piece of wood
a real compass

1. Half-fill the large bowl with water.
2. Place the wood in the water with the magnet on top, making sure they do not touch the sides.
3. When the wood is still, the magnet will be pointing to the North and South Poles. You can even check the position with a real compass.

By the 1400s, the Chinese were exploring the world. Their best explorer was a sailor named Zheng He. Zheng He used huge Chinese junks to sail right across the Indian Ocean as far as Africa. Wherever he went, Zheng He collected all kinds of precious stones, plants and animals to take back to China to show the emperor. The present that the emperor liked most was a giraffe from East Africa.

◀ The Chinese emperor was thrilled when Zheng He presented him with a live giraffe.

◀ A junk was a giant Chinese sailing ship, bigger than any other ships built at the time.

Zheng He's junks were the largest sailing ships on Earth. The biggest was 130 metres long and 60 metres wide. On a typical expedition, Zheng He would take 300 ships and more than 1000 crew members, as well as doctors, map-makers, writers, blacksmiths and gardeners. The gardeners grew fruit and vegetables in pots on the decks, so that there would be plenty of food for everyone.

Sailing around Africa

▼ Spices are cheap today, but in the Middle Ages they were worth their weight in gold – at least!

Ginger

Nutmeg

Mace

In Europe in the 1400s, people loved spices. They used the strong-tasting seeds and leaves to flavour food and make medicines. Nutmeg, cloves, ginger and pepper came from Asian countries such as India. The spices had to be transported on camels across Asia and Europe, which took a long time. They wanted to find a way to sail from Europe to Asia, to make the journey easier.

The best way to sail to Asia was around Africa. But nobody knew how. A Portuguese prince named Henry (1394–1460) started a sailing school to train sailors for the task and began sending ships around the coast of Africa. At first, the sailors were too scared to sail very far because they thought the Atlantic Ocean was too stormy and dangerous. But slowly they sailed further and further.

I DON'T BELIEVE IT!

Sailors were afraid to sail around Africa because of a myth that said if you went too far south in the Atlantic Ocean, the sun would burn you to ashes.

◄ Henry the Navigator never went exploring himself. He just organized expeditions and paid sailors to go on them.

In 1488, a captain named Bartolomeu Dias sailed around the bottom of Africa into the Indian Ocean. Dias had a rough journey, so he named the southern tip of Africa The Cape of Storms. It was renamed The Cape of Good Hope to make sailors think it was safe.

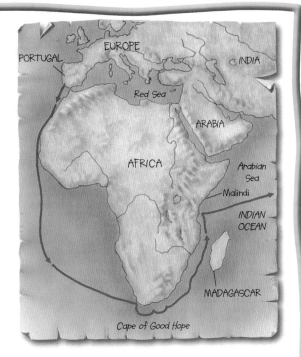

▲ Vasco da Gama sailed from Portugal, right around the southern tip of Africa and up the east coast, before crossing the Indian Ocean to India.

In 1497, a Portuguese sailor finally sailed around the coast of Africa. His name was Vasco da Gama. After sailing around the Cape of Good Hope, da Gama sailed up the east coast of Africa to Malindi. From there he crossed the Indian Ocean to Calicut in India. Here he hoped to buy spices, but the Rajah, Calicut's ruler, told da Gama he would have to come back with some gold. Da Gama went home empty-handed, but the king of Portugal was very happy. The sea route to Asia had been found, and many traders used it from then on.

◄ Besides being a sea captain, Vasco da Gama was a wealthy nobleman, as his grand outfit shows.

Discovering America

Lots of people think Christopher Columbus discovered America, but he didn't.
The Vikings were the first to sail there, in around the year 1000. They found a land with lots of trees, fish and berries, and called it Vinland. They didn't stay long – they went home after getting into fights with the native Americans. After that, many people forgot that Vinland existed.

▶ The *Santa Maria* was the leader of Columbus' fleet of ships. She was about 23 metres long and had three masts and five sails.

Almost 500 years later, Christopher Columbus found America – by mistake!
Columbus set sail from Spain in 1492, with three ships called the *Santa Maria*, the *Nina* and the *Pinta*. Columbus wasn't looking for a new land. Instead, he wanted to sail right around the Earth to find a new route to Asia, where he planned to buy spices. Although he was Italian, it was Queen Isabella of Spain who gave Columbus money for his trip.

When Columbus found land, he was sure he'd sailed to Japan. In fact, Columbus had found the Bahamas, which are close to American mainland.

Back in Spain, no one believed Columbus' story. They knew he couldn't have reached China in such a short time. Instead, they realized he must have found a brand new country. People called the new country the New World, and many more explorers set off at once to see it for themselves.

▲ Columbus and two of his men stepping ashore on the Bahamas, to be greeted by the local people.

America wasn't named after Columbus. Instead, it was named after another famous explorer, Amerigo Vespucci. In 1507, a mapmaker put Amerigo's name on a map of the New World, and changed it from Amerigo to America. The name stuck.

It's thanks to Columbus that Native Americans were known as Indians. Since he thought he was in Asia, Columbus called the lands he found the West Indies, and the people he met Indians. They are still called this today – even though America is nowhere near India.

The Conquistadors

'Conquistador' is a Spanish word that means conqueror. The Conquistadors were Spanish soldiers and noblemen who lived in the 1500s. After Christopher Columbus discovered America in 1492, the Conquistadors set off to explore the new continent. Many of them wanted to get rich by grabbing all the land, gold and jewels they could find in America.

▲ The Aztecs often used the precious stone turquoise in their art. This mask is covered in tiny turquoise tiles.

◄ Leoncico, Balboa's dog, was always at his master's side as he trekked through the forest.

Vasco Nuñez de Balboa was one of the first Conquistadors. He sailed to America in 1500 to look for treasure. In 1513, Balboa trekked through the jungle with his dog, Leoncico, and an army of soldiers. He was the first European to cross America and see the Pacific Ocean on the other side. Balboa loved his dog so much, he paid him a wage like the soldiers. But like most Conquistadors, Balboa could be cruel too – he killed many local people and stole their gold.

Hernan Cortes was a very cunning Conquistador. In 1519, he went to what is now Mexico, to conquer the Aztec people. When he arrived at their city, Tenochtitlan, the people thought he was a god. Cortes captured their king, Montezuma, and took over the city. Montezuma was killed by his own people. Then, after lots of fighting, Cortes took control of the whole Aztec empire.

QUIZ

1. What was Vasco Nuñez de Balboa's dog called?
2. What did the Aztecs do to make their gods happy?
3. What did the Inca king offer Pizarro in exchange for his freedom?

Answers:
1. Leoncico
2. Made human sacrifices
3. A roomful of gold

▼ The Spanish and the Aztecs fought fierce battles, but the Spanish won in the end — mainly because they had guns, and the Aztecs didn't.

To conquer the Inca people of Peru, Francisco Pizarro, another explorer, played a nasty trick. In 1532, he captured Atahuallpa, the Inca leader. Atahuallpa said that if Pizarro set him free, he would give him a room filled to the ceiling with gold. Pizarro agreed. But once Atahuallpa had handed over the gold, Pizarro killed him anyway. Then he took over Cuzco, the Inca capital city. Cuzco was high in the mountains, and Pizarro didn't like it. So he started a new capital city at Lima. Today, Lima is the capital city of Peru.

Around the world

▲ Ferdinand Magellan was a clever man who was very good at maths and science. These skills helped him on his exploration.

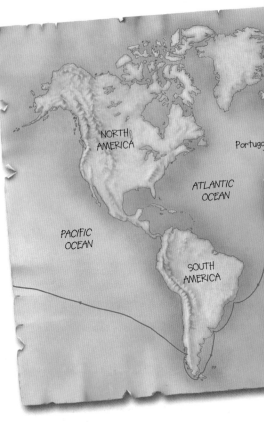

At the start of the 1500s, no one had ever sailed around the world.

Portuguese explorer Ferdinand Magellan wanted to sail past South America, and across the Pacific Ocean. It is possible that, like Columbus before him, Magellan thought he could get to Asia that way, where he could buy spices. Then he could sail home past India and Africa – a round-the-world trip.

Magellan fell out with the king of Portugal, but the king of Spain agreed to help him. The king paid for five ships and Magellan set off in 1519. Magellan sailed down the coast of South America until he found a way through to the Pacific Ocean. Sailing across the Pacific, many of the crew died from a disease called scurvy. It was caused by not eating enough fresh fruit and vegetables.

▲ Magellan set off from Spain on his round-the-world trip. X marks the spot where Magellan died, on the island of Mactan.

In the end, just one of Magellan's ships made it back to Spain. It picked up a cargo of spices in Indonesia and sailed home. Magellan had taken over 200 crew with him, but less than 20 of them returned. They were the first people to have sailed all the way around the world.

Another 55 years went by before anyone sailed around the world again. Queen Elizabeth I asked an English privateer (a kind of pirate) named Francis Drake to try a round-the-world trip in 1577. He made money on the way by robbing Spanish ships (the Queen said he could!). After his three-year voyage, Drake returned to England. Queen Elizabeth gave him a huge reward of £10,000.

Magellan made it across the Pacific – but then disaster struck. After landing in the Philippines in 1521, Magellan made friends with the king of the island of Cebu. The king was fighting a war and he wanted Magellan to help him. Magellan and some of his crew went into battle, and Magellan was killed. The rest of the crew took two of the ships and escaped.

QUIZ

Which of these foods would have helped to save Magellan's men from scurvy?

A. Lemon juice
B. Burger in a bun
C. Glass of milk
D. Cabbage
E. Chocolate cake

Answers:
A. and D.

Captain Cook

Captain James Cook spent just 11 years exploring, from 1768 to 1779. But he was still one of the greatest explorers. Cook sailed all over the Pacific Ocean and made maps that have helped sailors ever since. He also sailed around the world, north to the Arctic, and south to the Antarctic.

▼ As well as studying the planets, Cook took wildlife experts with him on his explorations. They collected plants that weren't known in Europe, and drew sketches and made notes about them.

Pen holder

Dividers

In 1768 the British navy asked Cook to go on an important mission. He was to go to the Pacific island of Tahiti, to make measurements and observations of the planet Venus passing in front of the Sun. After that, Cook went to look for a new continent in the far south – but he didn't find one. Instead, he explored Australia, New Zealand and the Pacific Islands and made new maps.

Parallel ruler

◄ Cook needed high-quality drawing instruments to help him make his measurements for maps.

Sector

Many people still believed there was an unknown continent in the south. So they sent Cook back to look for it again in 1772. He sailed further south than anyone had been before, until he found the sea was frozen solid. Cook sailed all the way around Antarctica, but he was never close enough to land to see it. It wasn't explored until 1820, nearly 50 years later.

For Cook's third voyage, he headed north.
He wanted to see if he could find a sea route
between the Pacific Ocean and the Atlantic
Ocean, across the top of Canada. After
searching for it in 1778, he went to spend
the winter in Hawaii. At first, the Hawaiians
thought Cook was a god named Lono!

I DON'T BELIEVE IT!
Captain Cook was the
first European to discover
Hawaii, in 1778. He called
it the Sandwich Islands.

Cook found his way around
better than any sailor before him.
An inventor named John Harrison
had created a new clock (called the
chronometer) that could measure the
time precisely, even at sea. Before
that, clocks had pendulums, so they
didn't work on ships. From the time
that the sun went down, Cook could
work out exactly how far east or
west he was.

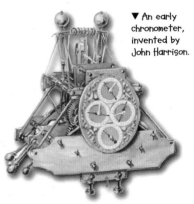

▼ An early
chronometer,
invented by
John Harrison.

Crossing America

The United States of America was created in 1776 — less than 250 years ago. At that time, there were huge parts of it that still hadn't been explored. In 1803, the third president of the USA, Thomas Jefferson, asked Meriwether Lewis to go exploring. Lewis asked his friend William Clark to go with him.

▼ After the Missouri grew too narrow for their boat, Lewis and Clark's team used canoes. Local Native American guides helped them to paddle and find their way.

Lewis and Clark planned to travel all the way across America to the Pacific Ocean. They built a special boat for sailing on rivers. The boat could be rowed, pushed along with a pole, or towed with a rope. It also had sails for catching the wind. They took a crew of about 40 men, and in May 1804, they set off from the city of St Louis, sailing along the Missouri River.

▶ It's thought that Sacagawea died a few years after the Lewis and Clark expedition, aged just 25 or 26.

In North Dakota, Lewis and Clark made a new friend — Sacagawea. She was a Shoshone Native American who joined the expedition as a guide. She helped Lewis and Clark to make friends with the Native American peoples they met during their trip. She knew where to find plants that they could eat and how to make tools. She also saved a pile of valuable papers that were about to fall into the river.

During the trip, Lewis and Clark were scared by bears. One day, Lewis was out hunting when a grizzly bear chased him. Lewis tried to shoot it, but he was out of bullets. The bear chased him into a river, but Lewis was in luck – the bear changed its mind and walked away.

MAKE A TOTEM POLE

You will need:
scissors cardboard tube paper
felt-tip pens glue
1. Cut strips of paper long enough to wrap around the tube.
2. Draw faces, monsters and birds on the strips, then glue them around the tube.
3. Make wings from paper and glue them to the back of the tube.
4. Make a beak by cutting out a triangle, folding it in half and gluing it to the front of the tube.

The crew paddled in canoes along the Columbia River to the sea. They reached the Pacific Ocean in November 1805 – then turned around and trekked all the way back. When they got home, Lewis and Clark were national heroes. The president gave them money and land.

As they crossed the Rocky Mountains, Lewis and Clark and their men almost starved. They couldn't find any buffalo or deer to hunt and eat, so they had to eat three of their own horses. They were only saved when they met a group of Nez Perce Native Americans who gave them food.

▶ Lewis and Clark were in danger of getting badly lost in the Rocky Mountains. The locals who showed them the way and gave them food saved their lives.

Exploring Africa

When Europeans began exploring Africa, they found it could be deadly. In 1795, Scottish doctor Mungo Park went to explore the Niger River, in West Africa. Along the way, Park was robbed, kept prisoner, had all his clothes stolen, almost died of thirst and fell ill with a fever. However, he still went back to Africa in 1805.

Mungo Park

▶ Livingstone made many of his journeys by boat. On one occasion, his boat collided with a hippo and overturned, causing him to lose some of his equipment.

Dr David Livingstone was one of the most famous explorers of Africa. He went there in 1840 as a missionary, to try to teach African people to be Christians. He trekked right across the dusty Kalahari Desert with his wife and young children and discovered Lake Ngami. He was also mauled by a lion, so badly that he could never use his left arm again.

Dr Livingstone kept exploring and became the first European to travel all the way across Africa. On the way, he discovered a huge, beautiful waterfall on the Zambezi River. The locals called it Mosi Oa Tunya, meaning 'the smoke that thunders'. Livingstone renamed it Victoria Falls, after Britain's Queen Victoria.

In 1869, Dr Livingstone went missing. He had gone exploring in East Africa and no one had heard from him. Everyone thought he had died. An American writer, Henry Stanley, went to look for Livingstone. He found him in the town of Ujiji, in Tanzania. He greeted him with the words: "Dr Livingstone, I presume?"

▼ It took Henry Stanley eight months to find Dr Livingstone in Africa.

▲ At their centre, the Victoria Falls are 108 metres high.

French explorer René Caillié went exploring in disguise. He wanted to see the ancient city of Timbuktu in the Sahara Desert, but only Muslims were allowed in. He dressed up as an Arab trader and sneaked into the city in 1828. He was the first European to go there and return home alive.

The source of the Nile

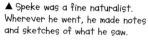

▲ Speke was a fine naturalist. Wherever he went, he made notes and sketches of what he saw.

In the ancient world, the Nile was an important river. It provided the Egyptians with water, and the Greeks and Romans knew about it, too. Ancient explorers tried to sail up the Nile to see where it went, but they kept getting stuck. An Egyptian named Ptolemy drew a map of the Nile, showing it flowing from a big lake in the middle of Africa.

In the 1800s, explorers still wanted to find the beginning, or 'source', of the Nile. In 1856, two British explorers named Richard Burton and John Speke set off to find it. They trekked across Africa to look for the big lake. Both men soon caught the disease malaria from mosquito bites. Burton became so ill he had to stop and rest.

▲ Richard Burton was an English army officer who learned to speak 29 languages.

▲ The Nile is the world's longest river. It flows across the entire length of the desert lands of Egypt.

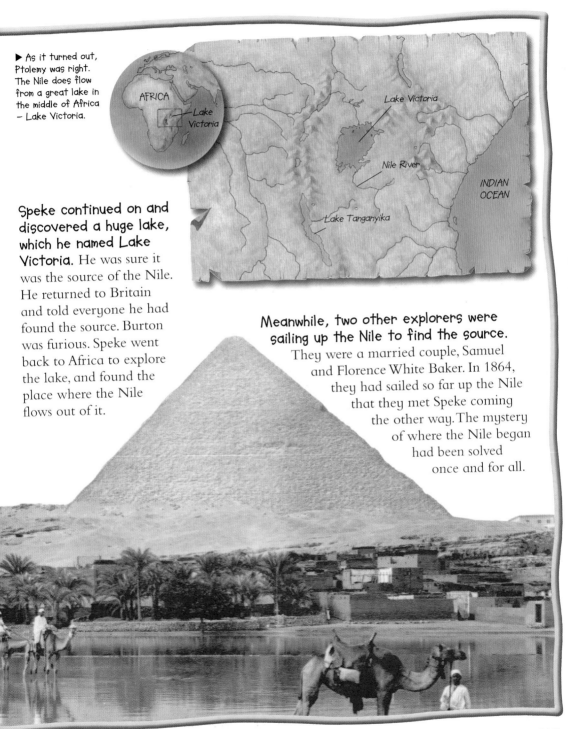

▶ As it turned out, Ptolemy was right. The Nile does flow from a great lake in the middle of Africa — Lake Victoria.

AFRICA
Lake Victoria

Lake Victoria

Nile River

Lake Tanganyika

INDIAN OCEAN

Speke continued on and discovered a huge lake, which he named Lake Victoria. He was sure it was the source of the Nile. He returned to Britain and told everyone he had found the source. Burton was furious. Speke went back to Africa to explore the lake, and found the place where the Nile flows out of it.

Meanwhile, two other explorers were sailing up the Nile to find the source. They were a married couple, Samuel and Florence White Baker. In 1864, they had sailed so far up the Nile that they met Speke coming the other way. The mystery of where the Nile began had been solved once and for all.

Exploring Australia

▶ The didgeridoo is a traditional musical instrument made from a hollowed out tree trunk. It is an important part of the historical culure of the aboriginal people.

People settled in Australia more than 50,000 years ago. The aboriginal people have lived there ever since. Just 400 years ago, in the early 1600s, sailors from Europe began to explore Australia. Britain claimed Australia for itself, and lots of British people went to live there.

European settlers were sure there was a huge sea in the middle of Australia. In 1844, a soldier named Charles Sturt went to look for the sea. He found that the middle of Australia was a hot, dry desert (now called the outback). His men got sunburn and scurvy, and their fingernails crumbled to dust. Sturt himself nearly went blind. But he had proved the mythical sea did not exist.

▼ Burke and Wills took more than 40 horses and camels on their expedition. The camels were from India, as they were well suited to Australia's dry climate.

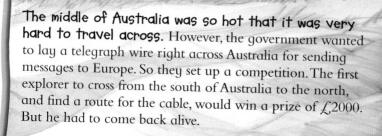

The middle of Australia was so hot that it was very hard to travel across. However, the government wanted to lay a telegraph wire right across Australia for sending messages to Europe. So they set up a competition. The first explorer to cross from the south of Australia to the north, and find a route for the cable, would win a prize of £2000. But he had to come back alive.

Irishman Robert Burke decided to try for the prize. He set off in 1860 with a team of horses and camels. Four men – Burke, William Wills, and two others – made it all the way across Australia. On the way back one man died, and they stopped to bury him. The rest of the team, waiting to meet them, gave up and went home. The three survivors were left alone in the desert, and Burke and Wills starved to death. Only one man lived – he was rescued by Aborigines.

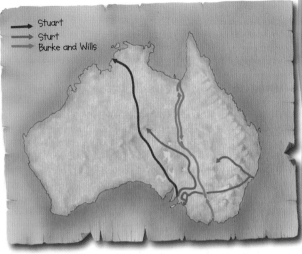

▲ Only Stuart's expedition was completely successful. His journey opened up the interior of Australia for settlement and farming.

Meanwhile, another explorer was racing Burke for the prize. John McDouall Stuart took a different route across Australia, further west than Burke's. Unlike Burke, Stuart made it back alive – but he almost died. When he came home to Adelaide to claim his prize, he was so sick he had to be carried on a stretcher.

QUIZ

The Aborigines could survive in the outback because they knew what foods to eat and where to find them. Which of these foods could Burke's men have eaten?
1. Bunya nut
2. Wichetty grub (a kind of baby insect)
3. Seaweed
4. Ostrich eggs
5. Wild honey

Answers:
1, 2 and 5. Not ostrich eggs, as ostriches are only found in Africa. Not seaweed, as it is only found in the sea.

Arctic adventures

The Arctic is the land and sea around the North Pole. Explorers first went there to search for the Northwest Passage – the sea-route leading from the Atlantic Ocean to the Pacific Ocean. They spent 400 years trying to find it, and many explorers died of cold or drowned in the Arctic Ocean.

Norwegian explorer Roald Amundsen was the first to sail through the Northwest Passage. Amundsen used a small fishing boat that made it easier to sail along shallow channels and between chunks of floating ice. But the journey still took him three years – from 1903 to 1906. Amundsen learned a lot about surviving in the cold from local peoples he met on the way.

There was still part of the Arctic where no one had been – the North Pole. Another Norwegian explorer, Fridtjof Nansen, built a ship called the *Fram*, which was designed to get stuck in the ice without being damaged. As the ice moved, it carried the *Fram* nearer to the Pole. Nansen almost reached the Pole in 1895 – but not quite.

Next, an American named Robert Peary and his assistant Matthew Henson, set off for the North Pole. Peary had always wanted to be the first to get there. After two failed attempts, Peary used dogsleds and Inuit guides to help him reach the pole in the year 1909.

When Peary announced that he had been to the Pole, he was in for a shock. Another explorer, Frederick Cook, who had been Peary's friend, said he had got there first! The two men had an argument. Then it was revealed that Cook had lied about another expedition. After that, nobody believed he had been to the North Pole either.

▲ Peary and Henson used traditional sealskin clothes for their journey, and paid local Inuit people to make their clothes and equipment.

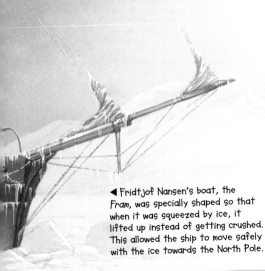

◄ Fridtjof Nansen's boat, the Fram, was specially shaped so that when it was squeezed by ice, it lifted up instead of getting crushed. This allowed the ship to move safely with the ice towards the North Pole.

I DON'T BELIEVE IT!

Some experts think Peary didn't actually reach the North Pole. If this is true then the first person at the North Pole was Wally Herbert, who walked there in 1969.

Antarctic adventures

Antarctica was explored less than 200 years ago. This large and mountainous continent is at the southern tip of the Earth. It is even colder than the Arctic and very dangerous. In the early 1900s, explorers such as Robert Scott and Ernest Shackleton tried to reach the South Pole and failed. In 1909, Shackleton came within 155 kilometres of the South Pole, but had to turn back.

In 1910, British explorer Robert Scott decided to set off for the South Pole again. He took motor sleds and ponies to carry all his supplies. He decided that when his men got near the Pole, they would pull their own sleds. In Antarctica, he also wanted to collect rock samples to study.

Meanwhile, Roald Amundsen was on his way to try to reach the North Pole. But when he heard that Robert Peary had already got there, he decided to race Scott to the South Pole instead. Amundsen used different methods from Scott – sleds pulled by husky dogs carried supplies.

▶ Amundsen's team used lightweight dogsleds. If a dog died or became too weak to go on, it was fed to the other dogs. This reduced the amount of food the men had to carry.

In 1911, both Scott and Amundsen reached Antarctica, and set off for the South Pole. Amundsen left first and got there quickly with his dogs. Scott's motor sleds broke down and his ponies died. His team trudged to the Pole, only to find Amundsen had been there first. On the way back, Scott's men got stuck in a blizzard. They ran out of food, and died of cold and hunger.

▲ When Scott's team reached the South Pole, they took photos of each other, but their faces showed how upset they were not to be there first.

Shackleton never got to the South Pole – but he had a very exciting Antarctic adventure.

He wanted to trek across Antarctica in 1914. But before he could start, his ship, the *Endurance*, was crushed by the ice. The crew were left on the frozen ocean with just three lifeboats. Shackleton left his men on an island while he took one tiny boat to get help. He had to cross a stormy ocean and climb over icy mountains before he found a village. All his men were rescued and came home safely.

Scientific searches

Lots of great explorers were scientists. Some went exploring to find rocks and minerals, or to study mountains or seas. Some were looking for new species (types) of plants and animals. Today, scientists explore in jungles, deserts and oceans to look for things no one else has found before.

▲ Darwin studied the many different types of finch on the Galapagos Islands.

Charles Darwin went on a round–the–world voyage on a ship called the Beagle, from 1831 to 1836. As the ship's naturalist (nature expert), it was Darwin's job to collect new species. He found all kinds of birds, plants, lizards, insects and other living things. He found many strange fossils, too. Back in England, Darwin wrote lots of important books about the natural world.

▲ Darwin made notes about his findings. He believed that plants and animals changed to suit their surroundings.

▼ The horses we know today developed gradually from smaller horselike animals over a period of about 55 million years. Darwin called this process of gradual change evolution.

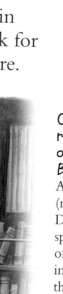

Eohippus

Mesohippus

Parahippus

Merychippus

Pliohippus

Equus

Henry Bates' favourite animals were bugs. In 1848, Bates went to the Amazon rainforest to study butterflies, beetles and other insects. He found more than 8000 species that no one had known about before. He also discovered that some harmless animals look like poisonous animals to stay safe. Today, this is called 'Batesian mimicry' (mimicry means copying).

◄ The hornet moth is an example of 'Batesian mimicry'. It is harmless but it mimics the hornet, which has a painful sting. This helps to scare predators away.

Hornet moth

Hornet

TRUE OR FALSE?

1. Henry Bates discovered more than 8000 species of insects.
2. Aimé Bonpland was an expert on local medicines.
3. Darwin's ship was called the *Basset*.
4. Mary Kingsley became caught in an animal trap.

Answers:
1.TRUE 2.FALSE Aimé Bonpland was a plant-expert.
3. FALSE Darwin's ship was called the *Beagle*.
4.TRUE

German scientist Alexander von Humboldt wanted to understand everything in the world. He and his friend, French plant-expert Aimé Bonpland, explored South America for five years between 1799 and 1804. They studied all kinds of things – poisonous plants, local medicines, ocean currents, rocks, rivers, mountains, and the stars at night. Later, Humboldt wrote a book, *Kosmos*, all about nature.

▶ Von Humboldt studied landscape extensively. The cold sea current that flows up the west coast of South America is named in his honour.

Mary Kingsley loved exploring rivers in Africa. She searched for new species – especially river fish – and studied the way of life of local rainforest people. On her travels, Kingsley fell into an animal trap full of spikes, got caught in a tornado, was cornered by an angry hippo and had a crocodile climb into her canoe.

Archaeological adventures

▲ The Nabataean people built many beautiful temples on the small plain at Petra.

Old ruined cities, palaces and tombs can stay hidden for centuries. Some get buried or covered with desert sand. Some are in faraway places where no one goes any more. When an explorer finds an ancient ruin, it can reveal lots of secrets about how people used to live long ago. Finding things out from ancient ruins is called archaeology.

Swiss explorer Johann Ludwig Burckhardt wanted to explore Africa. First he went to the Middle East to learn Arabic for his African trip. In 1812, in what is now Jordan, he discovered an amazing ruined city, carved out of red and yellow rock. It was Petra, the capital of the Nabataean people, built in the 2nd century. Burckhardt was the first European to go there.

The city of Troy, which you can read about in the Greek myths, really existed. In 1870, German archaeologist Heinrich Schliemann travelled to Turkey to see if he could find Troy. He discovered the ruins of nine cities, one of which he thought was Troy. He found it had been destroyed and rebuilt many times. Schliemann also dug up piles of beautiful gold jewellery from the ruins.

◀ Schliemann's wife, Sophia, wearing some of the jewels found in the ruins uncovered by her husband.

In 1911, American explorer Hiram Bingham found a lost city, high on a mountain in Peru. The local people knew about it, and called it Machu Picchu, meaning 'old mountain', but the outside world had no idea it was there. Bingham wrote a book about his discovery, and today, half a million tourists visit it every year.

▲ The cave paintings at Lascaux depict animals such as bison, deer and horses.

MAKE A CAVE PAINTING

You will need:
paper (rough beige paper looks best)
red and black paint   twigs
To make your painting look like real Lascaux cave art, use a twig dipped in paint to draw stick figures and animals such as cows, deer and cats. You can also try making patterns of spots using your fingertips.

Four teenagers exploring a cave stumbled upon some of the world's most important cave paintings. The cave was in Lascaux, France, and the four boys found it in 1940, after a tree fell down, leaving a hole in the ground. Inside were passages leading to several rooms. The walls were covered with paintings of wild animals and humans who had lived 17,000 years ago.

The highest mountains

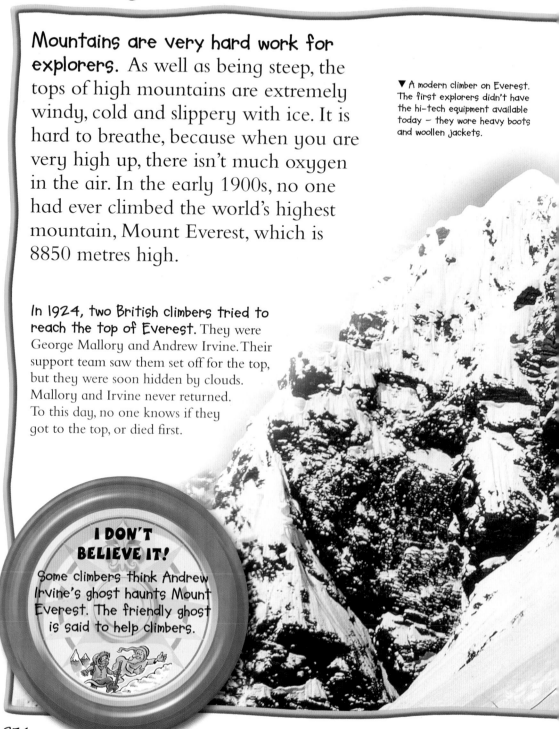

Mountains are very hard work for explorers. As well as being steep, the tops of high mountains are extremely windy, cold and slippery with ice. It is hard to breathe, because when you are very high up, there isn't much oxygen in the air. In the early 1900s, no one had ever climbed the world's highest mountain, Mount Everest, which is 8850 metres high.

▼ A modern climber on Everest. The first explorers didn't have the hi-tech equipment available today – they wore heavy boots and woollen jackets.

In 1924, two British climbers tried to reach the top of Everest. They were George Mallory and Andrew Irvine. Their support team saw them set off for the top, but they were soon hidden by clouds. Mallory and Irvine never returned. To this day, no one knows if they got to the top, or died first.

I DON'T BELIEVE IT!

Some climbers think Andrew Irvine's ghost haunts Mount Everest. The friendly ghost is said to help climbers.

In the 1950s, many countries were trying to send climbers to the top of Everest. A Swiss expedition nearly made it in 1952. In 1953, a British team set off. Two climbers, Evans and Bourdillon, climbed to within 90 metres of the summit, but had to turn back when an oxygen tank broke. Then, another two climbers tried. Their names were Edmund Hillary and Tenzing Norgay.

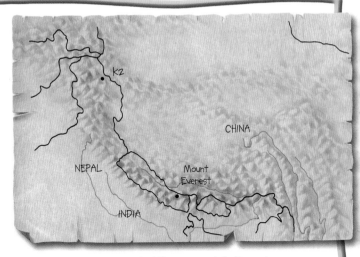

▲ Hillary and Norgay started their approach to Everest from its south side – which had been called unclimbable.

At 11.30 a.m. on 28 May, 1953, Tenzing and Hillary stood on top of Mount Everest. They hugged each other and took photos. They couldn't stay long, as they had to get back to their camp before their oxygen ran out. Hillary and Tenzing made it home safely, but many people have died trying to come back down Mount Everest after reaching the top.

There was still a mighty mountain yet to be climbed. K2, the world's second-highest mountain, is even more dangerous than Everest. People had been trying to climb it since 1902, and many had died. At last, in 1954, an Italian team succeeded. Lino Lacedelli and Achille Compagnoni were chosen to go to the top. Their oxygen ran out, but they kept going and reached the summit.

Under the sea

In 1872, a ship set out to explore a new world — the bottom of the sea. But the HMS *Challenger* wasn't a submarine. It measured the seabed, using ropes to find out the depth of the ocean. On its round-the-world voyage, *Challenger's* crew also found many new species of sea creatures.

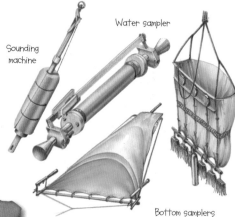

Water sampler

Sounding machine

Bottom samplers

▲ HMS *Challenger* and some of the equipment her crew used to measure the shape and depth of the seabed all around the world.

Lots of people still wanted to explore the seabed themselves. In 1928, an engineer, Otis Barton, and a wildlife professor, Wiliam Beebe, built the bathysphere, a round steel ball that could be lowered into the sea. In 1934, Beebe and Barton climbed inside and dived 923 metres down into the Atlantic Ocean.

Another inventor, Auguste Piccard, invented a craft called the bathyscaphe. It wasn't lowered from a ship, but could travel about by itself. In 1960, a bathyscaphe named *Trieste* took two passengers to the deepest part of the sea, Challenger Deep, in the Pacific Ocean. It is more than 10,900 metres deep.

▼ Chimney-shaped hydrothermal vents surrounded by giant tubeworms, which can grow more than one metre long.

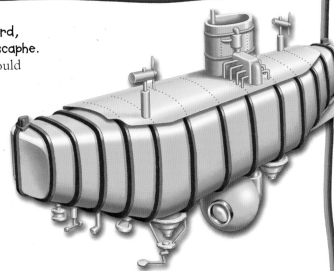

▲ The *Trieste*'s two passengers crouched inside the round part that you can see hanging below the main section.

In 1977, scientists discovered strange chimneys on the seabed and named them hydrothermal vents. Hot water from inside the Earth flowed out of these vents. The hot water contained minerals that living things could feed on. All around the vents were weird sea creatures that no one had ever seen before, such as giant tubeworms and giant clams.

The seas and oceans are so big, that parts of the undersea world are still unknown. There could be all kinds of strange sea caves and underwater objects we haven't found. Scientists think there could also be many new sea creatures, such as giant squid, sharks and whales, still waiting to be discovered.

Index

Index

Index

Index